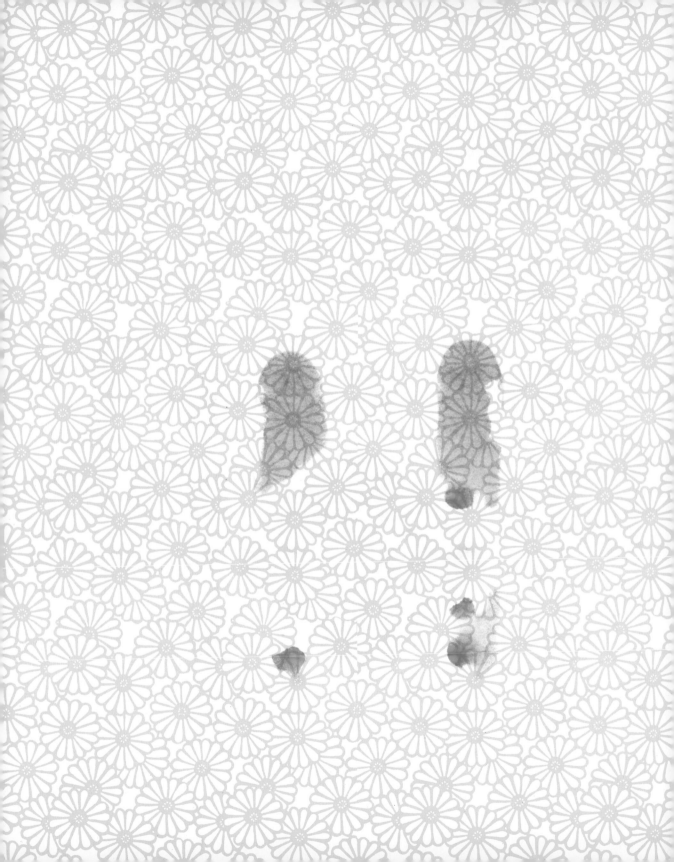

THE
ASIAN GRANDMOTHERS
COOKBOOK

THE
ASIAN GRANDMOTHERS
COOKBOOK

Home Cooking from Asian American Kitchens

Patricia Tanumihardja

SASQUATCH BOOKS
SEATTLE

Printed in China

Published by Sasquatch Books

Distributed by PGW/Perseus

15 14 13 12 11 10 09   9 8 7 6 5 4 3 2 1

Cover design: Rosebud Eustace

Cover photographs: © Rayshader | Dreamstime.com

© Densho: The Japanese American Legacy Project and the Seattle Buddhist Temple Archives

© *South Bend Tribune*

© Jeff Siddiqui

Interior design and composition: Rosebud Eustace

Interior photographs (food): Lara Ferroni

Interior photographs (grandmothers): © Patricia Tanumihardja (pages 44, 72, 100, 140, 176, 218, 292, 332)

© Scott Kushino (page 200)

© Susan C. Kim (page 252)

Original textile patterns: © Beth Wheeler (pages vi, 76, 176, 177, 218, 219, 252, 253, 256, 292, 293)

Stock patterns: © Dover Publications, Inc. *Traditional Japanese Stencil Designs*. Ed. Clarence Hornung. (pages i, 44, 45, 222, 296, 332, 333)

© Mandj98 (James Phelps) | Dreamstime.com (pages 48, 140, 141)

© Apollofoto (William Wang) | Dreamstime.com (pages 72, 73, 104)

© Ussr (Elena Andreeva) | Dreamstime.com (pages 30, 200, 201)

© Birdmanphoto | Dreamstime.com (pages ii, iii, 100, 101, 144)

Library of Congress Cataloging-in-Publication Data

Tanumihardja, Patricia.

   The Asian grandmothers cookbook : home cooking from Asian American kitchens / Patricia Tanumihardja.

      p. cm.

   Includes bibliographical references and index.

   ISBN-13: 978-1-57061-556-6

   ISBN-10: 1-57061-556-X

   1. Cookery, Asian. I. Title.

   TX724.5.A1T384 2009

   641.595--dc22

                        2009018162

Sasquatch Books

119 South Main Street, Suite 400

Seattle, WA 98104

(206) 467-4300

www.sasquatchbooks.com

custserv@sasquatchbooks.com

CONTENTS

Acknowledgments   *vii*

Introduction   *ix*

Using This Book and Menu Planning   *xi*

Techniques and Equipment   *xiii*

1. THE ASIAN PANTRY: A GLOSSARY OF INGREDIENTS   **1**

2. FOUNDATIONS: STAPLES AND STOCKS   **29**
   Profile of a Grandma: Kimiye Hayashi   44

3. TIDBITS, PURSES, AND PARCELS   **47**
   Profile of a Grandma: Ellen Shyu Chou   72

4. SAVORY SOUPS   **75**
   Profile of a Grandma: Merla See   100

5. ON THE SIDE   **103**
   Profile of a Grandma: Niloufer Gupta   140

6. THE CENTERPIECE   **143**
   Profile of a Grandma: Keo Choulaphan   176
   Profile of a Grandma: Daisy Kushino   200
   Profile of a Grandma: Nellie Wong   218

7. FEEDING A CROWD: POTLUCKS, PARTIES, AND FESTIVALS   **221**
   Profile of a Grandma: Sang Jung Choi   252

8. COMFORT FOOD AND ONE-WOK MEALS   **255**
   Profile of a Grandma: Alvina Mangrai   292

9. SWEETS, SIPS, AND SLURPS   **295**
   Profile of a Grandma: Gloria Santos   332

Beyond This Cookbook: Resources   *335*

Selected Bibliography   *337*

Conversion Tables   *339*

Index   *341*

ACKNOWLEDGMENTS

This book strikes a very sentimental chord with me.

For one, I never really knew my grandmothers, and growing up I envied friends who had grandma close by. My maternal grandmother passed away before I could remember her and my paternal grandmother lived in a completely different country. Because of this book, I now have multiple surrogate grandmothers!

Secondly, I have realized how very grateful I am to my mother, Juliana, who connected me to my cultural roots through food. Living in an adopted homeland, I was unconsciously linked to the country and culture I hardly knew through the food I ate every day. It is because of her that food plays such an important role in my life. I cannot thank her enough for the delicious and nutritious food she served us and for shaping me into the person I am today. I must also thank my father, Rudy, who has loved me unconditionally and supported me in everything I do. He also taught me a very important lesson: "You can't argue with taste!"

And of course I am eternally grateful to my loving husband, Omar, who patiently taste-tested every single recipe in this book, even if the dish looked or smelled "interesting" (his words exactly), and put up with my stressful months of writing, recipe testing, and editing.

And a very special thank you to the grandmothers I profiled in this book. They generously spent time with me, cooking and sharing words of wisdom and life stories: Sang Jung Choi, Ellen Shyu Chou, Keo Choulaphan, Niloufer Gupta, Kimiye Hayashi, Daisy Kushino, Nellie Wong, Alvina Mangrai, Gloria Santos, and Merla See. This book would not have been possible without you!

Additional thank yous:

To the wonderful team at Sasquatch Books: Publisher Gary Luke for putting the idea for this cookbook in my hands, Rachelle Longé for being a patient and thorough project editor, Deri Reed for meticulously copyediting the manuscript, Rosebud Eustace for designing a lovely book, and Lara Ferroni for her gorgeous photography. Thank you for helping me fulfill my dream.

To Irene Trantham and Melissa Chin for helping with edits and research.

And to all the wonderful people who cooked with me, shared recipes and stories, tested recipes, and/or helped me make connections:

Samia Ashraf

Byron Auyong, aunt Merla See

Eric Banh

Sophie Banh

Ivy Chan, father Kwok Sing Chan

Lynn Chang, mother Li Chang

Mary Lee Chin

Cathy Chun

Cathy Danh (gastronomyblog.com)

Olivia Dyhouse

Tisa Escobar

Wing Fong, grandmother Pearl Fong

Marvin Gapultos (burntlumpia .typepad.com)

Aaliyah Gupta, mother Niloufer Gupta

Desiree Haigh

Pranee Khruasanit Halvorsen

Luwei Hioe, mother Linawati Hioe

Dorothy Ho, mother Yuh-Wan Chiang

Churairat Huyakorn

Soyon Im, aunt Yangja Cho Im

Susan C. Kim, grandmother Sang Jung Choi

Katie Kiyonaga, mother Kimiye Hayashi

Shelly Krishnamurty, mother Champa Ramakrishna

Scott Kushino, mother Daisy Kushino

Eleanor Lee, mother Jean Lee

May Leong

Thanapoom Lertpanyavit, mother Panee Lertpanyavit

Tony Lew, mother Luisa Ines Taborda de Lew

Sharon Lim

Manda Mangrai, mother Alvina Mangrai

Yuki Morishima

Delia Lim Mota

Lisa Nakamura

Rin Nedtra

Huong C. Nguyen, mother Huong Thu Nguyen

Kim Khanh Nguyen

Mumtaz Rahemtulla

A. Rick Rupan

Roshita Shrestha

Jeff and Arman Siddiqui

Juana Stewart

Erica Sugita

Hiroko Sugiyama

Brigitta Suwandana

Phiroum Svy

Elaine Tay

Yi Thao

Leah Tolosa

Mike Tolosa

Lan Tran

Carol Vu, mother Thanh Nguyen

Ivy Wong, mother Pearlie Wong

Rachel Wong

Consolacion Mejia Yaranon

Angeline and Roxanne Yeo, mother Rosalind Yeo

RECIPE TESTERS:

Tuty Gunawan Alexander

Ann Marie Amarga

Matthew Amster-Burton

Katie Bashford

Julia Blanter

Susan Blee

Barb Bowen

Bri Brownlow

Angela Caragan

Diane Carlson

Jeffrey Chan

Tricia Cornell

Corinne Domingo

Jill Donnelly

Jennifer Fields

Jenny Fisk

Paula Forbes

Angela Fountas

Ada Fung

Marvin Gapultos

Ashley Gartland

Sharon Giljum

Joanna Harbaugh

Laura Navarra Haxer

Luwei Hioe

Cynthia Lannen

Kristel Leow

Jennifer Burns Levin

Hilary Lundquist

Nga Ly

Manda Mangrai

Angela Montgomery

Louise Mor

Diane Morissette

Christina Nevin

Eve Ng

Deanna Schneider

Heather Shannon

Carolyn Smith

Niki Stojnic

Danielle Sucher

Jesse and Laura Sycuro

Jess Thomson

Celeste Torres

Marie Tran

Sally Warn

Jora Atienza Washington

Tara Austen Weaver

Rose Wiegley

Ivy Wong

Sandy Yeung

INTRODUCTION

Grandmothers are the embodiment of love, comfort, and security. Many of us have fond memories of her kindly words of advice (elbows off the table!), the red packets filled with money she gave us at Lunar New Year and birthdays (how else could we fund our Barbie doll habit?), and the chicken rice porridge that gave us sustenance when we lay sick in bed (or just feigned illness to stay home from school). In Asian cultures, the grandmother's role is manifold, but one is of utmost importance: to ensure that grandchildren learn and preserve the many aspects of their ancestral culture. This is especially true in immigrant communities.

As an Indonesian Chinese living my formative years in an adopted country, food was a very vital link to my culture and heritage. In my case, my mother was the missing link as my sole surviving grandmother lived in a different country. Hence, for me and many others, grandmothers, mothers, and aunts are all custodians of home-cooked traditions.

More often than not, these women cook by instinct and their recipes are not recorded on paper. They hand down the secrets of the art of cooking verbally, and by example, from one generation to the next. By running around their knees or loitering at their elbows, generations of children and grandchildren have learned foodways and captured vivid memories of the how's and why's of cooking via osmosis—from the snap, crackle, and pop of spices roasting in the pan to the subtle balance of hot, sour, sweet, and salty on the tongue. These women link us to our heritage, particularly through food.

Today, life has changed. Instead of popping over to Grandma's place (she might even live on a different continent) or pulling out the wok to recreate our favorite family recipe, we head to any one of the Japanese restaurants down the block when we hanker for a savory *sukiyaki*. If we feel like a snack of crispy wontons, Chinatown beckons. Craving some *pho* (beef noodle soup)? Then we head for one of the Vietnamese restaurants that are competing for storefront space with coffee shops and yet another Thai eatery.

Just when did the restaurant become the keeper of our Asian food heritage? Perhaps the forced incarceration of Japanese Americans during World War II led subsequent generations of Asian Americans to distance themselves from their heritage. Maybe it was in the 1960s and '70s, when mothers fed the work force instead of their children. Or perhaps it was when migration—whether voluntary or forced—splintered families, scattering them around the world. The phenomenon could be perpetuated by nuclear families splitting apart thanks to increasing divorce rates.

We could also chalk it up to the inevitable watering-down of culture and heritage that comes with living in an adopted homeland over many generations. And who can blame refugee children for wanting to eat meatloaf instead of *canh* (Vietnamese soup) in an effort to embrace all things American and develop a sense of belonging?

Whatever the reason, modern times are making Asian home cooking a lost art in the United States, and many of the new generation of Asian Americans are now ignorant of these skills. That missing link to the past is a void that needs to be filled.

For this cookbook, I have interviewed, cooked with, and connected with grandmothers, mothers, aunties, and numerous people who have generously contributed their time, recipes, and stories. These recipes are family favorites that have been passed from mother to daughter to granddaughter, adapted, interpreted, and improvised according to the availability of ingredients and evolving palates. Some of the recipes are not to be found in print anywhere else. I've also included little tidbits of culinary wisdom that only a grandma can impart after years of cooking, as well as special family stories connected to the recipes.

Through research and a little detective work, I have also uncovered recipes from the annals of time that have been hiding in old church and community cookbooks. Often unattributed, but no less important, these recipes are also representative of our food heritage. The recipes meant a lot to the people who shared them and I want to record them before they disappear into the past forever.

I have compiled family recipes and stories from Asian communities across the spectrum. You'll find recipes from China, Japan, Korea, India, Pakistan, Nepal, Indonesia, Malaysia, Singapore, Laos, Cambodia, Vietnam, and Thailand. Many of these recipes have evolved from their original incarnation several fold, such as Indian curry from Guyana, Chinese-style shrimp toast from Vietnam, and a Dutch-influenced sweet (*klappertaart*) from Indonesia. Regardless of where in Asia they come from, these recipes represent a universal theme—they tell the story of our immigrant past.

In lieu of a real, live, and kicking person, I hope this book by your side will be like spending the day cooking with your very own Asian grandmother.

USING THIS BOOK AND MENU PLANNING

The first rule in Asian home cooking is that there aren't any hard and fast rules to follow. Consider the recipes and tips in this book as guidelines to help you discover your very own culinary footprint.

An Asian meal tends to be a communal affair with everyone around the table helping themselves to the various dishes and composing a personal meal. Hence, most of the recipes here are meant to serve 4 to 6 people as part of a multicourse family-style meal: typically a soup, one or two meat or seafood dishes, vegetables, and freshly steamed rice. Rice doesn't count as a dish but rather it is the blank canvas upon which the other flavors are highlighted and enjoyed.

Most of the recipes from various Asian cultures in this cookbook can be served family-style. You are at liberty to serve CLEAR SOUP WITH RED SPINACH AND SWEET CORN (page 79), WOK-FRIED PEA SHOOTS (page 121), and THAI BASIL PORK (page 174) in one meal. Just as long as the flavors don't clash on your tongue, why not mix and match?

Due to the creativity of home cooks (and often economic conditions), leftovers from one dish can be magically transformed into another, and variations and substitutions abound.

Then there is the one-wok meal. This is simply a single dish that constitutes an all-in-one meal. One caveat though: Don't count on just using one pot.

While there are a few dishes that are quite labor-intensive and comprise myriad herbs and spices that need to be ground and pounded (maids were a prominent feature in many Asian households earlier in the twentieth century), a systematic approach is what is needed when preparing these dishes. That's how you attain the complex, layer-upon-layer of flavors present in many Asian dishes. All it takes is some planning, and maybe a few extra hands to help out. The resulting dish will be well worth the effort.

COOK INTUITIVELY

The recipes in this cookbook have been gathered from home cooks, most—if not all—of whom cook intuitively, often measuring with a rice bowl, a handful, and of course, their taste buds. I have interpreted the recipes using American measurements (see page 339 for a metric conversion table) as best I could to act as a guide for cooks who may be unfamiliar with the cuisines. But don't be bound by precision. The recipes are merely acting as blueprints for you to discover how a dish is roughly supposed to taste. Feel free to personalize flavors to satisfy your personal preferences.

So even if a recipe calls for 1 tablespoon of soy sauce, take the liberty to subtract or add at will. The only limit is your palate. As I have discovered, no two people cook the same dish in exactly the same way.

Use your senses and be a kitchen vigilante. Smell seasoning pastes and taste coconut milk before you add it to a dish. Familiarize yourself with the visual clues, like the shimmer of oil when it's hot enough. Learn to listen to the sizzle of garlic or the gurgle of a curry to gauge when to move on to the next step. Most importantly, taste dishes to learn what you like and don't like. Experiment and discover how just a dash of salt or sugar can take a dish from blah to blessed!

Note that the recipes may use a lot of oil; fatty parts (pork belly!); or bone-in, skin-on chicken. Understand that these cuts of meat tend to be more economical. And, of course, fat adds lots of flavor! Yes, many of these dishes are not meant for the figure-conscious. Besides, there's nothing wrong with indulging for special occasions. However, you can always trim off all the fat or use a different cut of meat if you so choose. It's up to you to recreate the alchemy of each dish in your own kitchen.

By paying close attention to what you're doing and why, you'll understand how a dish comes together, as well as fine-tune your palate.

Lastly, you might not get some of the recipes right on the first try—or even second and third tries. But please, please don't give up. As many of the women I cooked with told me, it just takes practice.

If you need extra help, drop me a note at www.theasiangrandmotherscookbook .wordpress.com.

TECHNIQUES AND EQUIPMENT

While generations of women learned to cook from their grandmothers and mothers, several women I interviewed—perhaps because of circumstance or social status—didn't know how to cook before they got married. So how did they go from not knowing how to boil rice to becoming custodians of their food culture? Whether out of a need to feed their families, or because they yearned for the food of their homelands, they were motivated to learn. They picked up recipes and techniques from friends, cookbooks, TV, and cooking classes. And the most important lesson we can learn from them is: practice makes perfect! Just keep persevering, keep trying new things, and sooner or later you will perfect your techniques.

As early as two decades ago, there was a dearth of Asian cooking implements in the United States, so immigrants had to adapt. In actual fact, you don't need exotic equipment to cook Asian food. It can be prepared with the minimum of utensils, many of which are already found in a Western kitchen. Sure, if you already own a wok or a bamboo steamer, by all means use them—they can make cooking certain dishes easier. And if you would like to purchase the standard equipment used for each technique explained below, the items are readily available at Asian markets and specialty cooking stores.

DEEP-FRYING

Deep-frying involves immersing food completely in hot oil. Usually, you use 1½ to 2 inches of oil in the pan (about 3 cups of oil for a 14-inch wok) so that food is fully immersed in the oil and floating freely. However, be sure to allow space at the top of the wok for the oil to bubble and rise when the food is dropped in.

Pick an oil with a high smoke point—I use canola but peanut oil is a good alternative (see page 16). In the interest of economy, oil can be reused, but not more than twice in my opinion, and then only if you are cooking a similarly flavored food. So that means don't fry banana spring rolls in oil that was previously used to fry chicken! Filter the oil well through several layers of cheesecloth to remove any sediment, store it in a cool dry place, and reuse within a month or two at most. You'll know it has gone bad when it starts smoking at normal frying temperatures or if the color darkens.

When deep-frying, the empty pan doesn't need to be preheated. But the oil does need to be heated to an optimum temperature of 350 to 375 degrees F. I like to heat it over high heat: it heats up quicker, and then I can reduce it as needed. The temperature also depends on the type and size of the food being cooked. Vegetables and larger items can be deep-fried at lower temperatures. Remember, though, the temperature will drop slightly when you put in the food.

The key to successful deep-frying is knowing when the oil is at the right temperature. If the oil is too cool, the food will simply soak up grease without forming the nice brown crust we look forward to sinking our teeth into. Too hot, and the exterior will brown—and burn!—before the center of the food is cooked. If the oil starts smoking, it's way too hot and your food will truly taste burnt.

The easiest way to find the optimum temperature is to buy a deep-fry thermometer; a candy thermometer works too. One visual clue indicating the oil is hot enough: it will shimmer and swirl at the bottom of the wok. Or, plunge a wooden chopstick into the oil and if bubbles gather around it, the oil should be hot enough. You'll also smell the "hot oil" smell. However, these methods are not foolproof, so the best way is to test-fry a small portion of whatever it is you're frying or a bread cube—it should bubble gracefully to the surface and sizzle gently. If it just sits there soaking up oil, wait a couple more minutes before starting.

When the oil is ready, minimize splattering by gently sliding in the food with a pair of tongs or cooking chopsticks. Fry in batches so as to not overcrowd the wok. Overcrowding will lower the temperature and may lead to splattering or spillage. Turn the food occasionally so it browns evenly.

When done, remove the food with a wire mesh strainer or slotted spoon, shaking off any excess oil, and drain on a plate lined with paper towels to soak up the oil, or on a baking rack over a pan to allow the oil to drip down. Battered foodstuffs will often leave debris in the oil. Use a wire mesh strainer or slotted spoon to remove them from the oil and then bring the oil temperature back up again before frying the next batch.

Remember, properly fried food is not greasy at all. It will have a crisp exterior and a moist, tender interior. So take some care in getting this technique right.

In Asia, a wok is the most common vessel for deep-frying. A 14-inch wok will do for home cooking. A flat-bottomed wok works best for electric ranges and a round-bottomed one for gas (make sure the round-bottomed wok is securely in place in the wok stand). In addition, a heavy 12-inch skillet, 4-quart Dutch oven or heavy-bottomed pot work just as well. Some people feel safer sticking with a deep-fat fryer—just plug it in and fry away. A long handled wire-mesh skimmer is a great tool to have when deep-frying. It is used for removing noodles, wontons, dumplings, and the like from hot oil or boiling water. The wire mesh allows the oil to drip off the food, and the long handle protects your hand from the heat radiating from the wok. However, a slotted spoon works just as well.

Chinese cooks also use long, sturdy wooden chopsticks for turning over frying foods but this requires some dexterity. You might be happier with a pair of tongs.

STEAMING

Steaming is a gentle cooking technique that is perfect for showcasing the natural flavors of ingredients. It is also a very healthy method of cooking. In Asia, it is more common to steam than bake sweets, such as CANTONESE-STYLE STEAMED CAKE (page 299).

Steaming baskets, which come in various sizes, are stackable, so you can steam food in two or three baskets at the same time. There are generally two types: bamboo steamers are placed in a wok; metal steamers come with a bottom vessel to hold the water.

Sometimes you can place items directly in the steamer, like LOLA'S SWEET RICE ROLLS (page 330), but most of the time you'll have to put the food on a heatproof rimmed plate (a Pyrex glass pie dish works well) before setting it in the steamer basket or rack. Make sure it is at least 1 inch smaller than the width of the steamer basket.

Fill the wok or bottom vessel with a generous amount of water, perhaps 3 or 4 inches depending on its size (see page xvi for differences in bamboo and metal steamers). Cover and bring the water to a rolling boil over high heat. Reduce the heat to medium until you are ready to steam.

To steam, set the steamer basket on top of the water. Adjust the heat to the steaming temperature called for in the recipe and cover. You should constantly see steam escaping from underneath the lid.

From experience, I have learned that a constant stream of steam is not any indication of water level. So be sure to monitor the water level by reducing the heat to low and carefully taking a peek at the level. Replenish, if necessary, with boiling water, raise the heat back up, and continue steaming. After a few times, you'll know how long it takes before you need to replenish the water.

When done steaming, turn off the heat and wait for the steam to subside before lifting the lid. Lift it away from you to prevent scalding yourself and hold it so as to keep condensation from dripping onto the food. Carefully remove the steamer basket containing the food and set it on the counter. Use a spatula to lift out the dish, aided with a potholder and set it aside to cool.

Bamboo versus Metal Steamer

A bamboo steamer has a plaited cover to absorb moisture. As the steam circulates, the condensation collecting under the lid is minimized, thus preventing water from dripping onto the food, which can spoil the taste and appearance of the dish. The pretty baskets can also double as serving trays for steamed foods. Set a 10- to 12-inch basket right into a 14- to 16-inch wok (make sure the bottom rim is just covered by water, as the baskets scorch easily; replenish with boiling water as needed). Bamboo steamers cost from $15 to $20 and are widely available. They are pretty but are prone to mildew and scorching and not as sturdy.

I prefer metal steamers. They are often stainless steel, have heat-resistant plastic handles, and are sturdy, long lasting, and easy to clean. A metal steamer usually has three tiers. The bottom pan is for the water, and the top two baskets have holes with different sizes for steaming different types of foods: bigger holes for meat and smaller holes for delicate foods like sticky rice. I recommend filling the bottom pan about half to three-quarters full.

With a metal steamer, condensation can be an issue, although the dome-shaped lid encourages water to slide down the sides instead of onto the food. This problem can be further curtailed by placing a tea towel over the top basket before covering the steamer to absorb any dripping liquid. Choose a 10- to 12-inch steamer for the greatest versatility—it will reduce overall cooking time and you won't have to steam in batches. If you would like to invest in one—especially if you're planning on steaming often—these nifty steamers are available in Chinatown for about $50. Larger 16-inch steamers are great for steaming whole fish or chickens.

But keep in mind that you don't have to go out and buy a steamer to make the recipes in this book. You can easily steam most foods in a stockpot with a pasta insert or in an asparagus steamer.

Or you could experiment with common implements you might already have in your kitchen. All you need is a vessel to hold water, a vehicle to suspend the food over the water, and a lid to keep the steam in. Here are some possible combinations:

- Set three 2- to 3-inch-tall cans (tuna cans are perfect) with both ends removed (or use the removable rim of a cheesecake pan) into a deep wide pan with a lid. Top the cans with a round cake rack and place a pie plate on it.

- Place a collapsible vegetable steaming rack in a skillet or wok.

- Crisscross four wooden chopsticks (tic-tac-toe fashion) inside a wok and add enough water to almost reach the chopsticks. Bring to a boil and balance a plate of food on the chopsticks.

- Place a trivet or a small inverted bowl in a wok or a large wide pot. Place a pie plate on top. Pour in enough water so that just the trivet legs are submerged. And don't worry if you hear the trivet knocking against the bottom of the wok as the water boils.

STIR-FRYING

Stir-frying is one of the most prolific Asian cooking techniques. Using a minimal amount of oil, ingredients are tossed in a hot wok and kept moving to evenly distribute the heat.

To achieve wok-searing action and flavor, always preheat the wok. This also eliminates any water droplets that will spatter when you add the oil. I choose to heat my wok to medium-high heat and raise or reduce it if I need to. If you're adding garlic first, it will burn very quickly if the wok is too hot, so adjust appropriately, and vegetables only require a medium-high heat. But if you are stir-frying meat first, you need it very hot so that the meat is seared as soon as it touches the wok surface, sealing in the juices.

Preheating takes about a minute or so, but how can you tell when it's hot enough? Sprinkle some water into the wok—the beads should dance on the surface and vaporize within a couple of seconds of contact. Or hover your palm about 2 inches above the wok surface; you should feel the heat tickling your palm (similar to the warmth of a hot radiator). The wok should also give off a wisp of smoke.

Next, pour in the oil and swirl it around the wok by tilting the wok from side to side, back and forth, to coat the bottom evenly. Wait for about 30 seconds for the oil to heat up. Here's how you know when it's hot enough: When you first pour the oil into the pan, it will be thick and syrupy. But once it heats up, it will thin out into a runny liquid, start to shimmer, and separate from the edge of the pan.

You can also test by throwing in your first ingredient, usually garlic. If it sizzles gently and bubbles gather around its edges, the oil is ready. If it fries aggressively and starts burning, the oil is too hot. If it sits still, the oil is not hot enough. If at anytime the oil gets too hot and starts to smoke uncontrollably, remove the pan from the heat for a few seconds and lower the heat.

The secret to stir-frying is not to overcrowd the wok. If too many ingredients are in the wok, the temperature will dip and the food will cook too slowly to attain the distinctive high heat "burnt" taste. Most home kitchen electric stoves aren't designed to produce the extreme high heat of a powerful gas stove, so woks hardly reach the optimum temperature required anyway. To achieve best results, add the ingredients gradually, in small handfuls, or stir-fry smaller amounts of food at a time.

Once the stir-frying begins, be a vigilant temperature monitor to protect the temperature in the wok from dropping too drastically. Adjust the heat to compensate for the addition of colder temperature foods or liquids. Above all, listen to the sizzle in your pan. Too much sizzle means you should decrease the temperature; too little sizzle means you need to increase it.

Keep things moving swiftly around the wok; slide your spatula to the bottom and keep turning and tossing ingredients up and over one another. Make sure they all have contact with the oil and hot surface of the wok and that the sauces and seasonings cover them evenly.

Other tips for stir-frying: Have all your ingredients prepared and cut to similar size so they'll cook evenly. Make sure the food is dry; a wet or soggy ingredient can lower the heat in the wok (after washing greens, always dry them thoroughly in a salad spinner). When done, spread the stir-fried food out in a large serving platter and serve immediately because ingredients continue to cook even after they're off the heat.

While technique is important, a successful stir-fry also relies on the wok or pan you use. The wok (called *kuali* in Indonesia or *kadai* in India) is the standard stir-fry tool and is ideal for stir-frying (as well as deep-frying, making sauces, braising, and other cooking methods). Because of its shape, the wok distributes heat evenly while sloping sides ensure food falls back inside rather than over the edge. But skillets, sauté pans, and even Dutch ovens work well.

Avoid aluminum or Teflon-coated woks. Instead, go for a heavy cast-iron wok that won't tip easily, or modern carbon steel flat-bottom woks that conduct heat well and accommodate both large and small amounts of food.

Other accessories include: a wok lid, which is ideal for finishing off a stir-fry, and a wok spatula—a long-handled utensil used for stirring and shifting the food in the wok. The spatula has a wide, slightly curved metal blade that is specially designed to avoid scratching a seasoned wok. Another option I like is a wooden spoon or spatula. Finally, a wok ring is used to stabilize a round-bottomed wok on the stove and bring it as close to the heat as possible.

CLAY POT COOKING

Clay pot dishes are the Asian equivalent of Western casseroles, but instead of baking in the oven, a clay pot is heated on top of the stove. It imparts a deep, smoky flavor to foods and is good for slow-braising recipes. There are two pot styles: one with a thick handle and another with two smaller ones. Both come in small and large sizes. Big pots are good for cooking dishes requiring lots of steam, like CLAY POT LEMONGRASS-STEAMED FISH (page 205).

Clay is a porous material so it readily soaks up moisture. As the pot warms, it releases the moisture as steam. The food inside the clay pot retains its moisture because it is surrounded by steam, resulting in a tender, fragrant dish. When cooking, set the clay pot right on the gas stove, then raise the heat gradually. Use a heat diffuser with an electric range. To prevent cracks, avoid setting a cold pot on a very hot stove and cook on medium, not high, heat. And never plunge a hot pot in cold water. Over time, the pot will blacken and develop a few unharmful cracks.

MORTAR AND PESTLE

In Southeast Asia, a variety of ingredients are pounded in a mortar with a pestle. This task requires quite a bit of muscle power, but when making seasoning pastes you will be rewarded with a smooth paste that's gently massaged and not pulverized. Start with hard spices such as coriander and lemongrass. When these have been reduced to a smooth powder or paste without any gritty or sinewy bits, add softer ingredients—chilies, ginger, garlic, and shallots.

Some mortars and pestles are carved from granite to pound hard, dry spices; others are fashioned from wood or clay for pounding softer ingredients like green papaya, fresh chilies, garlic, and more.

If you'd rather not spend an arduous half hour pounding, a 3- or 4-cup food processor is a fine substitute for a mortar and pestle. Your ingredients won't be ground properly in a processor that is any bigger. Use a spatula to scrape down the side and pour in drizzles of water gradually if the paste is not turning over as expected. Be observant and feel the texture of the paste between your fingers.

1

2

3

6

5

4

7

10

11

12

8

9

13

14

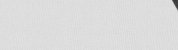

1

THE ASIAN PANTRY: A GLOSSARY OF INGREDIENTS

Myriad ingredients are used in Asian cuisine. Some are easy to find: ingredients such as chilies, ginger, and even soy sauce are readily available at most supermarkets, and gourmet markets often carry specialty items like whole spices and lemongrass. As for the others, you may have to hunt for them at an Asian market or elsewhere (see page 336 for online and mail-order resources).

Shopping for Asian ingredients in Chinatown or Little Saigon may require sleuthing, some deductive-reasoning skills, and lots of patience. Very often you can't rely on English translations—if they're even provided—and completely different products can share the same English name on their packages.

So what's a reader to do? The extensive glossary and accompanying photographs in the following pages should fill in the blanks. The entries will help you identify the physical characteristics of ingredients and the packages they come in.

Before you trek out to shop, be prepared. Read the glossary and do additional research online. Write down the phonetic pronunciation or bring a picture of the hard-to-find item with you when you shop, and if you need help, do ask a salesperson or a fellow shopper who looks like they know the lay of the land.

1. Thai palm sugar
2. Indonesian palm sugar
3. Dried shrimp paste
4. Tamarind pods
5. Star anise
6. Black shrimp paste
7. Dried shrimp

8. "Wet" tamarind
9. Dried black mushrooms
10. Ajowan seeds
11. Asafetida
12. Chinese salted black beans
13. Wood ear mushrooms
14. Broad bean sauce

Agar Agar (*Kanten* [Japanese], China Grass)

Agar agar is the Asian answer to gelatin. Made from seaweed, it's an integral ingredient in puddings and custards. High in fiber and practically fat-free, it is gaining popularity in the West as a vegetarian gelatin substitute. But unlike gelatin, agar agar doesn't need refrigeration to set (although it is now often chilled in the refrigerator). It comes as a whitish powder in small packets or as colorful dried strips. My mom has been using yellow packets of Swallow Globe brand forever and it's my choice as well.

Azuki Beans (Red Beans, Adzuki Beans, or Aduki Beans)

Azuki beans are naturally sweet beans mashed and cooked with sugar to form a paste (see page 310) that's used in cookies, cakes, and kanten (Japanese agar agar). Black azuki beans or red kidney beans can be substituted.

Banana Leaves

In Southeast Asia, banana leaves act like aluminum foil, not only protecting sweet and savory foods while grilling or steaming, but also imbuing them with a mild grassy fragrance and pale green color. Banana leaves are most often available frozen; you can sometimes find them fresh—if you're lucky or live in Hawaii. Partially defrost frozen leaves at room temperature before unfurling. Use scissors to cut off a section and refreeze any unused portions (they'll keep for up to a year). Rinse and then wipe dry with a paper towel to remove any white residue. Remove the center spine, trim off any brown edges, and cut to the required size. Particularly stiff leaves can be dipped in boiling water to soften.

Basil, Thai (*Bai Horapa*)

Though it may look like Italian basil, Thai basil has a very different flavor, much like that of licorice. With white flowers and purple stems, they are milder in flavor than holy basil (*bai gkaprow*) and can be found in Asian markets and even some larger supermarkets.

Bok Choy (Chinese White Cabbage, Pak Choy)

A member of the cabbage family, this Chinese vegetable staple is a stir-fry favorite. Of its many varieties, Shanghai bok choy is probably most familiar to Westerners. With pale green spoonlike stems, the vegetable is harvested young and often found in Western supermarkets labeled as "baby bok choy." In Asian markets, what is simply called bok choy comes with broad white stems and large green corrugated leaves. It is usually about the size of Swiss chard but there are "baby" varieties as well. Choose bok choy with tightly closed buds and avoid yellowing leaves and brown stems. Refrigerate wrapped in paper towels in the crisper.

Bonito Flakes (*Katsuo Bushi*)

Bonito—skipjack tuna—is dried and shaved into thin, pinkish flakes, then used primarily to prepare the Japanese cooking stock dashi (see page 40). It can also be used to season sushi and sashimi. Store in an airtight container and use fairly quickly as the flakes lose their flavor if kept for too long.

Broad Bean Sauce or Paste (Brown or Yellow Bean Sauce)

This is a thick purée made from fermented soybeans, wheat flour, salt, and sugar. Available in cans and jars, it can be refrigerated for 4 to 6 months after opening.

Broccoli, Chinese (Chinese Kale)

Chinese broccoli, known commonly by its Cantonese name *gai lan*, has thick, round stems and broad, deep green leaves. The stalks often have clusters of edible yellow blossoms attached. Mature gai lan (with stems about ½ inch thick or more) have a stronger, woody taste and should be peeled and halved before cooking. Baby gai lan, with slimmer stalks, are more tender. The slimmer stems do not require peeling and can be stir-fried. Refrigerate in an unsealed plastic bag for up to 5 days.

Cabbage, Chinese (Napa Cabbage, Peking Cabbage)

With a distinctive long, barrel shape and mild, neutral flavor, Chinese cabbage is often used in stir-fries. It ranges in color from white to light green and has crisp, crinkly leaves. Choose firm, light-colored heads and refrigerate wrapped in paper towels.

Cardamom, Green, Black, and White (*Elaichi* [Hindi])

Cardamom seeds are encased in protective pods that help preserve their pungent, smoky flavor. It is best to buy cardamom seeds still in their pods. Seeds alone tend to lose their flavor quickly. In South Asian cooking, green cardamom is used in both savory and sweet dishes. Slightly larger than its green sibling, black cardamom is popular in African and Middle Eastern cooking. It has a unique smoky flavor because it is traditionally dried over open flames, and it is rarely used in desserts. Use green cardamom pods if you can't find black ones. When cooking, throw cardamom into a dish, pod and all, or crush the seeds in a mortar and pestle before using.

Chilies

Chilies are a very important component of Asian cooking, adding both perfume and heat. Try to obtain a good balance of the two when picking chilies, remembering that size and color are not good indicators of potency. In all the recipes in this book, the amount of chilies you use is optional, depending on your personal capsaicin-o-meter (capsaicin is the compound that makes chilies hot). The seeds are the most potent part of the chili, so remove them if desired. One caveat: Don't add so much chili that you cannot taste the sweet, salty, and sour flavors of a dish.

I don't use rubber gloves when working with chilies (and no, I have not come across a grandmother who does), as I prefer the tactile sensation of ingredients in my hands. However, I am careful not to wipe my face or rub my eyes and promptly wash my hands thoroughly with soap and warm water after handling chilies. I advise beginners to use gloves.

Holland chilies (Dutch chilies, finger chilies), a crimson-red hybrid with narrow bodies that end in pointed tips, are about 4 inches long and ½ inch in diameter at their thickest girth. They resemble cayenne peppers in flavor and heat. Sold fully ripened and deep red, they are available fresh all year. They are sold in small plastic bags or in bulk. Store them in a closed paper bag in the refrigerator for up to 2 weeks or in plastic in the freezer for 3 months. Fresno (sometimes called red jalapeño), cherry bell, Anaheim, or cayenne chilies make excellent substitutes.

Korean green chilies (*kochu, gochu*) are bright green with slightly curved bodies that taper to a point. Measuring 3 to 5 inches in length and ¾ inch in diameter, they give heat to the spicy dishes Korean cuisine is known for. If you can't find them, substitute jalapeños.

Thai chilies are only 1½ to 2 inches long and ¼ inch in diameter at their widest, but the fiery specimens pack a lot of heat into their little bodies. They are used both fresh and dried, and are extremely spicy. When the green immature chilies ripen, they turn red. Refrigerate in a paper bag for up to 2 weeks, or freeze them fresh and they should keep well for up to 3 months. Substitute bird chilies (bird's eye chilies, *cili padi* [Malay]), which are even tinier and spicier (so use less), or de arbol chilies.

Chili paste, or **sambal** in Malay or Indonesian, is a popular condiment in Southeast Asian cuisine and is often made fresh. It also conveniently comes in a bottle. Indonesian *sambal oelek* is my favorite. Named for the mortar the paste is traditionally pounded in, it comprises a mixture of fresh chilies, vinegar, and salt. The result of this fiery mixture is powerful flavor that complements almost any dish. If you cannot find sambal oelek, pound fresh Holland chilies with salt into a coarse paste. Alternatively, any other type of chili paste may be used as a substitute. Keep sambal oelek in your refrigerator and it will last indefinitely.

Chinese Salted Black Beans (Fermented Black Beans, *Dow See* [Cantonese])

Chinese salted black beans are actually soybeans preserved in salt. Ubiquitous in Chinese stir-fries, marinades, and sauces, they develop their dark color, salty flavor, and slightly bitter aftertaste through oxidation. Look for shiny, firm beans available in clear cellophane packages in the dried beans section (Mee Chun brand). They need no refrigeration and keep well for about a year in a tightly sealed container away from light. Before cooking, soak in hot water for about 10 minutes, or at least rinse in several changes of cold water to remove excess salt.

Chives, Chinese (Garlic Chives, *Koo Chye* [Cantonese])

There are three types of Chinese chives, all of which possess a distinct garlic tinge. **Green chives** are fatter than their Western counterparts, with long flat blades that are between 10 and 16 inches long. **Yellow chives** (also called blanched chives), similar to green chives, are grown in the dark. They wilt quickly, but their milder flavor is prized by the Chinese and hence they cost more. **Flowering chives** have stiff stems 8 to 12 inches long with a tiny ½-inch-long pale green bud at its tip. Avoid chives that are wilted and give off a pungent smell. To store, wrap all varieties well in paper towels, slip into a plastic bag, and refrigerate. Use quickly as their strong smell will stink up your fridge.

Cilantro (Chinese Parsley, Coriander Leaf)

Refreshing and fragrant, chopped cilantro leaves are often sprinkled over hot dishes as a garnish right before serving. Cilantro roots (which are muskier and more pungent) and the bottom stems are smashed and added to soup stocks and stews, minced to make curries and chili pastes, and tossed into marinades such as the one for CHINESE BARBECUED PORK (page 165). Look for whole cilantro plants with roots at farmers markets or grow your own. If roots are unavailable, the bottom stems will do.

Coconut Milk

Coconut milk is the creamy, sweet liquid pressed from the freshly grated flesh of mature, brown coconuts. In Southeast Asia, it is prepared fresh right before cooking. This is hardly convenient in the United States, where time is of essence and good coconuts are hard to come by. The good news is that high-quality canned coconut milk is available (Chaokoh and Mae Ploy are recommended brands). Avoid coconut milk containing guar gum as well as light coconut milk: either may alter the consistency of the final dish. You can also find frozen or powdered coconut milk, but these are not my first choices. Always buy unsweetened coconut milk and certainly not cream of coconut. Stir the contents of the can before measuring: the richer coconut cream usually rises to the top, leaving thinner milk below. Coconut milk spoils quickly so use as soon as possible (it only keeps for a day or two in the refrigerator). Or freeze any unused portions and defrost as necessary.

Coconut Water (Coconut Juice)

Coconut water, also called coconut juice, is the clear, mildly sweet liquid swishing inside young, green coconuts. It is used in many Southeast Asian dishes and is a popular drink on its own. Don't confuse coconut water with coconut milk. While fresh coconut water is relatively translucent, coconut milk looks much like thick, creamy evaporated milk. Coconut water is available in cans (with bits of coconut meat in it) shelved with the rest of the canned drinks, and also in clear bags in the frozen section.

Coriander, Vietnamese (Laksa Leaves, *Rau Ram* [Vietnamese])

Though it looks nothing like cilantro and is unrelated, Vietnamese coriander smells like cilantro with citrus undertones and a refreshing, peppery bite. Use as you would cilantro, shredded or torn then thrown into soups, noodles, and stir-fries. Compared to cilantro, Vietnamese coriander withstands cooking better and can be added to a dish halfway through cooking to imbue subtle flavor. The oval shaped leaves with pointy tips and a mauve horseshoe imprint in the center are sold in small plastic bags and will keep 4 to 5 days in the refrigerator.

Coriander Seeds (*Dhania* [Hindi])

There are two types of coriander seeds, but the tiny round, tan ones with a lemony taste are most common. As with all spices, they are best when bought whole. Find the seeds at South Asian markets and store in a tightly sealed jar for up to 6 months.

Culantro (Mexican Coriander, Saw-Tooth Herb, Saw Leaf)

Culantro and cilantro are related, but they look nothing alike. With serrated leaves (hence its other monikers) 4 to 5 inches in length on either side of a prominent central ridge, it also has a stronger aroma than its relation. Culantro is usually sold in small plastic bags under the Vietnamese name of *ngo gai*. Store wrapped in paper towels and then in a plastic bag in the warmest part of the refrigerator. Cilantro is a fine substitute.

Curry Paste

Curry paste is a moist blend of ground or pounded herbs and/or spices. Thai curry pastes are made from fresh aromatics such as lemongrass, galangal, and chilies that are pounded together. Red curry paste, like that used in SHRIMP AND PINEAPPLE RED CURRY (page 209), may also include red chilies, shallots, coriander root, shrimp paste, and kaffir lime leaves. Homemade pastes yield the best flavor but take a lot of effort, so store-bought pastes such as the Mae Ploy brand (in 14-ounce tubs) are very good in lieu. Japanese curry pastes tend to be a milder version of Indian spice blends (see Curry Powder entry).

Curry Powder

Curry is an Anglicized term coined by the British for *kari*, a Tamil word meaning sauce; curry powder refers to a masala, or spice blend, used to make curries. It is a mixture of ground spices that varies widely in composition but usually contains turmeric (which gives it its yellow color), cumin, coriander, and cardamom. Other seasonings, such as ginger, garlic, cinnamon, cloves, mustard seeds, and red and black pepper, can be added, depending on the family recipe and the dish being cooked. Madras curry powder, a mixture favored in the southern Indian state of the same name, typically contains a blend of curry leaves, turmeric, coriander, cumin, cinnamon, cloves, chilies, bay leaves, fenugreek, allspice, and black pepper. Vietnamese brands of curry powder are based on this Madras blend.

Dates, Red Dried (Chinese Dates, Jujubes)

About the size of large olives, these leathery fruits are usually packaged in plastic bags already pitted. With a smell akin to raisins and a crisp, sweet flavor, they are often used in Chinese cooking for both savory and sweet dishes. Soak dried red dates in water before using in sweet soups or braises. Store in an airtight container to keep for several months.

Dumpling Skins

Dumpling skins, or wrappers, are small, thin wrappers made with wheat flour, water, and/or eggs that are available in different shapes (usually square or round) and thicknesses. Once filled, they can be fried, boiled, steamed, and even baked, taking on different textures: crispy, springy, chewy, or soft as clouds. Dumpling skins are usually labeled to indicate their use: wontons, pot stickers, *shiu mai*, or gyoza. Keep dumpling skins in the refrigerator for up to a week. Beyond that, you can freeze them for up to 2 months. Defrost frozen wrappers overnight in the refrigerator before using. Here's a great tip when assembling dumplings: Cover the stack of dumpling skins with a damp towel to keep them moist.

Fish Sauce (*Nam Pla* [Thai], *Nuoc Mam* [Vietnamese], *Patis* [Tagalog])

Indispensable in Southeast Asian kitchens, fish sauce is used the same way you'd use soy sauce in Chinese cooking. Instead of soybeans, it's made by fermenting fresh fish (most often anchovies and sometimes other fish and shellfish) with salt in large earthenware jugs, wooden casks, or vats. A good fish sauce (usually from the first extraction) is a clear, golden-red liquid that's slightly oily with a deep, rich flavor that isn't overly salty. Once opened, fish sauce can be left on the shelf. A wide variety of brands are available in Asian markets but there are some favorites: Three Crabs or Squid brand (Vietnamese), or Tiparos (Thai).

Five-Spice Powder

Five-spice powder is a blend of spices including star anise and cinnamon, as well as any combination of cloves, fennel, ginger, nutmeg, and Sichuan peppercorns. The pungent spice combination is a wonderful flavor enhancer for stews, barbecued pork, and even desserts. Use sparingly and store in a cool, dry place for about 6 months.

Galangal (Galanga, *Laos* [Indonesian])

Related to ginger, this plump rhizome has tannish-yellow skin encircled with brown rings enrobing creamy white flesh. Gala. has an earthy aroma and a pine-like flavor with a faint hint of citrus (though some people find it somewhat medicinal). As one of Southeast Asia's most popular aromatics, galangal pieces are tossed into curries, soups, stews, as well as fresh chili pastes (sambals) and sauces. Be sure to remove large bits before serving, as it has a hard, chewy texture. Wrap galangal well and it will stay fresh for up to 3 weeks in the refrigerator; or freeze for up to 6 months. Although it is available dried or ground, fresh has much more flavor.

Garam Masala

Garam masala is an aromatic blend of spices meant to "warm" the body, hence the phrase's literal meaning, "hot spices." While not a standardized mix, garam masala traditionally has black pepper, cinnamon, cumin, cloves, nutmeg (and/or mace), and green or black cardamom. Seasoned cooks make their own, but you can buy prepared blends from a South Asian market. Garam masala comes in two forms: as individual whole spices or a commercially ground mix.

Garbanzo Bean Flour (Besan, Gram Flour, or Chickpea Flour)

Garbanzo bean flour can be found in South Asian markets and some health food stores. To make it at home, lightly roast dried garbanzo beans and then grind in a blender until the consistency of flour. Lightly ground roasted dried yellow split peas may be used as a substitute.

Ghee (Clarified Butter)

Ghee is made by simmering unsalted butter until all the water has boiled off and the milk solids have settled to the bottom. The top golden layer is then spooned off. Unlike butter, ghee can be stored for extended periods without refrigeration, provided it is kept in an airtight container and remains moisture-free. Ghee is sold in jars at South Asian markets.

Ginger, Fresh

Perhaps one of the most versatile and widely used ingredients in Asian cooking, fresh ginger has a warm, zesty flavor and fragrance that adds a spicy bite to both sweet and savory dishes. The rhizome is used smashed, grated, sliced (always against the grain of the sinew running through it), chopped, shredded, and even juiced. Look for rhizomes that are firm and glossy-skinned, without wrinkles. Wrap ginger in paper towels, slip into a plastic bag, and refrigerate. The recipes in this book call for fresh ginger pieces that are about 1 inch in diameter.

Kaffir Lime (Kieffer Lime, *Makrut* [Thai])

While the glossy dark green leaves of this wonderful aromatic most often find their way into Southeast Asian dishes, the pebbly rind and juice of the fruit are used as well. All lend a citrusy undertone to coconut milk dishes, soups, and braises. Kaffir lime's double-barrel leaves are unmistakable, and are best when fresh or frozen. Don't buy them dried if you can help it as they lack aroma and flavor. Kaffir lime leaves keep for 10 days in the refrigerator and up to 6 months in a zip-top bag in the freezer.

Kalamansi (Calamansi, Calamondin)

Sometimes described as a native of the Philippines or other areas of Southeast Asia, the kalamansi tree is in fact a hybrid and unknown in the wild. The small orange fruit resembles a round key lime and its acidic juice has the fresh, floral aroma of tangerines. Fragrant Meyer lemons are a great substitute. Kalamansi juice is used as a souring agent to season meats and FILIPINO FRIED NOODLES (page 233) and is also made into drinks. The juice is available frozen in small packets at Asian markets, and the shrub is sold by specialty citrus growers.

Lemongrass (*Serai* [Malay], *Sereh* [Indonesian])

These variegated yellowish-green stalks have stiff, lance-like leaves and imbue many soups, curries, and stir-fries with a delicate, citrus flavor. Choose plump stalks that are firm and tight with no signs of mildew or rot. Store fresh lemongrass wrapped in moist paper towels in the refrigerator for up to 2 weeks. Or freeze in a sealed plastic bag for 3 months.

❧ PREPARING LEMONGRASS FOR COOKING ❧

Trim about an inch from the hard root end of the stalk and chop off the woody top where it just starts to turn from green to pale yellow. You should have 6 to 7 inches of lemongrass stalk remaining. Peel off the loose, tough outer layers to expose the tender white core, then bruise the entire length of the stem with a meat pounder, large knife, or heavy glass to release the aroma and oils. Lemongrass (as well as ginger and galangal) have tough fibers running through them. Mince the stalks to avoid chewing long stringy pieces and chomping down on hard, fibrous bits. To mince, cut the stalks crosswise into very thin ringlets (as thin as you can possibly cut them). Then rock your knife blade over the pieces to chop them into confetti-sized flakes. Or whirl in a food processor. You should get about 3 tablespoons from one stalk. For convenience, frozen ground lemongrass can be found in tubs in the freezer section of Asian markets.

Mirin

Mirin is a pale gold, spirit-based liquid (sometimes called sweet rice wine) used in Japanese cooking to add subtle sweetness to salad dressings, marinades, and stews. Look for *hon-mirin* (true mirin), a naturally brewed elixir containing natural sugars and avoid *aji-mirin* or any bottle labeled "sweet cooking seasoning" which usually contains sweeteners and other additives like salt. Opened bottles of mirin can be left on the shelf for about 6 months or in the refrigerator for up to 1 year.

Miso

Miso is a thick, rich paste made by fermenting soybeans, rice, barley, and/or wheat. There are various grades, colors, and strengths, but the general rule is the darker the miso, the saltier it will be, and the lighter the miso, the sweeter. Two types of miso are used in this book. White miso, which is actually pale gold in color, is mild and sweet. Caramel-brown red miso (also known as just "miso"), on the other hand, has a higher salt content and an earthier flavor. Misos are often interchangeable in recipes—simply adjust to be more sweet or salty as desired. After opening, miso keeps for 6 months to 1 year in the refrigerator.

Mizuna

With tender, feathery leaves, this Japanese green has a delightful peppery flavor suited for salads, simmered dishes, and soups. If you can't find mizuna, baby mustard greens or arugula may serve as substitutes.

Mung Beans, Whole and Hulled

Whole mung beans, tiny green, oval-shaped beans, are used in sweet and savory dishes. The beans can also be hulled to reveal the yellow inner germs (they look like egg yolk–colored flakes) that are used widely in Indian and Southeast Asian cooking. When nurtured, mung beans become bean sprouts. Mung bean starch, extracted from ground beans, is used to make cellophane noodles. Both whole (green) and hulled (yellow) mung beans can be found in 14-ounce packages in the dried goods aisle at Asian markets.

Mushrooms, Dried Black (Chinese Black Mushrooms, Dried Shiitakes)

Despite their name, dried black mushrooms range in shade from pale to dark brown and vary in size from 1 to 3 inches. Succulent and smoky, they are very popular in Japanese, Chinese, and Chinese-influenced cooking. The large light-colored mushrooms with cracked surfaces are of the highest quality (and have an accompanying high price tag) but the mid-range mushrooms work well too. The mushrooms are sold in cellophane packages, boxes, and in bulk. Store them in a cool, dry place in an airtight container.

 USING DRIED BLACK MUSHROOMS

Rinse then soak the mushrooms in warm water for about 30 minutes to reconstitute them (you may have to soak larger ones for a couple of hours). If you can plan ahead, soak them for 8 hours for an unsurpassed soft, spongy texture. After soaking, cut off their tough stems and cut up the plump caps as required. The water used to soak the mushrooms is often used in cooking to enhance the flavor of your dish, but discard the last few tablespoons specked with grit. In Japanese recipes, add a pinch of sugar to the soaking water.

Mushrooms, Wood Ear

Wood ear mushrooms are quite neutral in flavor; their appeal lies in their texture. The firm, almost rubbery texture adds contrast to soups and stuffings. They are most often available dried, either whole or shredded (much more convenient!), but can sometimes be purchased fresh. Sold in cellophane packages (sometimes labeled "auricularia"), the surface of the delicate crinkly mushroom is black and the underside is grayish. When soaked, the flesh turns dark purplish gray to almost black in color. Before using, soak dried wood ear mushrooms in warm water for at least 15 minutes. Then, rinse several times and trim the stem where it was attached to the tree. Once rehydrated, store in the refrigerator for up to one week. Cloud ear mushrooms are thicker, but they can be used as a substitute.

Mustard Greens, Asian (Mustard Cabbage, *Gai Choy* [Cantonese])

Just as its name implies, this vegetable has a sharp, peppery bite. It works well in soups and stir-fries. Two varieties of mustard greens are commonly available. The more common one has thick, curving leaf ribs springing from a central stalk that blossom into large ruffled leaves. This variety is used for pickling as well as in soups and stir-fries. The other, called bamboo mustard cabbage (*jook gai choy*), has skinnier stems and longer and thinner frilly-edged leaves. Trim the base of each stem and separate the leaves before washing thoroughly to remove the grit that gathers there. As with any green leafy vegetable, look for firm stalks and fresh bright leaves with no sign of yellowing. Refrigerate in a plastic bag for up to a week.

Noodles

There are so many varieties of Asian noodles available—made from rice or wheat flour, with or without eggs, and sold fresh, dried, cooked, or uncooked. Even I get confused at the dizzying array available! Find fresh noodles in the refrigerated section at Asian markets; depending on the type, they will keep from several days to a few weeks. Dried noodles will keep indefinitely if stored in a cool, dry place.

Recipes often require noodles to be boiled first. Most types cook quickly (1 to 3 minutes), but follow the package directions and your own taste. After boiling, dump noodles into a colander and flush with cold water to stop further cooking and to expel excess starch. Drain completely, then sprinkle with oil and toss them about to prevent sticking. Just like pasta!

Cellophane noodles (mung bean threads, glass noodles, *sai fun* [Cantonese]), made from mung bean starch, are translucent and have a smooth, slippery texture, making them perfect for noodle-in-soup dishes. Soak the delicate noodles in hot water or soup until soft and pliable (5 to 10 minutes); never boil them. Snip noodles into shorter lengths for stir-fries and stuffings. They are commonly sold dried in packages with 8 to 10 bundles, each ranging from 1.3 to 2 ounces.

Chinese egg noodles are made with eggs and wheat flour. The noodles come dried or fresh in various shapes and widths (fresh chow mein noodles are one example). Dried "egg" noodles often don't contain any egg, only yellow food coloring, so I prefer fresh noodles. Look for pale yellow strands that are dry, supple, and dusted with cornstarch to prevent sticking. Uncooked noodles keep in the refrigerator for about a week, and in the freezer for 3 months. Don't thaw frozen noodles before cooking or they will turn soggy. Simply boil them for a little longer than directed.

E-fu noodles (yifu noodles, *yi mien* [Cantonese]) are flat egg noodles that have a springy, spongy texture thanks to the carbonated water used in making the dough. The noodles are usually available formed into 8-inch round patties and dried. Cook briefly in boiling water, then drain and use as directed in the recipe. Fresh Shanghai noodles or even linguine can be substituted.

Pancit canton, the Filipino adaptation of Chinese noodles, are dried yellow strands that are used to make FILIPINO FRIED NOODLES (page 233). They come in rectangular blocks and are made with wheat flour, coconut oil, and yellow food coloring. Substitute e-fu noodles as needed.

Rice noodles made from rice flour and water are extremely popular across all Asian cuisines. The myriad shapes and sizes are used in soups, stir-fries, and braised dishes.

Dried rice sticks or noodles can be roughly classified as small (⅛ inch or less in width, such as *banh pho*), medium (¼ inch, such as *chantaboon* or pad Thai noodles), and large (½ inch). Before use, soak rice sticks in warm water until soft but still somewhat firm. This will take anywhere from 3 minutes to 30 minutes. It is better to undersoak than oversoak them. Flush with cold running water and drain. Then stir-fry, or dunk in boiling water briefly before pouring soup over them.

Fresh wide rice noodles (rice ribbon noodles, *sen yai* [Thai], *sha ho fun* [Cantonese], *kway teow* [Fujian]) come already cut in ¾-inch strands. Or purchase the fresh rice sheets that can be cut to the desired width. Rinse under cold running water before adding to stir-fries or soups. Purchase fresh noodles only if they are soft and springy at room temperature, and try to use them the same day. If refrigerated, they will harden and break apart easily.

Rice vermicelli (fine rice noodles, *maifun* [Cantonese], *sen mee* [Thai], *pancit bihon* [Tagalog]) looks very much like bean threads when dry but has a starchier texture and becomes opaque when cooked. They are sometimes called

1. Asian mustard cabbage
2. Mustard greens
3. Ginger
4. Galangal
5. Culantro
6. Pandan leaf
7. Mizuna
8. Holland chili and Korean green chili
9. Thai chilies
10. Kaffir lime leaves
11. Thai basil
12. Salam leaf
13. Pea shoots
14. Lemongrass

1. Small round rice noodles (*bun*)
2. Small dried rice sticks (*banh pho*)
3. Medium dried rice sticks (*banh pho*)
4. Large dried rice sticks (*banh pho*)
5. Fresh wide rice noodles
6. Fresh rice sheets
7. Dried pancit Canton (Filipino-style Chinese egg noodles)

8. Somen
9. Rice vermicelli
10. Fresh thin Chinese egg noodles
11. Lumpia wrappers
12. Korean sweet potato noodles
13. Cellophane noodles
14. Jasmine long-grain rice
15. Japanese short-grain rice

16. Shiu mai dumpling skins
17. Chinese spring roll wrappers
18. Brown basmati long-grain rice
19. Black and white glutinous rice
20. Wonton dumpling skins

rice sticks. Before using, soak the dried noodles in warm water until they're soft (about 10 to 15 minutes), then cook briefly. The large rectangular blocks often come in 17.5-ounce packages.

Round rice noodles (*bun* [Vietnamese], *pancit palabok* [Tagalog]) come in various sizes ranging from small to extra-large. The small noodles bear a very close resemblance to rice vermicelli; place the two side by side and you'll be able to tell that rice vermicelli is skinnier. They are sold dried as wiry flat skeins or straight sticks in clear plastic packages.

Somen are delicate Japanese wheat noodles that are sold in small distinctive bundles tied together with colored tape or string. These very skinny strands (about ¹⁄₁₆-inch) are usually served cold and come in a variety of colors. Green somen is made with green tea powder, bright yellow somen with egg yolk, and pink somen gets its tint from red shiso oil. Boil briefly or the soggy strands will clump together.

Oils, Vegetable

With their neutral flavor and high smoke points, vegetable oils (canola, corn, peanut, safflower, soybean, sunflower) are the best choices for Asian cooking. However, more than one grandmother has recommended mild olive oil for stir-fries. Don't use extra-virgin olive oil though, its fruity taste is too pronounced for Asian cooking. I usually opt for canola oil because it's versatile and low in saturated fat, but feel free to use your choice of oil. Note that different oils add slightly different flavors to your dishes, so it's best to experiment with a variety of oils for different purposes. These are the two most popular in Asian cooking:

Canola oil has become popular among health-conscious Asians in recent years. It is low in saturated fats and contains omega-3 fatty acids. It's also neutral in taste and ideal for wok or high-heat cooking.

Peanut oil has been a long-time favorite as an all-purpose cooking oil because of its clean taste and high smoke point (it can reach around 500 degrees F before smoking or burning). Cold-pressed peanut oil is of high quality (akin to extra-virgin olive oil) with a pleasant but not overwhelming peanutty aroma.

Oyster Sauce

Made from oysters, water, and salt, this is one condiment a Chinese kitchen cannot do without. It serves well as a multipurpose seasoning for everything from meat or vegetables to noodle dishes. Chinese cooks recommend Amoy, Lee Kum Kee, and Hop Sing Lung high-quality brands, which usually come in glass bottles. I like Mae Krua, a Thai brand with no MSG. Once opened, oyster sauce will keep indefinitely when refrigerated.

Palm Sugar

Used in sweet and savory dishes alike, palm sugar is an effective neutralizer of salty soy and fish sauces and spicy chilies. You will find two distinct types of palm sugar. Dark reddish-brown Indonesian (*gula jawa, gula merah*) or Malaysian (*gula melaka*) palm sugar is made from the sap of the fruit of the sugar palm. Complex and smoky, its flavor is similar to, but far surpasses, dark brown sugar. It is sold in a distinctive package with two 8-ounce cylinders. It is almost impossible to cut into a block of gula jawa straight out of its package. First remove the packaging and soften it in the microwave on medium for 15 to 20 seconds. Use a chef's knife to shave off pieces and then finely chop. Less complex in flavor, Thai palm sugar is light tan in color and comes in 2-inch disks that are rounded on one side and flat on the other. While brown sugar may be used as a substitute in a pinch, it does not carry the same flavor complexity as palm sugar. Store palm sugar in an airtight container or wrapped tightly in plastic in a cool, dry place to avoid a sticky mess.

Pandan Leaves (Pandanus Leaves, Screwpine Leaves)

Often called the vanilla of Southeast Asia, pandan leaves are long, grass-like blades measuring 1 to 3 inches across at their widest and up to 2 feet long. They have a sweet, floral aroma and a slightly grassy taste that's reminiscent of coconut. The fragrant leaves are used to flavor sweets as well as savory curries and rice. Scrape each leaf with the tines of a fork to release its fragrance and then tie into a knot (so the fibers don't come loose) before throwing into a pot. Fresh or frozen leaves are found in Asian markets and keep well in the refrigerator for 2 to 3 weeks, or in the freezer for months. Pandan extract with its bright green color (food coloring!!) and artificial fragrance is no substitute for fresh or frozen leaves.

Peppercorns, Sichuan

Though they resemble black peppercorns, Sichuan peppercorns are actually berries and not related. They have a spicy, slightly woodsy flavor and leave a numbing sensation on the tongue. They are usually toasted in a skillet and then crushed before use. The dried pink berries are sold in plastic bags, and while they lose flavor over time, keeping them in an airtight jar in a cool place helps preserve their flavor.

Red Pepper Paste, Korean (*Koch'ujang, Gochu-jang*)

Korean red pepper paste is made from fermented soybean powder, glutinous rice, red chili peppers, and malt. Read labels and buy a brand that does not contain any artificial coloring, cornstarch, vinegar, MSG, or other additives. Store in the refrigerator after opening; it will stay fresh indefinitely.

Red Pepper Powder and Flakes, Korean (*Koch'u Karu, Gochu-garu*)

Made from hot Korean red chili peppers, this powder is a brilliant, flaming red with a pungent sweet smell. In some stores you can find three grades of the powder. Fine ground powder is used for cooking and making Korean red pepper paste, coarse ground for making kimchi, and crushed flakes for cooking and as a garnish. Store in a tightly covered jar or plastic bag in the refrigerator where it will stay fresh for several months. Once it loses its pungency, discard.

Rice

The number of different types of rice you can find in an Asian market is mind-boggling. Most rice, whether long-grain or short-grain, comes in both white and brown varieties. Brown rice is unmilled or partially milled rice with a chewy texture and mild, nutty flavor. For the most part, white and brown rice can be used interchangeably (just vary the time and amount of water when cooking) but do not substitute regular rice for glutinous rice, or vice versa! There are no hard and fast rules as to what type of rice goes with certain dishes, but Chinese and Southeast Asian dishes tend to use jasmine long-grain rice (and sometimes glutinous long-grain rice), Japanese short-grain rice goes with Japanese and Korean dishes, and basmati rice is reserved for South Asian meals. At the Asian market, rice usually comes in 5-pound bags or larger. Don't worry if you're not an avid rice eater. Rice can be stored for several months in a cool dry cupboard in its original bag, or preferably in an airtight container. Note that 1 cup raw rice yields about 3 cups cooked rice.

Jasmine long-grain rice is named for its mild floral aroma (which has nothing to do with the flower) and cooks up light and fluffy. *Hom mali* is a strongly scented hybrid developed in Thailand that is widely available in Asian markets in the United States. Jasmine rice is my preferred long-grain rice, but you may favor another variety. Golden Phoenix and Royal Umbrella are recommended brands.

Basmati long-grain rice has a slightly longer grain than jasmine rice and is especially popular in South Asian cooking. Extremely aromatic and fluffy, it tastes great in biryanis and pairs perfectly with curries.

Japanese short-grain rice (sushi rice, sweet rice) has a gummier, stickier texture in comparison to long-grain rice, which is why short-grain rice is sometimes called sticky rice. But don't confuse it with glutinous rice (below) even though they both have a similar shape and color when uncooked. (Note that Japanese glutinous short-grain rice is called *mochigome*.) Cook short-grain rice the same way you would long-grain, but with slightly more water. There are some good brands from California, such as Kokuho Rose and Kagayaki.

Traditional Japanese cooking relies heavily on quality ingredients and water is a very important factor, especially when cooking rice. Hiroko Sugiyama, a Japanese culinary instructor, uses pure spring water to make rice (as well as tea and soups), as she believes any off odors or tastes in tap water will be transferred to the final dish. She follows this credo not just for special occasions but for everyday consumption. Several times a month, she makes the 30-mile trek to a wellspring that's certified pure by the city, bringing home ten 2-gallon containers. Although Hiroko swears by her spring water, she acknowledges that sometimes you just have to compromise and use the best you can find, such as filtered tap water.

Glutinous rice (sticky rice, *naw mai* [Cantonese], *malagkit* [Tagalog]), when raw, is fat and opaque compared to regular long-grain rice, which is skinny and translucent. Once cooked, white glutinous rice turns translucent and clumps together, while regular long-grain rice separates. Black glutinous rice has a sweet, nutty taste; cooking turns the raw brown-black rice grains into a deep purple. Before cooking glutinous rice (steaming is the ideal method), rinse the raw rice well and soak it overnight. Glutinous rice's mildly sweet flavor is excellent in desserts and snacks.

Rice Flour (Rice Powder)

Rice flour, ground from regular long-grain rice, is used to make rice noodles as well as savory cakes like turnip cake and taro cake. Be careful not to confuse regular rice flour with glutinous rice flour. They are not interchangeable. Glutinous rice flour looks much like cornstarch and is used to make savory and sweet cakes, dumplings, and many Asian desserts. *Mochiko* is the Japanese version of glutinous rice flour. Store in a cool, dark place and a bag of rice flour should keep for up to a year.

Rock Sugar, Yellow (Rock Candy)

Golden chunks of yellow rock sugar are made from a combination of crystallized white sugar, brown sugar, and honey. It is used to flavor both sweet and savory dishes, leaving a translucent sheen to them. It usually comes in 1-pound plastic packets or boxes and can be store indefinitely in a cool, dry place. Break rock sugar into smaller chunks with a meat pounder or a heavy glass before using.

Sake

An alcoholic beverage made by fermenting cooked ground rice, sake has a clean, dry flavor somewhere between vodka and dry sherry. Sake comes in many grades. Drinking sake tends to be more refined and clear while pale amber sake is used for cooking. Sake and mirin are sometimes used interchangeably in cooking but keep in mind that mirin is sweet so adjust seasonings accordingly.

Salam Leaves (*Daun Salam* [Indonesian], Indian Bay Leaves)

A member of the cassia family, the salam tree is native to Indonesia and Malaysia. Its leaves, used fresh in Asia, have a spicy, woodsy scent. Fresh leaves are not available in the United States, but the dried leaves are sold in Asian markets in cellophane bags usually labeled "Daun Salam—Indian Bay Leaves." Measuring 3 to 4 inches, the brittle leaves are a dusty green. Despite the English name, bay leaves are not a substitute.

Sausage, Chinese (*Lap Cheong, Lop Cheung*)

Made from pork, pork fat, sugar, and spices, wrinkled Chinese sausages look like skinny salami but taste sweet and slightly smoky. The long skinny sausages are sold connected by a thick cord in vacuum-packed packages. If kept in the fridge, Chinese sausage can last a few weeks. Freezing will preserve them for months. They are very hard and can be difficult to cut unless steamed briefly.

 STEAMING CHINESE SAUSAGE

Steaming Chinese sausage makes it easier to cut and removes excess fat as well. You can use a stovetop steamer, but it's easier to use the microwave. Place sausages on a rimmed plate and add enough water to reach about half way up the sides of the sausages. Microwave on medium-high for 1 minute then drain the fat and water.

Seaweed

Seaweed is eaten in many coastal communities and is an integral part of Japanese and Korean cooking. Enjoyed for both its delicate flavor and healthful properties, seaweed is widely available farmed or foraged from the wild. The following types are used in this book:

Kombu (*konbu*, sea cabbage, kelp) is a very dark forest green—almost black—seaweed with a sweet, ocean-fresh scent. It is sold dried in ⅛-inch-thick pliable sheets. Kombu is used to make DASHI (page 40), a key ingredient in miso soup.

Choose sheets that are very dark. Before using, wipe them to remove any grit but don't rub off the white residue as it is safe and actually incredibly flavorful. Stored in a cool, dark place, kombu keeps indefinitely.

Nori (dried laver seaweed) is most familiar as the wrapper for sushi rolls. It comes in crisp, thin sheets precut for this purpose and ranges in color from dark green to deep purple. It is not only used to wrap sushi, but also as a condiment or garnish for tempura batter and soups. Keep nori in a cool, dark place and wrapped in plastic.

Sesame Oil

Thick, amber-colored sesame oil is pressed from toasted or roasted sesame seeds. The darker the color, the stronger the fragrance and flavor. Unlike other oils, sesame oil is rarely used for cooking (although Japanese and Korean cooks sometimes mix it with lighter tasting oils). Instead, it is used sparingly as a seasoning because its rich aroma and flavor can overpower other ingredients. Use it in marinades, sauces, dressings, stir-fries, or as a finishing drizzle for steamed vegetables and soups.

Sesame Seeds

Tiny white, cream, or black sesame seeds are often toasted to bring out their nutty flavor. They're available already toasted but you can easily do it at home.

 TOASTING SESAME SEEDS

In a small dry cast-iron (best) or heavy skillet, toast a few tablespoons of sesame seeds at a time over medium heat, shaking the pan or stirring often to ensure they brown evenly. Once the seeds start popping and turn golden brown and fragrant, 2 to 3 minutes, they're ready.

Shallots, Asian

Measuring just 1½ inches long and 1 inch wide, and weighing ½ to ¾ ounce each, Asian shallots are babies compared to their larger European counterparts. They grow in oval clusters of 2 or 3 bulbs attached to a single root. Scrape off the papery copper skin to reveal purplish-pink layers of flesh. In contrast to European shallots, they are milder and sweeter. However, both will work fine in the recipes in this book. Just be sure to use the correct measured amounts.

Shallots, Fried

Fried shallots, generously sprinkled over everything from soups to stir-fries, add a wonderful crunch and flavor to savory dishes. You can buy them in plastic containers at Asian markets but they're easy to fry at home.

FRYING SHALLOTS

Cut 8 shallots (about 6 ounces) lengthwise into paper-thin slices. Pour oil to a depth of about 1 inch into a medium heavy skillet or saucepan. Heat over medium-high heat until very hot but not smoking (about 350 degrees F). Tip in as many shallot slivers as will fit comfortably in the skillet (small batches are easier to monitor). The oil will foam and froth because of the moisture, but the bubbles should die down as they cook. Using a slotted spoon or wire mesh strainer, stir continuously to ensure the shallots brown evenly—but don't burn! They will soften and wilt before turning light golden and crispy, 2 to 3 minutes. The timing depends on how hot the oil is and how thin the slices are. If the shallots start to burn, adjust the heat accordingly. Once they are uniformly brown, remove immediately (if they overcook, they will turn dark brown and taste bitter) and drain on paper towels. The limp shreds will eventually crisp up. Store in an airtight container for up to one week in a cool, dry place.

Shaoxing Rice Wine (Shao-hsing Rice Wine)

This aromatic wine made by fermenting glutinous rice is the standard Chinese cooking spirit, finding its way into most stir-fried and braised dishes. Don't confuse it with Chinese rice wine vinegar, and avoid Shaoxing cooking wine or Shaoxing cooking sherry which are heavily salted. Only pale, dry sherry is a suitable substitute, never sake or white wine. The Pagoda brand is recommended.

Shrimp, Dried (*Ha Mai* [Cantonese], *Hae Bee* [Fujian], *Goong Haeng* [Thai])

Whole dried shrimp adds its distinctive, fishy scent and flavor to many Asian dishes and should be used sparingly. The salted, sun-dried baby shrimp are ½ to 1 inch in size. Choose dried shrimp that are orangey-pink and soak them for about 10 minutes to soften, unless the recipe calls for ground shrimp. Regardless, always rinse them thoroughly under cold running water to clean them. Find dried shrimp in

8-ounce plastic packages, imported mostly from Thailand and China. Ground dried shrimp can also be found in little jars. Store in a covered container in a cool, dark place. If keeping for over a month, refrigerate them.

Shrimp Paste, Black (*Petis* [Indonesian], *Hae Ko* [Fujian])

Made from shrimp, salt, sugar, and water, black shrimp paste is used as a condiment as well as a sauce when diluted with water. Be careful not to confuse petis with *patis*, which is Filipino fish sauce. Store indefinitely in the refrigerator.

Shrimp Paste, Dried (*Belacan* [Malay], *Trassi* or *Terasi* [Indonesian])

Dried shrimp paste comes in various forms and ranges from pinkish- to dark reddish-brown. The dried shrimp paste used in this book is the Indonesian or Malay variety. Tiny shrimp are first fermented with salt before being ground into a smooth paste, then shaped into small bricks or cylinders and sundried. It is never eaten raw and only in small quantities, usually shaved into thin slices and mixed with other spices to make sauces and seasoning pastes. Once cooked, its pungent, fishy smell transforms into a delicate aroma and flavor that adds an unmistakable nuance to many Southeast Asian dishes. Dried shrimp paste is sold in rectangular blocks (ranging from 8 to 20 ounces) wrapped in paper or plastic and labeled "belacan" or "trassi" (or some variation). After opening, wrap tightly in plastic and/or store in an airtight container to prevent its smell permeating other food; refrigerate for up to 6 months. Substitute Thai shrimp paste (*gapi*), which is softer and moister and a little less pungent.

Soy Sauce

Soy sauce may be a Chinese invention but it has been used for generations throughout Asia. Made from fermented roasted soybeans and ground wheat, there are many different varieties manufactured in different countries. Keep in mind that not all soy sauces are the same. I suggest trying them for yourself to see which you prefer. In this book, I use the following:

Thai black soy sauce has a slightly sweet flavor characteristic of the darker sauces. It is sometimes labeled "soy superior sauce."

Citrus soy sauce (*toyomansi*) is a distinctive Filipino product: regular soy sauce flavored with kalamansi (see page 9). It is used in marinades and FILIPINO FRIED NOODLES (page 233). To substitute, use one part Japanese soy sauce and 1 part kalamansi, Meyer lemon, or key lime juice.

Dark soy sauce, aged longer than regular soy sauce, is rich and robust with a touch of sweetness. Molasses is added at the end of the process, giving the sauce a rich, black-brown color and caramelly flavor. It's often added to braises to tint the gravy and meat a beautiful chocolate-brown.

Indonesian sweet soy sauce (*kecap manis*) has the addition of palm sugar so it is a thick, syrupy elixir reminiscent of smoke and honey. It is used in marinades, stir-fries, and stews, as well as a dipping sauce at the table. Cap Bango is my favorite brand, but ABC is cheaper and more widely available.

MAKING SWEET SOY SAUCE

Mix 1 tablespoon water, 1 tablespoon regular soy sauce and 3 tablespoons brown sugar together in a small bowl. Microwave on medium for 20 to 30 seconds. Stir to mix. The flavor is similar but the consistency will be thinner than store-bought. Makes ¼ cup.

Japanese soy sauce (*shoyu*) tends to be sweeter and less salty than Chinese soy sauce because it contains more wheat and less soybeans. It is used as a condiment and a dipping sauce. Tamari, a naturally-fermented thick, dark, and sweet Japanese soy sauce is usually wheat free. But check labels to be sure. In Japanese recipes, I use Japanese soy sauce exclusively. Kikkoman is a good brand and available even in mainstream supermarkets.

Regular soy sauce is sometimes called light soy sauce or thin soy sauce; but don't confuse it with "lite" soy sauce, which usually means reduced-sodium. It is used as a seasoning to flavor stir-fries and braised dishes as well as soups. I primarily use Chinese soy sauce for cooking (except for Japanese recipes) but the Thais, Filipinos, and Malaysians all have their own versions. Pearl River Bridge or Lee Kum Kee make good soy sauces across the board.

Star Anise

Star anise is an eight-pointed star-shaped pod that imbues braises and soups with an intense licorice flavor and fragrance. It is usually removed before serving. The hard and reddish-brown pods are packaged in plastic and sometimes mislabeled star aniseed. They should be stored in an airtight jar away from light and heat.

Tamarind

Tamarind is a popular souring agent in Southeast and South Asian cooking. With a mellow sweet-tart tang, its flavors are more complex than lime or lemon. It is used in curries, pickles, and spicy soups and is also popular in drinks and desserts. Whole tamarind pods are becoming more common, but I prefer using "wet tamarind." Sold in plastic packages, the sticky coffee-colored pulp is removed from the pods, seeds and all, and compressed into semi-pliable rectangular blocks. The pulp must be soaked in hot water to form a paste before using. Tamarind concentrate—processed pulp in a jar or tub—is convenient, but the flavor cannot compare! In a cool, dry place, tamarind pods and pulp will last almost forever.

 PREPARING TAMARIND PASTE

Use ½ cup of hot water for every 3 tablespoons of tamarind pulp and soak for 5 to 10 minutes. When cool enough to handle, rub the pulp with your fingers until the seeds are free of pulp and fiber. Grab the seeds and fiber, squeeze out any liquid, and discard. Push the pulp through a sieve with a wooden spatula to yield about 6 tablespoons of glossy brown paste. Discard the seeds and fibers. Leftover prepared paste can be refrigerated for up to 1 week.

Tapioca Starch (Tapioca Flour)

Made from the tuber tapioca (also called cassava, manioc, and yucca), tapioca starch is similar in appearance to cornstarch; both can be used to thicken sauces and in marinades. In fact, many Southeast Asian cooks prefer using tapioca starch to cornstarch as tapioca starch thickens at a lower temperature. Be sure to work fast as it tends to thicken liquids fairly quickly.

Tofu (Bean Curd, *Dofu*, *Dauhu*)

Tofu is a high-protein, low-fat wonder that is made by coagulating fresh soy milk with a calcium compound until it curdles. The curds are then pressed together to form cakes. Tofu comes in a number of varieties ranging from silky soft and fragile to firm and dense. What type you use depends on the cooking method, and sometimes your taste.

Silken tofu is almost custardy and the most delicate of tofus. As such, it is only suitable for soups, braises, and desserts. Don't try to deep-fry silken tofu because it can react dangerously with hot oil.

Firm and extra-firm tofu can be sliced, diced, and cubed and is sturdy enough for stir-fries and deep-frying. Extra-firm is drier and less silky than firm. The Japanese have *momen* ("cotton") tofu, a dense textured tofu that stays together well for stir-fries and stews.

House, Sunrise, and Sun Luck are good tofu brands available in many markets, both specialty and mainstream, but seek out fresh locally made tofu at Asian markets. Tofu usually comes in 12- to 16-ounce packages with a single large block, or two smaller blocks, sitting in a water-filled plastic tub (the water keeps the tofu moist). If the tofu is locally made, it is sometimes sold in open containers or buckets. Tofu is extremely perishable; any unused portions should be transferred to a bowl filled with water, wrapped in plastic wrap, and refrigerated immediately. If stored for more than a day (but not more than 3 days), change the water regularly. Once the tofu turns yellowish and/or the water looks cloudy or smells sour, it's time to throw it out.

DRAINING TOFU

Draining tofu or excess moisture before using is important especially when deep-frying. Cover a cutting board or rimmed plate with 2 layers of paper towels or non-terry kitchen towels. Place the tofu on top and cover with 2 more layers of towels. Carefully place a heavy weight, such as a book or bowl, on the tofu. Drain for 15 minutes, changing the towels as required.

Fried tofu or **tofu puffs** are golden triangles, rectangles, or cubes of tofu that have been deep-fried. They are added to braises and happily soak up the flavors of the sauce they're cooked in. They're sold in plastic packages or Styrofoam trays of 12 to 18 pieces.

Turmeric

Turmeric gives curries a gorgeous golden color and imbues a peppery, musky flavor. The fresh rhizome has a rich orange tint and gingery taste that is lacking in the ground powdered form. For convenience, the recipes in this book call for only the ground powdered version. Look for turmeric powder that is a pure deep yellow or gold. Store in an airtight container and refrigerate for up to a year.

Watercress

Peppery watercress is used both in Western and Asian cooking, but while it is mostly eaten raw in the West, it is often cooked in Asia (used in soups, stir-fried, or blanched). Watercress is highly perishable so be sure to buy it fresh when you need it. Refrigerate watercress with the stems submerged in water and the leaves covered with a plastic bag for no more than 2 days.

Wrappers

Made with any combination of wheat flour, water, and oil, these paper-thin wrappers are very versatile. (See also dumpling skins on page 7.) Two different kinds are used in this book.

Lumpia wrappers, sometimes called Shanghai-style wrappers, are used to prepare LUMPIA (page 61) and BROWN SUGAR BANANA SPRING ROLLS (page 324). The Simex brand has nine ½-inch-round wrappers packaged in flat boxes sold in the frozen section. Lumpia wrappers can be eaten fresh or fried. Chinese spring roll wrappers (below) are the best replacement but thicker egg roll wrappers will work. Do not use Vietnamese rice paper (used to make fresh Vietnamese spring rolls).

Chinese spring roll wrappers are thin, beige, 4- to 8-inch squares used for most other versions of fried spring rolls. Though commonly sold frozen, they are sometimes available freshly made in the refrigerated sections; these don't keep longer than 2 to 3 days. Choose paper-thin, translucent wrappers.

Store all of the above in the refrigerator or freezer, but let them come to room temperature before using. While assembling, cover the stack of wrappers with a damp cloth to keep them moist. The wrappers are very delicate and are prone to tearing. If possible, buy the ones that are already separated, and always buy extra!

2

FOUNDATIONS: STAPLES AND STOCKS

Rice, the staple of most Asian cuisines, provides a canvas to appreciate the various courses that are eaten at a meal, absorbing flavors and offering contrasts in texture. It also acts as a filler. I have heard from more than one grandmother that they don't feel full if they don't eat rice. In fact, it is such an indispensable part of the Asian diet that the first Japanese immigrants to Hawaii built terraces in an attempt to grow rice, but to no avail.

How to cook rice is the first lesson a novice cook learns in the kitchen. While most Asian homes have rice cookers (even grandmothers prefer this convenience), pillow-soft and fluffy rice is easy to make in a pot. Take note that different rice varieties have divergent properties. A quick walk through the rice aisle of an Asian market reveals a mind-spinning array of varieties: jasmine, basmati, Japanese, glutinous, black, and more. (See page 18 for descriptions of the different varieties.) I prefer to pair fragrant jasmine rice with Southeast Asian recipes and Japanese short-grain rice for Japanese and Korean recipes. But the choice is yours. Most varieties can be cooked in a pot on the stove but glutinous rice is most often steamed.

In this chapter, you'll also find recipes for stocks, which form the base for many delicious soups and can be added to stir-fries as well.

1. Regular soy sauce
2. Japanese soy sauce
3. Fish sauce
4. Oyster sauce
5. Sambal oelek

6. Thai black soy sauce
7. Citrus soy sauce
8. Dark soy sauce
9. Indonesian sweet soy sauce

Staples
Garlic Fried Rice (*Sinangag*)
Japanese Rice Cooked in a Clay Pot (*Gohan*)
Purple-Dyed Glutinous Rice
Stove-Top Jasmine Rice
White Glutinous Rice

Soup Stocks
Dashi (Japanese Kelp and Fish Stock)
Homemade Chicken Stock
Korean Beef Stock (*Komt'ang*)

❧ Staples ☙

Garlic Fried Rice (*Sinangag*)

Like SPECIAL INDONESIAN FRIED RICE (page 279), this dish is best made with refrigerated leftover rice. The cold rice is firm and won't turn mushy when fried in oil. Serve hot with CHICKEN ADOBO (page 182).

Time: 15 minutes
Makes: 4 servings

> 4 cups cooked long-grain white rice
> ¼ cup vegetable oil
> 6 cloves garlic, minced (2 tablespoons)
> 1 teaspoon salt

❧ With wet fingers, break up any large clumps of rice and separate the grains. In a large wok or skillet, heat the oil over medium heat until it becomes runny and starts to shimmer. Add the garlic and cook until golden brown and fragrant, 30 to 45 seconds. Adjust the heat as necessary to prevent the garlic from burning.

❧ Tip in the rice and sprinkle with the salt. Slide a spatula along the bottom of the wok and toss the rice up and over to coat the grains evenly with oil and garlic. Use the spatula to break up any clumps. Cook, stirring constantly to prevent the rice from sticking to the wok, until the rice is heated through and the grains are shiny with oil but not mushy, 8 to 10 minutes.

Japanese Rice Cooked in a Clay Pot (*Gohan*)

Whenever Hiroko Sugiyama, a Japanese culinary instructor living in Seattle, Washington, craves rice with a slightly burned bottom (*okoge*), she uses a Japanese clay pot called *donabe*. This basic recipe is so easy. Unfortunately, once the rice cooker was introduced, most Japanese no longer cooked rice in this traditional manner. If you don't have a donabe, cook the rice in a rice cooker using the same proportions. But do not use this method to cook rice in a regular pot on the stove.

Time: 20 minutes (10 minutes active) plus draining
Makes: 4 to 6 servings

> 2¼ cups Japanese short-grain rice
> Scant 2⅔ cups spring or filtered water (see page 19)

❧ In a large bowl, wash the rice in 3 or 4 changes of water until the water almost runs clear (see page 37). Drain in a colander for 1 hour.

❧ Combine the rice and water in a Japanese clay pot (donabe) and cover tightly with the lid. Set the pot over high heat. As soon as you see steam escaping from the hole in the lid, set a timer for 3 minutes (don't reduce the heat). When the time is up, remove the pot from the heat. Let the rice stand for 5 to 10 minutes. Lift the lid carefully. Stir the rice gently with a Japanese rice paddle (*shamoji*) and transfer it to a wooden rice container (*ohitsu*) if you have one, or lay a cotton cloth (*fukin*) over the rice and cover with the lid.

Pat's Notes: Hiroko prefers the Tamaki brand of *haigamai* (partially milled, short-grain white rice): the brown bran has been removed but the nutrient-laden germ (*haiga*) is left intact. Haigamai maintains many of the vitamins, minerals, and dietary fiber present in brown rice, but it tastes and cooks just like white rice.

If you have a 180-cc Japanese rice cup, use 3 cups rice and 2¾ cups of water.

Purple-Dyed Glutinous Rice

Black glutinous rice is sometime called purple glutinous rice. But this rice from Yi Thao, a young Hmong mother of four children between the ages of fifteen and twenty-four, is actually white glutinous rice dyed a purple hue. In this typical Lao method, the purple dye doesn't really add much except a lovely color. As Yi says, it is "for color and to make pretty." Yi tosses the black rice because she doesn't like its texture and taste but you can save it for BLACK GLUTINOUS RICE PORRIDGE (page 317).

Time: 45 minutes (25 minutes active) plus soaking
Makes: 4 to 6 servings

> 1 cup black glutinous rice (see page 19)
> Water
> 2 cups white glutinous rice (see page 19)

❧ In a large saucepan, bring the black glutinous rice and 6 cups water to a boil over high heat. Reduce the heat to medium and simmer until the water turns an inky dark purple, 10 minutes.

❧ Pour the mixture through a sieve, straining the black rice and collecting the colored water in a large bowl. Reserve the black rice for another use or discard.

❧ Soak the white glutinous rice in the colored water for at least 1 hour, preferably 4 hours. The white rice grains will absorb the purple color. Drain and follow instructions for steaming WHITE GLUTINOUS RICE (page 38).

Pat's Notes: Do not presoak the white glutinous rice or it will not absorb the purple "dye."

Stove-Top Jasmine Rice

Cooking rice in a pot can be tricky, as the ratio of rice to water varies depending on how old the rice is. The older the rice, the drier it is, and the more water you'll need for it to come out tender. As a general rule, new-crop rice uses a one-to-one ratio, but older rice needs 1 cup rice to 1¼ cups water. New crop rice is usually labeled as such on the bag. Regardless, always pay attention to the rice-to-water ratio the first time you make rice from a new bag, even if it is your favorite brand that you've been buying for decades. If the rice is too dry, add more water, a few tablespoons at a time, and continue cooking. If it's too soggy, decrease the water gradually the next few times you cook. You may have to make a few mediocre pots before you get perfect rice, but it will be worth it! Look for Thai or North American jasmine rice—they are of the highest quality.

Time: 40 minutes (10 minutes active)
Makes: 2 servings

> 1 cup jasmine long-grain rice
> 1¼ cups water

❧ In a medium heavy-bottomed saucepan with a tight-fitting lid (preferably glass so you can observe the changes), wash the rice in at 2 to 3 changes of water, until the water almost runs clear (see page 37). Drain.

❧ Pour in the water, swirling the rice with your hands, and let the grains settle evenly at the bottom of the saucepan. Set the saucepan over high heat and bring the water to a simmer. Bubbles will gather around the edge of the saucepan. Reduce the heat to the lowest possible setting and cover the saucepan tightly with the lid. Cook for 15 to 18 minutes, or until all the water is absorbed.

❧ Turn off the heat and let the rice steam, lid intact, for another 10 minutes. Lift the lid and gently fluff the rice with a fork or a pair of chopsticks. The rice should not be lumpy and the individual kernels should be separate. Keep the rice covered until ready to serve. Serve hot.

Variation: To cook Japanese short-grain rice, follow these directions, but use 1½ cups rice and 2 cups water. Allow the rice to stand in the water for at least 30 minutes before cooking on the stove.

RICE: TO WASH OR NOT TO WASH?

The act of washing uncooked rice is a tradition dating back to when it was essential to remove bits of debris, rice hulls, and, yes, bugs. Back then, rice was also coated with talc and washing removed most traces of the powder. Today, the U.S. Food and Drug Administration mandates that all milled white rice be fortified with an enrichment coating (i.e., vitamins and minerals)—that's what causes the water to turn white and cloudy when you wash your rice. Some believe that washing breaks down the starchy surface, producing shiny, pearly grains of rice that are the fluffiest and tastiest when cooked. In the end, it's all about personal preference. I wash my rice out of habit more than anything else but if you are concerned about washing away the nutrients, you don't have to do it.

To wash rice, measure it into your cooking container, be it a saucepan or a rice cooker bowl. Fill halfway with cold water. Using your fingers, swish and slosh the rice grains until the water becomes a cloudy white. Tilt the container over the sink to drain the water out, cupping your free hand along the container's edge to prevent rice from falling out. Repeat two or three times until the water comes out mostly clear. It's okay if it's still a little cloudy. Drain the water completely and cook according to recipe instructions.

White Glutinous Rice

In Cambodia, Laos, and northern Thailand, glutinous rice—instead of jasmine rice—is the staple food. When steamed properly, the rice grains have a firm, chewy texture and stick together in a clump, but not to your hands. Glutinous rice is best eaten with your hands and isn't messy at all when done correctly. Pull off a bite-sized chunk and roll the rice with your fingers and palm of your right hand to form a football-shaped clump. Then dip the ball in sauce and/or pick up a small chunk of meat or vegetable and stuff everything in your mouth!

Time: 30 minutes (10 minutes active) plus soaking
Makes: 4 to 6 servings

> 2 cups white glutinous rice (see page 19)

❧ Wash the rice once (see page 37). Put in a large bowl and add enough water to cover by 2 inches. Soak for at least 4 hours, preferably 12 hours. (Like beans, the longer the rice soaks, the less time it takes to cook). The rice grains will absorb the water, expand, and be soft enough to break into pieces when pressed between the fingers.

❧ Set up a steamer (see page xv for other steaming options). Fill the steamer pan half full with water and bring to a rolling boil over high heat. Reduce the heat to medium until you are ready to steam.

❧ Drain the rice and spread the grains evenly on a rimmed platter that will fit inside the steamer without touching the sides. Set the platter of rice in the steamer basket or rack. Return the water in the steamer to a rolling boil. Set the steamer basket or rack on top of the steamer pan. Cover and steam over medium heat until the grains are translucent and soft and chewy to the bite, 20 to 25 minutes.

❧ When done, turn off the heat and wait for the steam to subside before lifting the lid. Lift it away from you to prevent condensation from dripping onto the rice and keep from scalding yourself. Carefully remove the rice from the steamer. Serve warm with Southeast Asian dishes such as LAO SAUSAGE (page 168), THAI BASIL PORK (page 174), or LAO CHICKEN AND HERB SALAD (page 185).

Pat's Notes: Traditionally, cooked sticky rice is spread out on a piece of canvas (usually an old rice bag) to cool so it doesn't clump together.

To cook larger quantities, I recommend using a special glutinous rice steaming basket and pot set (it looks like an inverted cone-shaped straw hat balanced on a spittoon-shaped pot), available from Southeast Asian markets. This set-up ensures that the mass of grains cooks evenly. Steam for 30 minutes, flipping the rice halfway when it is soft on top.

Some methods recommend steaming glutinous rice on a piece of cheesecloth lining the steamer rack. I've found that the cloth absorbs much moisture and turns the layer of rice touching it into mush.

Grandma Says: To reheat glutinous rice, wrap the desired amount in a damp paper towel and microwave for 1 minute. Do not reheat the same batch of rice more than twice.

✄ Soup Stocks ✄

Dashi (Japanese Kelp and Fish Stock)

Dashi is the basic stock that provides the underlying flavor to most Japanese dishes. Look for high-glutamate kelp, labeled *Rishiri* or *Makobu kombu* which will greatly enhance the flavor of all dishes you make with the stock.

Dashi can be made from any combination of kelp and/or dried fish flakes. But there are always two grades of the stock: Dashi I (*ichiban dashi*) has a fragrant aroma and a delicate flavor and is used mainly in the clear soups that begin classic Japanese meals; Dashi II (*niban dashi*) is less refined but is used more often for simmering, sauces, and thick soups. Unless Dashi I is specified in a recipe, use either Dashi II or instant dashi (see Pat's Notes).

Time: 45 minutes plus soaking
Makes: 15½ cups Dashi I, plus 7½ cups Dashi II

> 6 quarts plus ¼ cup spring or filtered water, divided
> One 43-gram sheet dried kelp (*kombu*), wiped with a damp cloth
> 8 cups (50 grams) dried bonito flakes (*katsuo bushi*)

✄ In a large stockpot, soak the kelp in 4 quarts of the water for 30 minutes to allow the kelp to gradually infuse the water with its flavor.

✄ To make Dashi I: Place the stockpot over medium-high heat. Watch very carefully and don't let the liquid boil as it will become bitter. After 20 to 25 minutes, bubbles will gather around the edge of the pot (the only way to determine the correct timing is to try this procedure a few times; it all depends on your pot and your stove). Remove the kelp and reserve it for making Dashi II. Add ¼ cup cold water to stop the stock from boiling and immediately add the bonito flakes. Give the stock a gentle swirl, then strain it through a cheesecloth or paper towel into a large container. Reserve the bonito flakes. The stock will be a clear, amber liquid.

✄ To make Dashi II: Return the reserved kelp and bonito flakes back to the same pot. Add 2 quarts of the water and bring to a boil over medium-high heat. Reduce the heat to medium and simmer for 10 minutes. Strain through a cheesecloth into another container. This time, gently squeeze as much liquid as possible from the kelp mixture into the container.

❀ Store Dashi I and Dashi II in separate containers in the refrigerator for about 3 days, or freeze for up to 2 weeks.

Pat's Notes: The best dashi is, of course, homemade. But several authentically flavored instant dashi powders are available. Simply mix with water. Ask for *dashi-no-moto* or *hon-dashi* in Japanese markets and well-stocked supermarkets. Check the list of ingredients before you buy as many brands contain monosodium glutamate (MSG).

Homemade Chicken Stock

Store-bought chicken stock just cannot compare to homemade, and considering how simple it is to prepare, why shouldn't you always have some on hand? Not only is homemade stock an excellent base for soups and stews, it also imparts flavor to stir-fries and other dishes. Chicken backs, necks, and breast bones produce the best stock, but you can save and freeze any chicken parts in any amount until you have enough for a big pot of stock. Some butchers sell the off-cuts as soup pieces as well. There is some confusion between a stock and a broth. Technically, a stock is made with bones, and a broth is made from protein. You can make chicken broth by following this recipe but using meaty chicken parts instead.

Time: 2¼ hours (15 minutes active)
Makes: 14 cups

> 2 pounds chicken bones, carcass, and/or parts, or the same weight in chicken pieces
>
> 1 gallon water
>
> 4 cloves garlic, smashed with the flat part of a cleaver or large knife
>
> 1-inch piece fresh ginger, cut into 4 coins
>
> 2 green onions, white and green parts, each cut into thirds

✻ Rinse the chicken bones in cold running water to remove any traces of blood and reduce the amount of residue in the stock. In a large stockpot, combine the chicken bones and/or parts, the water, garlic, ginger, and green onions and bring to a boil over high heat. Reduce the heat to medium-low and skim off any scum or foam that rises to the surface. Cover and simmer, skimming when necessary, for a minimum of 2 hours and up to 4 hours.

✻ Let the stock cool, then strain and discard all solids. Skim off as much fat as possible. Use the stock immediately, or refrigerate overnight in a sealed container.

✻ The next day, skim the congealed fat off the surface. Return to the refrigerator until needed. Use refrigerated stock within 5 days, or freeze to keep indefinitely.

Pat's Notes: Make a large quantity of stock to freeze for later use—it's a great time saver.

Try pork bones instead of chicken, or a combination of the two (pork and chicken blend well together) which will give the stock a rich depth of flavor.

Korean Beef Stock (*Komt'ang*)

Unlike Chinese cooking, which mainly uses chicken or pork stock as a base, Korean cuisine relies on beef stock for soups and stews, and as a flavor-enhancer in meat dishes and stir-fries. Beef bones are simmered (sometimes for half a day) to produce a mineral-rich stock laden with calcium and phosphorus. Vegetables such as daikon radish can also be added.

Time: 3 hours (10 minutes active)
Makes: 8 to 9 cups

> 1 pound assorted beef knuckles, bones, or brisket
> 10 cups water
> 6 cloves garlic, smashed with the flat part of a cleaver or large knife
> 3 tablespoons soy sauce

- Rinse the bones thoroughly in cold running water to remove all traces of blood and reduce the amount of residue in the stock.

- In a large stockpot, bring the beef bones, water, garlic, and soy sauce to a boil. Reduce the heat to medium-low and simmer for 2 to 3 hours or up to 12 hours. Occasionally skim off any scum or foam that rises to the surface. Strain through a sieve lined with cheesecloth. Scrape off any meat from the bones and use in your recipe if desired.

Pat's Notes: The beef stock will keep in an airtight container in the refrigerator for a few days or in the freezer for a few months.

Profile of a Grandma: KIMIYE HAYASHI

 Petite in stature and crowned with a silver head of shoulder-length curly hair, Kimiye Hayashi exudes grandmotherliness.

With five children, six grandchildren, and three great-grandchildren, she's had lots of practice. Kimiye lives with her daughter and son-in-law Katie and Gary Kiyonaga and their two sons in a large house in the Seattle suburb of Bellevue. When I asked her what she does everyday, she quipped with a smile, "I cook and clean—I have to earn my keep." She's also a grand-mother with a great sense of humor!

This *nisei*, or second generation Japanese, was born in December, 1922, in Pueblo, Colorado, to Japanese parents from Hiroshima. When she was five, her family moved to Southern California where she lived out the next decade in the fishing community of Terminal Island in Los Angeles County.

"It was just like a Japanese village really," Kimiye explains. Many Japanese settled on the island and were employed by Van Camp's and French's canneries. Like most of the men on the island, her dad was a fisherman. Hence fish was a major part of their diet. During the Depression, Kimiye and her family ate simply. Their meals consisted mostly of rice, fish, vegetables, and lots of soy sauce. And while it's hard to imagine, Kimiye says, "You get tired of sashimi if you eat it all the time."

The women all worked in the canneries. Even Kimiye had her turn, working there the summer she was sixteen. "I only worked a couple of weeks, I couldn't stand it." She grimaces, remembering the fish guts and livers she had to remove. "It was the lowliest job."

At eighteen, right out of high school, Kimiye married Shibo Hayashi. But their happy marriage was short-lived once the United States entered World War II the following year. After Pearl Harbor was attacked on December 7, 1941, the FBI rounded up all the adult males on Terminal Island and sent them to detention centers. Shibo and Kimiye, with her four younger brothers and sisters in tow, escaped the island and stayed on an abandoned farm in Torrence, California.

Eventually, Kimiye and her family ended up in the Rohwer War Relocation Center in Arkansas where she gave birth to her oldest daughter. After one year, they were allowed to leave the camp and worked for some Dutch farmers in Imlay City, Michigan. "We were a curiosity to them but they treated us well," says Kimiye.

After the war, the Hayashis found a farm to lease and settled in Michigan. In 1960, they moved to Seattle where Shibo worked on a farm in the suburbs. All this while, Kimiye was a stay-at-home mom, looking after their five children and cooking both American-style foods—spaghetti with meatballs, fried chicken, and hamburgers—and Japanese dishes palatable to her kids like teriyaki and JAPANESE BEEF AND VEGETABLE HOT POT (page 271). Although Kimiye took home economics in high school, she doesn't credit her cooking skills to those lessons. Cookies and roast chicken do not a skilled home cook make.

Instead Kimiye scoured Japanese cookbooks, especially the ones published by different churches, and "just picked it up," she says modestly. "You want to eat something you want, you just learn how to do it."

She does miss sashimi though. "I wasn't that crazy about sashimi back then but now I seldom eat it and it's so expensive."

3

TIDBITS, PURSES,
AND PARCELS

Asians love to snack. They love eating small bites, or what I call tidbits. Just take a look at the immense variety on display at any Asian market or listed at the beginning of a restaurant menu. In Asia, snack food is easily purchased from street vendors; customers either eat standing beside the cart or have their food wrapped up to take home. Americans are most familiar with the small bites known collectively as dim sum (*dianxin*). In China, and Chinese communities all over the world, dim sum is eaten at breakfast or lunch.

At home, grandmas and moms prepare these tidbits as after-school snacks, small bites to serve visitors, or as mini meals for small appetites. The morsels also make great finger foods for parties. However they are served, these small, varied bites are delightful. And true to the chapter's title, many of these items come wrapped in bundles of all shapes and sizes.

Shrimp Toast

Tidbits

Marbled Tea Eggs

Seaweed and Sesame Rice Crackers (*Furikake Mix Arare*)

Sesame Seed Chicken Wings

Shrimp Toast (*Banh Mi Tom Chien*)

Purses and Parcels

Crispy Shrimp Rolls

Fragrant Grilled Beef Bundles (*Bo Nuong La Lot*)

Lumpia (Filipino Eggrolls)

Shanghai Soup Dumplings (*Xiao Long Bao*)

Shiu Mai (Pork and Shrimp Cups)

Thai Stuffed Omelet (*Kai Yad Sai*)

✂ Tidbits ✄

Marbled Tea Eggs

Tea eggs, served warm or cold, are a common Chinese snack. The eggs are twice-cooked: After the first boiling, the shells are gently cracked and then the eggs are simmered in an aromatic "tea." The eggs absorb the delicate flavors of soy sauce and star anise and reveal an attractive crackle glaze once peeled. Not only are tea eggs nutritious and delicious, they're also pleasing to the eye.

Time: 2¼ hours (15 minutes active) plus steeping
Makes: 8 eggs (4 servings)

> 8 eggs
> ½ cup soy sauce
> 4 star anise pods
> 3 black tea bags, strings removed (English Breakfast or Assam, or for a smokier flavor, lapsang souchong)

✄ In a large saucepan, arrange the eggs in a single layer. Cover with water and bring to a rolling boil over medium-high heat. Remove the pan from the heat, cover, and let stand for 15 minutes. Drain and cover the eggs completely with fresh cold water. Allow to cool.

✄ When the eggs are cool enough to handle, tap each one gently with the back of a teaspoon to make fine cracks on the surface of the shell. Try to keep the shells intact.

✄ In the same saucepan, bring 3 cups of fresh water to a boil over high heat. Add the soy sauce, star anise, and tea bags. Reduce the heat to medium-low. Use a spoon to carefully lower the eggs one by one into the tea. If the eggs are not completely submerged, add more water. Cover and simmer for 2 hours.

✄ Remove the saucepan from the heat and let the eggs sit in the tea liquid on the stove for 1 hour. Transfer to the refrigerator to steep for at least 2 more hours, or preferably 12 hours.

✄ Peel a small portion of the shell to see if the eggs have attained a dark enough color. If the crackle glaze isn't obvious enough, steep the eggs longer.

⚓ Drain the eggs, peel them and serve whole, halved, or quartered. Unpeeled eggs can be refrigerated in a covered container for up to 4 days.

Pat's Notes: Cook the eggs longer for a stronger flavor and deeper color.

Seaweed and Sesame Rice Crackers
(*Furikake Mix Arare*)

Making homemade *kaki mochi*, Japanese rice crackers coated with a sweet and savory glaze, is a lot of work. First, the dough is rolled out paper thin and cut into tiny strips. Then the strips are deep-fried, individually dipped in syrup, and baked. Fortunately, there is a solution courtesy of Katie Kiyonaga. Her Auntie Shiz came up with a jiffy version that is much, much easier to make—and just as tasty!

Time: 1¼ hours (15 minutes active)
Makes: 2½ cups

> ⅓ cup sugar
>
> ¼ cup (½ stick) butter
>
> ¼ cup vegetable oil
>
> ¼ cup light corn syrup
>
> 1 tablespoon Japanese soy sauce
>
> 12-ounce box rice or corn cereal (such as Crispix or Chex)
>
> ½ cup (one-half to three-fourths of a 1.76-ounce bottle) seaweed and sesame seed topping (*nori furikake*) (see Pat's Notes)

⚓ Preheat the oven to 250 degrees F. Line two 15- by 10- by 1-inch jelly roll pans with foil.

⚓ In a medium saucepan, heat the sugar, butter, oil, corn syrup, and soy sauce over medium-low heat, stirring until the sugar dissolves completely and a smooth, thick syrup is formed, 2 to 3 minutes.

⚓ Put the cereal in a large bowl and pour the syrup over. Sprinkle with the seaweed and sesame topping and mix gently with a wooden spoon until the cereal is sticky and lightly coated with the syrup and topping. Spread the cereal evenly in the prepared pans. Bake, stirring every 15 minutes, for

1 hour. Remove from the oven and give it another stir. Cool the mix completely before storing in airtight bags or containers.

Pat's Notes: Nori furikake is a Japanese dried seasoning mix made of dried seaweed, white and black sesame seeds, salt, and sugar. It comes in different varieties and is used to flavor steamed rice with sweet, salty, and crunchy accents. It is available in 1.76-ounce bottles at Asian markets and some well-stocked supermarkets. Look for one that doesn't contain MSG or salt. Shirakiku and Urashima are good brands.

Sesame Seed Chicken Wings

Ideal for picnics, potlucks, and everyday snacking, these Japanese-influenced chicken wings were Erica Sugita's favorite childhood snack. Erica and her siblings would sneak into the kitchen while their mom was cooking to steal a wing or two, fresh from the sizzling oil. They could never get enough of the crispy, sesame-speckled wings!

Time: 1 hour plus marinating
Makes: About 1 dozen wings (4 to 6 servings)

> 2 eggs
> ¼ cup Japanese soy sauce
> 2 green onions, green parts only, chopped
> 2 cloves garlic, smashed with the flat blade of a cleaver or large knife
> ½ cup cornstarch
> ¼ cup all-purpose flour
> ¼ cup sugar
> 2 tablespoons sesame seeds
> 1½ teaspoons salt
> 3 pounds chicken wings, separated at the joints into wings and drumettes (10 to 12 wings)
> 3 cups (or as needed) vegetable oil for deep-frying

❀ In a large bowl, mix together the eggs, soy sauce, green onions, garlic, cornstarch, flour, sugar, sesame seeds, and salt. Add the chicken wings and toss to coat evenly. Cover and marinate in the refrigerator for at least 8 hours, or preferably 12.

Preheat the oven to 250 degrees F. Line a plate with paper towels. In a large wok, heavy skillet, or Dutch oven, heat the oil over high heat until it reaches 375 degrees F on a deep-fry thermometer (see page xiii for deep-frying tips).

Reduce the heat to medium-high. Using tongs, pick up the chicken pieces one by one and allow the excess marinade to drip off. Gently lower into the oil and fry in a batch of 4 or 5 pieces until tender and evenly golden brown, 10 to 15 minutes. Remove the chicken with a slotted spoon, shaking off the excess oil, and drain on paper towels. Keep warm in the oven.

Use a slotted spoon or a wire mesh strainer to remove any debris from the oil and bring the oil temperature back to 375 degrees F before frying the next batch. Repeat with the remaining chicken. Serve hot.

Shrimp Toast (*Banh Mi Tom Chien*)

Essentially an Asian canapé, this Vietnamese version of Chinese shrimp toast comes from Cathy Danh, a first generation Vietnamese American food writer who learned how to cook by shadowing every woman in her family. She picked up shrimp toast from her Aunt Phuong. The tasty morsels are crispy (the toasts) and chewy (the shrimp) at the same time; no wonder they're considered Aunt Phuong's signature appetizers and are such a hit at family gatherings! In a few easy steps, they can be yours too.

Time: 1 hour plus marinating
Makes: 60 toasts (10 to 12 servings)

Salt

1 pound unpeeled medium (36/40 count) shrimp

2½ tablespoons fish sauce

1 egg white

3 green onions, white and green parts, finely chopped

2 cloves garlic, minced (2 teaspoons)

1½ tablespoons sugar

1 teaspoon freshly ground black pepper

Ten 4- by 5-inch slices of white bread

3 cups (or as needed) vegetable oil for deep-frying, plus more for brushing

꙳ Fill a large bowl with water and stir in about ½ teaspoon salt. Rinse the shrimp in the salted water. Discard the water and repeat the process 3 or 4 times with fresh batches of salted water. Peel and devein the shrimp. Drain the shrimp in a colander and pat dry with paper towels.

꙳ In a large bowl, mix the fish sauce, egg white, green onions, garlic, sugar, and pepper together. Add the shrimp and toss to mix. Cover with plastic wrap and marinate in the refrigerator for at least 30 minutes, or preferably 12 hours.

꙳ Meanwhile, position a rack in the middle of the oven and preheat to 200 degrees F. Trim the crusts from the bread and cut each slice into 6 equal rectangles (about 2 by 1⅔ inches). Arrange the rectangles on a baking sheet and toast in the oven for 10 minutes. They don't need to be brown, just dry and crisp.

🥄 Put the marinated shrimp in the work bowl of a food processor and whirl until a thick, coarse paste is formed. Spread 1 teaspoon of shrimp paste on each piece of toast. The paste should be as thick as the toast and cover the entire rectangle from edge to edge. Lightly brush with oil.

🥄 Line a plate with paper towels. In a large wok, heavy skillet, or Dutch oven, heat the oil over high heat until it reaches 350 degrees F on a deep-fry thermometer (see page xiii for deep-frying tips).

🥄 Reduce the heat to medium-high. Using tongs, gently lower the shrimp toasts, shrimp-side down, into the oil one by one. Fry in a batch of 5 or 6, turning them occasionally so they cook evenly and don't stick together, until the shrimp is orangey-pink and the toast is golden brown, 1½ to 2 minutes. Remove the toasts with a slotted spoon, shaking off any excess oil, and drain on paper towels.

🥄 Bring the oil temperature back to 350 degrees F before frying the next batch. Repeat with remaining toasts or freeze for later (see Pat's Notes). Serve immediately.

Pat's Notes: In her cookbook, *Into the Vietnamese Kitchen*, Andrea Nguyen proposes a solution for the grease-averse: bake the shrimp toasts instead of frying. Follow instructions as above but bake at 350 degrees F until the shrimp turns light orangey-pink, 10 to 12 minutes.

To freeze, arrange assembled uncooked toasts on a baking sheet and freeze until solid, about 2 hours. Tip frozen toasts into a zip-top bag and freeze for up to 1 month. To serve, thaw to room temperature, brush with oil, and proceed as above.

Crispy Shrimp Rolls

These Vietnamese fried rolls make great appetizers for parties—you can easily adjust the numbers up or down depending on how many people you're feeding. Be warned, these bite-sized nibbles go fast! Serve with Thai sweet chili sauce or mayonnaise for dipping.

Time: 30 minutes or longer (depending on how fast you can wrap the rolls)
Makes: 25 rolls (4 to 6 servings)

> 25 (about ½ pound) small (41/50 count) shrimp with tails on, peeled and deveined
>
> Salt
>
> Freshly ground black pepper
>
> 25 (4- by 4-inch) square spring roll wrappers or wonton skins
>
> 2 cups (or as needed) vegetable oil for deep-frying

❧ Sprinkle the shrimp liberally with salt and pepper on all sides.

❧ Prepare a small bowl of water. Carefully peel one wrapper from the stack (cover the remaining wrappers with a damp cloth to keep them moist). Lay the wrapper on a dry work surface with one corner pointing toward you to make a diamond. Fold the diamond vertically in half (right corner over left corner) to form a triangle. Place one shrimp parallel to your body about an inch above the bottom corner with the tail sticking over the edge. Fold the bottom corner over the shrimp and roll once or twice. Fold the left corner in and continue rolling the shrimp into a tight tube until you reach the end of the wrapper. Before you reach the end, dab some water along the top edge to seal the roll. You'll get a mini spring roll with a shrimp tail sticking out. Lay the roll seam side down on a lightly floured plate or sheet pan. Repeat with the remaining shrimp and wrappers.

❧ Line a plate with paper towels. In a large wok, heavy skillet, or Dutch oven, heat the oil over high heat until it reaches 350 degrees F on a deep-fry thermometer (see page xiii for deep-frying tips).

✻ Reduce the heat to medium-high. Using tongs, gently lower the shrimp rolls into the oil one by one; fry in a batch of 9 or 10 until both sides are evenly golden brown, 1 to 2 minutes. Remove the shrimp rolls with a slotted spoon, shaking off excess oil, and drain on paper towels.

✻ Bring the oil temperature back to 350 degrees F before frying the next batch. Repeat with remaining shrimp rolls. Serve immediately.

Pat's Notes: If you prefer, you can remove the shrimp tails and roll the shrimp rolls the same way you'd roll LUMPIA (page 61). It makes it a less-messy finger food that way!

Be sure to buy spring roll wrappers meant for frying, not the ones used for making fresh Vietnamese spring rolls. If you can't find small spring roll wrappers, you can cut the larger ones to size.

Fragrant Grilled Beef Bundles (*Bo Nuong La Lot*)

This fragrant, seasoned beef bundle wrapped in wild betel leaf (*la lot* or *piper sarmentosum*) and grilled over a charcoal fire is a favorite Vietnamese snack, usually chased with cold beer or white wine. Shiny on one side and matte on the other, the soft, pliable wild betel leaf doesn't have much character as is. But once heat is applied, it releases its sweetly spicy, incense-like fragrance. Traditionally, the filling contains ground beef. Sophie Banh, chef and co-owner of Monsoon restaurant in Seattle, has a contemporary take on this dish—she uses flank steak instead.

Time: 1 hour plus soaking and marinating
Makes: 20 bundles (4 servings)

8 ounces flank steak

1 plump stalk lemongrass, trimmed and finely chopped
   (3 tablespoons) (see page 10)

1½ tablespoons honey

1 tablespoon fish sauce, plus more for serving

1 tablespoon vegetable oil, plus more for brushing

4 cloves garlic, 1 clove minced and 3 cloves sliced paper thin

1½ teaspoons kosher salt

1 teaspoon five-spice powder

5 ounces wild betel leaves, enough to yield 40 to 50 large leaves (see Pat's Notes)

4 ounces (½ small) jicama (Mexican turnip), peeled and cut into 40 julienne pieces the same length as the steak strips

20 Thai basil leaves

Green Onion Oil (recipe follows)

2 tablespoons crushed roasted peanuts

⚜ Soak 10 wooden skewers in water for at least 1 hour.

⚜ Handle the beef partially frozen so that it is easier to cut (if it's fresh, place in the freezer for about 30 minutes). Cut the beef along the grain into 1½-inch-thick strips. Then, with your knife at an angle almost parallel to the cutting surface, slice the meat diagonally across the grain into ⅛-inch-thick slices for a total of 20 slices.

⚜ In a bowl, toss the steak with the lemongrass, honey, fish sauce, oil, minced garlic, salt, and five-spice powder. Marinate for 15 minutes.

⚜ Pluck the betel leaves from their center stalks. Snip off any protruding stems. Lay two overlapping leaves matte-side up on a work surface with the tips of the leaves facing the outer edges. Together the leaves must form a wrapper big enough for the sides to come up and over a steak strip to completely enclose it. Place a steak strip in the center of the leaves. Layer 2 pieces of jicama, 1 basil leaf, and 2 garlic slices on top of the meat. Fold the sides of the leaves in over the ingredients and roll into a secure bundle. Make a second bundle. Thread the two bundles horizontally onto a skewer, making sure they are secure and hold their shape. Repeat with the remaining leaves, meat, vegetables, and skewers.

⚜ Preheat a gas grill to medium, or prepare a medium charcoal fire (you can hold your hand over the rack for only 4 to 5 seconds), which is the traditional way of cooking the bundles.

⚜ Brush all sides of the bundles with oil. Grill them, turning often to prevent the leaves from burning, until the leaves are lightly charred but not burnt, 6 to 8 minutes.

🌿 Pour the green onion oil onto a serving plate and place the beef bundles on top. Sprinkle with crushed peanuts. Serve as an appetizer or snack with fish sauce in dipping dishes.

Variations: Wild betel leaves are sometimes hard to come by. While the fragrance is lacking, you can substitute with red perilla (*shiso*) or grape leaves.

You can also broil the bundles in the oven or grill them on a stovetop cast-iron grill (over low heat).

Pat's Notes: Wild betel leaves are sold in many Asian markets. Look for leaves with a healthy green color. A few holes here and there are okay. At home, snip off the bottom ½ inch of stem and put the leaves in a small container partially filled with water. Loosely cover with a plastic bag and refrigerate for up to 4 days.

Green Onion Oil

Gently infused with the flavor of green onions, this flavoring oil is so versatile—drizzle it over grilled meats and roasted vegetables as well as serving with the beef bundles.

Time: 5 minutes plus chilling
Makes: ¼ cup

> 2 green onions, green parts only, finely chopped
> ¼ cup vegetable oil
> ½ teaspoon kosher salt

🌿 Place the green onions in a heatproof bowl. Heat the oil in a small saucepan over medium heat until it starts to bubble gently, 2 to 3 minutes. Don't let it smoke. Remove the saucepan from the heat and pour the oil carefully over the green onions. It might sizzle and splatter so stand back. Sprinkle with salt and mix well. Cover and refrigerate to help preserve the green onions' bright green color. Remove after 10 minutes and set aside at room temperature until ready to serve.

Lumpia (Filipino Eggrolls)

Tisa Escobar, a Filipino American attorney who grew up in California, learned to make *lumpia* from her mom, Victoria, who is a stickler for what goes into them. Victoria doesn't believe in using ground meat, which is common in many traditional recipes. She also has two tips for all potential lumpia makers out there: don't add too much soy sauce because it will make the filling soggy, and the smaller the lumpia, the easier it is to cook them and keep the wrappers crispy.

Time: 1½ hours or longer (depending on how fast you can wrap the rolls)
Makes: About 2 dozen eggrolls (10 to 12 servings)

> 2 teaspoons salt, divided
> 1 pound skinless, boneless chicken breasts
> 1 tablespoon vegetable oil
> 1 medium onion, finely chopped (1 cup)
> 3 cloves garlic, minced (1 tablespoon)
> 3 medium carrots, shredded (1½ cups)
> 1 cup (4 ounces) finely chopped green beans
> 1 teaspoon soy sauce
> Freshly ground black pepper
> 30 lumpia wrappers (have a few extra on hand just in case)
> 1 egg white, beaten, or water for sealing
> 3 cups (or as needed) vegetable oil for deep-frying
> Sweet and Sour Sauce (recipe follows)

❧ Fill a medium saucepan half full with water. Add 1 teaspoon of the salt and bring to a boil over high heat. Carefully add the chicken breasts, making sure they are entirely submerged. When the water returns to a boil, reduce the heat and simmer until the chicken is just cooked through, 10 to 12 minutes. Test by cutting into a piece: it should not be pink. Let cool and shred the meat along the grain into tiny shards with your fingers, or chop into a confetti-sized dice. Reserve the stock for another use or discard.

❧ Meanwhile, in a small skillet, heat the 1 tablespoon oil over medium-high heat until it becomes runny and starts to shimmer. Add the onion and garlic and cook until the onion is soft and light golden, 4 to 5 minutes. Set aside to cool.

❧ When the chicken and the onion-garlic mixture are completely cooled, mix them together in a large bowl with the carrots and green beans. Add the soy sauce, remaining salt, and 1 teaspoon pepper (or to taste).

❧ To assemble the lumpia, carefully peel one wrapper from the stack (cover the remaining wrappers with a damp cloth to keep them moist). Lay the wrapper on a dry work surface. (If you are using a square spring roll wrapper, lay it like a diamond with one corner pointing toward you.) Place 2 tablespoons of filling just below the center line of the wrapper parallel to your body. Shape it into a mound 1 by 3 inches, leaving about 2½ inches on either side. Fold the edge of the circle (or corner) closest to you over the filling and tuck it in snugly. Roll once, then fold the left and right sides in to form an envelope. Continue to roll the filling tightly into a fat tube until you reach the end of the wrapper. Before you reach the end, dab some egg white or water along the top edge to seal the lumpia. The lumpia should measure 4 to 5 inches in length and 1 to 1½ inches in diameter. Repeat with the remaining filling and wrappers.

❧ Preheat the oven to 250 degrees F. Line a plate with paper towels. In a large wok, heavy skillet, or Dutch oven, heat the 3 cups oil over high heat until it reaches 350 degrees F on a deep-fry thermometer (see page xiii for deep-frying tips).

❧ Reduce the heat to medium-high. Using tongs, gently lower the lumpia into the oil one by one; fry in a batch of 5 or 6 until both sides are evenly golden brown, 45 seconds to 1 minute. Remove the lumpia with a slotted spoon, shaking off excess oil, and drain on paper towels. Keep warm in the oven.

❧ Bring the oil temperature back to 350 degrees F before frying the next batch. Repeat with the remaining lumpia. Serve immediately with sweet and sour sauce.

Pat's Notes: Lumpia are best eaten when freshly fried. If left overnight, they get soggy and the wrappers lose their crisp shell.

However, you can freeze assembled but uncooked lumpia for up to a month. To serve, simply deep-fry them (for an extra minute or so) straight from the freezer.

Sweet and Sour Sauce

Adjust the amounts of vinegar and sugar to suit your palate.

Time: 5 minutes
Makes: ¾ cup

> 3 tablespoons rice or distilled white vinegar
>
> 2 tablespoons sugar
>
> 1 tablespoon ketchup
>
> 1 teaspoon soy sauce
>
> 2 teaspoons cornstarch dissolved in ¼ cup water to form a slurry

In a small saucepan, bring the vinegar, sugar, ketchup, and soy sauce to a boil over medium heat. Stir the cornstarch slurry and add to the pan, stirring constantly until the sauce thickens, about 1 minute. Pour into a small bowl and serve with lumpia.

Shanghai Soup Dumplings (*Xiao Long Bao*)

The Chinese name for soup dumplings comes from the little baskets (*xiao long*) they are steamed in. But what makes them so special is the gelatinized stock in the filling that liquefies into soup once steamed—thus you get soup-in-a-dumpling! Gelatinized stock is similar to aspic. Collagen from the marrow and fat thickens the stock, but you can use gelatin as a shortcut. Use two envelopes (1 tablespoon) of unflavored powdered gelatin per 2 cups of chicken stock, and follow package directions. There are many ways to eat soup dumplings but be aware the contents are very hot. I pick a dumpling up with chopsticks, dip it in the vinegar sauce, and then nestle it in a soupspoon. You should carefully bite into the dumplings to release some steam and soup, blow on them to cool the contents a little, and enjoy!

Time: 3 hours plus simmering, resting, and chilling time
Makes: About 40 dumplings (8 to 10 servings as a snack or appetizer)

Gelatinized Stock:

> 2 pounds pig's feet and ham hocks with skin
>
> 1 pound chicken parts (necks, backs, bones, or carcass)
>
> 1-inch piece fresh ginger, cut into 4 or 5 coins
>
> 2 green onions, each tied into a knot
>
> 2 quarts water or chicken stock
>
> Salt

Dough:

> 2 cups all-purpose flour, plus more for dusting
>
> ½ cup boiling water
>
> ¼ to ½ cup cold water

Filling:

> 1 pound ground pork
>
> 2 green onions, white and green parts, finely chopped
>
> 1 tablespoon soy sauce
>
> 1 tablespoon Shaoxing rice wine or dry sherry
>
> 1 teaspoon sesame oil
>
> ½-inch piece fresh ginger, minced (1 teaspoon)
>
> ½ teaspoon sugar
>
> Chinese cabbage leaves or parchment paper for lining the steamer
>
> Black Vinegar Dipping Sauce (recipe follows)

❧ To make the gelatinized stock, wash the pig's feet and ham hocks well. Use a knife to scrape the surface of the skin to clean it further and remove fine hairs. For a clean and clear soup, parboil the pig and chicken parts: place the parts in a large stockpot, pour in enough water to cover, and bring to a boil. Boil for 1 minute, then drain and rinse with cold water. Rinse the stockpot as well to get rid of scum.

❧ Return the pig and chicken parts to the stockpot; add the water, ginger, and green onions; and bring to a boil. Reduce the heat and simmer gently, uncovered, for at least 6 hours, skimming off any scum that rises to the surface. The stock is ready when it can solidify at room temperature. To test, spoon some stock into a small bowl and let it cool. If it solidifies like Jell-O, it is ready.

❧ Strain the stock through a fine mesh strainer and season with salt to taste. Discard all solids. You should have about 2½ cups of stock. Reserve 1½ cups of stock for the filling and pour into a large container with a tight-fitting lid. Save the remaining stock for flavoring sauces or stir-fries. Let the stock cool to room temperature, then cover and refrigerate until solid, 3 to 4 hours. It is best to make the stock ahead, but use it within 3 days.

❧ To make the dough, combine the flour and ½ cup boiling water in a large bowl. Mix quickly with a wooden spoon until it becomes crumbly. Slowly add ¼ cup cold water and mix well with the spoon. With your hands, form the dough into a rough ball, adding more cold water 1 tablespoon at a time (no more than 2 to 3 tablespoons total), until the dough comes together. You want the dough to be pliable but not sticking to your fingers. Sprinkle with a little more flour if the dough becomes too wet. The dough will not feel smooth at this point. Set the dough back in the bowl, cover with a damp towel, and let rest for 1 hour.

❧ To make the filling, use a pastry cutter or a large fork to run through the reserved gelatinized stock, breaking it up into small shards. Place the gelatinized stock, ground pork, soy sauce, rice wine, sesame oil, ginger, and sugar in a medium bowl. Mix well with chopsticks or clean hands. Cover with plastic wrap and refrigerate until the dough is ready. You can prepare the filling a day ahead.

❧ To form the dumpling skins, knead the dough on a lightly floured surface until it is smooth all over, about 5 minutes. Divide into 4 equal balls. Knead each ball individually for about 30 seconds. Roll each portion into a log about 10 inches long and ¾ inch in diameter. Working with one log at a time (keep the others covered with a damp cloth), pinch off 10 even, walnut-sized pieces. Dust with flour as needed to prevent them from sticking to the work surface.

❧ Roll a piece into a ball and flatten into a disk between your palms. Place the flattened disk on a well-floured surface. Using a Chinese rolling pin (see Pat's Notes on page 238), start at the bottom right edge of the disk and roll from the outside of the circle in. Use your right hand to roll the pin over the edge of the disk as your left hand turns it counterclockwise. (Do the opposite if you are left-handed). Keep rolling and turning until it becomes a circle about 3 inches in diameter. Don't worry about making a perfect circle. Ideally, the skin will be thicker in the middle than at the edge. Repeat to make the remaining skins. Dust the skins with flour so they won't stick to each other. Cover them with a damp cloth as you make the dumplings.

❧ Cup a dumpling skin in the palm of your left (or non-dominant) hand and spoon about 2 teaspoons filling into the center of the skin. Gather the skin edges at the top to form a loose pouch, letting the filling sag in the middle. Hold the edges with your right thumb and forefinger and pleat around the circumference, turning the dumpling in the palm of your left hand as you do so. Twist the pleats together at the top, leaving a tiny hole in the center to allow steam to escape. The sealed dumpling should look like a bulb of garlic with pleats. (Traditionally, 18 pleats are made but don't worry about this.)

❧ On a parchment-lined tray dusted lightly with flour, set the dumpling firmly down. Repeat until all the dough or filling is used.

❧ Set up your steamer, preferably bamboo (see page xv for other steaming options). Fill a wok with 2 to 3 inches of water and bring to a rolling boil over high heat. Reduce the heat to medium until you are ready to steam.

❧ Blanch the cabbage leaves in hot water for about 30 seconds, drain, and use to line the bottom of the steamer basket. Arrange the dumplings on the leaves about 1½ inches apart (you may have to steam them in batches).

❧ Return the water in the steamer to a rolling boil. Set the steamer basket in the wok. Cover and steam over medium heat for 5 to 7 minutes, or until the dumping skin is no longer doughy and the pork is cooked through.

❧ When done, turn off the heat and wait for the steam to subside before lifting the lid. Lift it away from you to prevent scalding yourself and to keep condensation from dripping onto the dumplings. Carefully remove the steamer basket. Serve the dumplings in the basket immediately with the dipping sauce.

Pat's Notes: Soup dumplings cannot be frozen, nor can they be refrigerated overnight, as the skins will crack and the stock will leak out. The dumplings should be served immediately and eaten all at once. Save this dish for entertaining large groups or only make a half recipe.

Black Vinegar Dipping Sauce

If you can't find black vinegar, use rice vinegar and soy sauce in a one-to-one ratio. Use any leftover sauce within 2 days.

Time: 10 minutes
Makes: ¾ cup

> 2-inch piece fresh ginger, peeled
> ½ cup Chinese black vinegar
> ¼ cup soy sauce
> 1 teaspoon sesame oil

❧ Using a sharp paring knife, cut one end of the ginger crosswise to create a flat surface. Stand the ginger firmly on a cutting board and cut thin, vertical, lengthwise slices. Stack the slices and cut into long, thin shreds in the direction of the fibers.

❧ Combine the ginger shreds with the black vinegar, soy sauce, and sesame oil in a small bowl. Let the mixture sit for at least 10 minutes to allow the flavors to meld.

Pat's Notes: Chinese black vinegar, made from glutinous rice and malt, is the Asian equivalent of Italian balsamic vinegar. It is mild and sweet, with a complex flavor and aroma. Chinkiang vinegar, originating in its namesake city, is considered the best of the black vinegars. Gold Plum or Koon Chun are good brands.

Shiu Mai (Pork and Shrimp Cups)

Dried black mushrooms give these tidbits an earthy flavor while water chestnuts add crunch. And this dim sum staple is easier to make than you may think. Look for fresh or frozen round *shiu mai* skins in Asian markets—the thinner the better. If you can't find shiu mai skins, thicker gyoza or wonton skins (trim off square corners before using) will do. The skins come in packs of about 50.

Time: 2½ hours
Makes: 3 dozen (10 to 12 servings)

> 1 pound ground pork
>
> 6 medium dried black mushrooms, rehydrated (see page 11) and finely chopped (½ cup)
>
> 8 ounces shrimp, peeled, deveined, and chopped with a food processor or cleaver
>
> ⅓ cup finely chopped water chestnuts (about 5 canned pieces or 3 peeled fresh pieces)
>
> ¼ cup finely chopped green onions, white and green parts (4 stalks)
>
> 1 tablespoon cornstarch
>
> 1 teaspoon sesame oil
>
> 1 teaspoon soy sauce
>
> 1 teaspoon Shaoxing rice wine
>
> 1 teaspoon sugar
>
> 1 teaspoon salt
>
> ½ teaspoon ground white pepper
>
> 12-ounce package dumpling skins

❧ In a large bowl, combine the pork, mushrooms, shrimp, water chestnuts, green onions, cornstarch, sesame oil, soy sauce, rice wine, sugar, salt, and pepper.

❧ Set the dumpling skins on a floured work surface and cover with a damp towel. Make a circle with your left thumb and index finger (right if you're left handed). Place a dumpling skin over the circle and scoop 1 tablespoon filling into it. Let the filling drop halfway through the hole and gently squeeze your hand to shape it into a cup, leaving the top open. Put the dumpling on the work surface and gather the edges of the skin around the filling, pleating the edges to form petals. The top should remain open. Stand the dumplings upright ½ inch apart on a greased plate that will fit in your steamer. (The size of your steamer will determine how many dumplings you can steam at a time.) Repeat until all the filling is used. Brush the tops of the dumplings with oil.

※ Set up your steamer (see page xv for other steaming options).

※ Fill the steamer pan half full of water and bring to a rolling boil over high heat. Reduce the heat to medium until you are ready to steam.

※ Return the water in the steamer to a rolling boil. Set one plate of the dumplings in the steamer basket or rack. Cover and steam over high heat for 15 minutes, or until the pork is no longer pink. Pierce a dumpling with a sharp knife to check doneness. Turn off the heat and wait for the steam to subside before lifting the lid. Lift it away from you to prevent scalding yourself and to keep condensation from dripping onto the dumplings. Carefully remove the dumplings and set aside to cool. Repeat as many times as necessary.

※ When the dumplings are cool enough to handle, transfer to a serving platter and serve immediately.

Thai Stuffed Omelet (*Kai Yad Sai*)

With just a few ingredients, anyone can recreate this Thai street food favorite at home for a snack or easy weeknight supper. Make the omelets as described here, or follow the lead of Panee Lertpanyavit, a Thai native from the suburbs of Bangkok and a soon-to-be grandmother. She makes one large, thin omelet that's easy to fold. She doesn't flip the omelet either, preferring to leave the inner layer a little undercooked to allow the flaps to stick and leaving the residual heat from the filling to cook the egg completely. If you have trouble making a folded parcel, just place the pork mixture right on top of the omelet and serve.

Time: 30 minutes
Makes: 4 appetizer or 2 main-course servings

> 3 eggs
> 1¼ teaspoons fish sauce, divided
> Ground white pepper
> 2 tablespoons plus 2 teaspoons vegetable oil, divided
> 4 ounces ground pork
> 1 small firm tomato (preferably Roma), finely chopped (¼ cup)
> 4 green beans, finely chopped (¼ cup)
> 2 Asian shallots, finely chopped (2 tablespoons)
> 1 teaspoon sugar
> ¼ teaspoon soy sauce
> Cilantro sprigs for garnish

※ In a small bowl, beat the eggs with ¼ teaspoon of the fish sauce and a dash of pepper. Set aside.

※ Preheat an 8- to 10-inch nonstick skillet over medium-high heat for 1 minute. Swirl in 2 tablespoons of the oil and heat until it becomes runny and starts to shimmer. Stir in the pork and cook until it loses its blush, 1 to 2 minutes. Reduce the heat to medium and add the remaining the fish sauce, the tomato, green beans, shallot, sugar, soy sauce, and ¼ teaspoon white pepper. Stir and cook until the green beans are cooked and the tomato juices thicken the mixture a little, 5 to 6 minutes. Remove the mixture to a bowl and cover to keep warm while you make the omelets.

❀ Wipe the skillet clean with a paper towel and heat 1 teaspoon of the oil over medium heat. Swirl in half the egg mixture to coat the base of the skillet in a thin, even layer. Cook until the omelet is still a little soggy on the surface and the underside is light golden, 45 seconds to 1 minute. Lift the edge to check. If desired, flip to cook completely on both sides. Scoop half of the stuffing into the center of the omelet. Fold the two opposite sides toward the middle and then fold in the remaining two sides to form a neat square parcel. Flip the parcel onto a serving plate, folded-side down.

❀ Repeat with the remaining oil, egg, and stuffing. Garnish with cilantro sprigs. Cut each omelet in half and serve with freshly steamed rice.

Pat's Notes: You can also cook the omelets first and transfer them to a plate before adding the stuffing and folding into a parcel.

Profile of a Grandma: ELLEN SHYU CHOU

After living in the United States for more than three decades, Ellen Shyu Chou (or *Shyu Huann-ming*) now considers both Taiwan and the United States home.

Ellen was born in Hubei Province in China but moved to Taiwan at the age of five when the Communists took over in 1948. Growing up, Ellen wasn't allowed in the kitchen. "My mom never went to school and her dream for me was to get as much education as possible," she explains. "So she chased me out of the kitchen."

It was during home economics classes at school that Ellen learned to cook some common Chinese foods such as FROM-SCRATCH POT STICK-ERS (page 236). "We cleared the Ping-Pong table and everyone stood around it making dumplings," she recalls with a smile. Dumplings were also a major feature of her childhood Chinese New Year celebrations. While her mom and aunts huddled together to fill and fold dumplings for breakfast, Ellen and her cousins were playing with dough and making a mess!

Ellen's mother needn't have worried—Ellen more than fulfilled her mother's dreams. She studied journalism at the Political Staff College in Taipei and became a well-respected journalist, working for the *China Daily* newspaper and the Central News Agency for several years.

In 1968, she pursued a master's degree from the Missouri School of Journalism (University of Missouri) and returned to Taiwan three years later in 1971. That same year, she married her college classmate, David.

In 1974, David decided to enter the Missouri School of Journalism as well, and the Chous, together with their young daughter and son, left for the United States, but not for the same city. While David was studying hard in Missouri, Ellen worked in Washington, D.C., as a feature writer with Central News Agency–affiliate Far East News Agency, and also looked after the children. After six months of long-distance family life, Ellen called it quits. "My husband was so skinny and my son needed a father figure," she laments. She realized that perhaps her dream to be a successful journalist wasn't meant to be pursued and that she "should put more emphasis on taking care of my children and husband."

Both Ellen and David decided to change course and they started a business. In 1980, they opened Chou's Buffet in Columbia, Missouri.

Running the restaurant was very hard work. They worked seven days a week and even the children joined in the production: their oldest, Hsiao-Ching, started making wontons when she was eight, younger brother Sam peeled shrimp, while baby David slept upstairs in the office. However, the restaurant bound them together as a family and provided the sustenance to keep them going both emotionally and financially.

Ellen has no regrets. "I gave up my dream because I love my children," she says firmly. "If you don't see your children, all of a sudden they're grown up and you miss everything. Being with them was more precious than pursuing our own dreams."

They closed the restaurant in 2003 and at the same time, a long chapter in Ellen's life ended.

Sadly, David passed away two years later. Ellen was devastated. For the first time ever, she couldn't bring herself to cook. But eventually her love for her children and grandchildren kept her going. "My husband not only left me behind but also his sons, and grandsons," she says wistfully. "We have to go on."

Ellen has three grandkids now. She recently moved from Missouri to Seattle, Washington, to help look after her youngest granddaughter, Meilee, Hsiao-Ching's first child. "Hsiao-Ching needs me," she explains, ever the loving mother. As always, Ellen is thinking of her children first.

4

SAVORY SOUPS

Soups play a significant role in Asian cuisine. During the main meal of the day, soup is almost always one of the items on the table. Instead of being served in individual bowls as a first course, a big bowl of soup is usually placed in the center of the table alongside the other dishes and shared by everyone. During an informal meal, everyone dips a soup spoon into the communal bowl. When guests are present or on special occasions, soup is ladled into smaller bowls for diners to enjoy throughout the meal.

Asian soups come in two forms: clear, light soups that involve simple ingredients (CLEAR SOUP WITH RED SPINACH AND SWEET CORN, page 79), and fuller, richer soups that are meat-based and contain coconut milk and/or various spices (CHICKEN COCONUT SOUP, page 84). Light soups are served on hot days and richer soups during the cooler months. Often, a few spoonfuls of soup are added to rice to soften it. A hearty soup poured over a mound of rice can be eaten as a meal.

Rice soup (*jook* [Cantonese], or *congee* [from the Dravidian word *kanji*]), like chicken soup, is considered a curative. HEALING PORK AND SHRIMP RICE SOUP (page 92) and HERB-SCENTED CHICKEN SOUP (page 94) are both examples of healing soups that are perfect for a sick child or adult.

Clear Soup with Red Spinach and Sweet Corn

Light Soups

Clear Soup with Red Spinach and Sweet Corn (*Sayur Bening*)

Hot and Sour Soup (*Suan La Tang*)

Sweet and Sour Fish Soup (*Canh Chua Ca*)

Richer Soups

Chicken Coconut Soup (*Tom Ka Kai*)

Colonial Curried Chicken Soup (Mulligatawny Soup)

Hearty Beef and Vegetable Soup

Red and White Miso Soup (*Awase Miso Shiru*)

Healing Soups

Healing Pork and Shrimp Rice Soup (*Kao Tom Moo*)

Herb-Scented Chicken Soup (*S'ngao Chruok Moan*)

Nepalese Nine-Bean Soup (*Kawatee*)

Watercress and Pork Rib Soup

Clear Soup with Red Spinach and Sweet Corn
(*Sayur Bening*)

The key ingredient in this light and delightful soup from Indonesian grandmother Juliana Suparman is a rhizome called Chinese keys or fingerroot. Other names include *temu kunci* (Indonesian) and *krachai* or *kachai* (Thai). Widely cultivated in Southeast Asia, it adds a subtle, spicy flavor. It has fleshy rounded rootlets that look like a bunch of beige baby carrots. Its English name, Chinese keys, denotes this growth configuration which suggests a large bunch of keys. If not available fresh, buy whole Chinese keys preserved in brine in jars usually labeled krachai, kachai, or (mistakenly) lesser galangal. After opening, store it in the refrigerator. If you can't find Chinese keys, substitute galangal or ginger, but the soup will have an entirely different nuance.

Time: 45 minutes
Makes: 6 to 8 first-course servings

3 quarts water

¼ cup plus 2 tablespoons sugar

5 Chinese key rootlets, smashed

4 Asian shallots (3 ounces), peeled, trimmed, and smashed

4 salam leaves (see page 20)

2 teaspoons salt

3 medium ears sweet corn, kernels scraped off (3 cups)

1 small (8-ounce) orange sweet potato or yam, cut into ¾-inch cubes

1 pound red spinach (see Pat's Notes), 4 to 5 inches trimmed off the bottom end, leaves plucked, and stems cut into 1-inch lengths

2 medium ripe tomatoes (8 ounces), halved and cut into quarters

❧ In a large stockpot, bring the water to boil over medium-high heat. Add the sugar, Chinese keys, shallots, salam leaves, and salt. Return to a boil. Reduce the heat to medium and toss in the corn, sweet potato, and spinach stems. Simmer until the sweet potato is tender, 9 to 10 minutes. Taste and adjust seasonings. It is supposed to be exceptionally sweet for a savory soup, but feel free to adjust the seasonings to your taste.

% Raise the heat to high and return to a boil. Toss in the spinach leaves and tomatoes. Cover, turn off the heat, and let the soup sit for 5 minutes. Fish out the Chinese keys, shallots, and salam leaves and discard. Serve hot with freshly steamed rice and a meat dish.

Variation: Chopped carrots can be used instead of sweet potatoes.

Pat's Notes: Sturdier and more flavorful than regular spinach, red spinach is available at Asian markets and some farmers markets. If you can't find it, use regular spinach.

Hot and Sour Soup (*Suan La Tang*)

Hot and sour soup is a staple of many Chinese restaurants, but it's also common in Chinese and Taiwanese homes around the globe. Don't be scared off by the many unusual ingredients used in this recipe from Grandma Ellen Shyu Chou (see page 72). If you can't find any of them, or don't want to use them all, the soup will taste just as good with just a few basic ingredients.

Time: 45 minutes
Makes: 6 to 8 first-course servings

> 1 tablespoon oil
>
> 2 ounces pork loin or chop, cut into slivers (¼ cup) (optional)
>
> Soy sauce
>
> 8 cups chicken stock (recipe on page 42), pork stock, or water
>
> ⅓ cup white vinegar
>
> 2 teaspoons ground white pepper
>
> 6 ounces medium or firm tofu, cut into 2- by ¼- by ¼-inch strips (¾ cup)
>
> 5 ounces fresh or canned bamboo shoots, cut into julienne pieces (½ cup)
>
> ¾ ounce (½ cup) dried wood ear mushrooms, rehydrated, cleaned (see page 12), and chopped

1 ounce (¼ cup) dried lily buds, rehydrated (see Pat's Notes)

4 medium dried black mushrooms, rehydrated (see page 11) and cut into thin slices (½ cup)

¼ cup cornstarch dissolved in ½ cup water to make a slurry

3 eggs, beaten

Sesame oil

Chopped green onions for garnish

Chopped cilantro for garnish

❧ Preheat a small skillet over medium-high heat for 45 seconds to 1 minute. Swirl in the oil and heat until it becomes runny and starts to shimmer. Stir in the pork and add a splash of soy sauce for color. Stir and cook for about 1 minute.

❧ In a large saucepan, combine the stock, ⅓ cup soy sauce (or to taste), vinegar, and white pepper. Add the pork, tofu, bamboo shoots, wood ear mushrooms, lily buds, and black mushrooms. Bring to a boil over high heat. Reduce the heat to medium. Pour the cornstarch slurry slowly into the soup, stirring constantly until it thickens and returns to a boil, 1 to 2 minutes. Turn off the heat.

❧ Moving in a circular motion around the pot, pour the egg into the soup through the tines of a fork or a pair of chopsticks to help it flow in a slow, steady stream. You want the egg to form wispy strands, not one lumpy mass. Gently stir in one direction to integrate the egg into the soup.

❧ Taste and adjust seasonings if desired. Drizzle with sesame oil and garnish with green onions and cilantro.

Pat's Notes: Dried lily buds (golden needles, lily flowers, or tiger lily buds) are the dried unopened flowers of day lilies. Before cooking, soak the buds in warm water for about 30 minutes until softened. Then strip the hard knobby ends and tie a knot in the middle of each bud to prevent it from opening during cooking. Look for dried lily buds that are golden rather than brown and brittle.

Grandma Says: If you don't have stock on hand, water makes a good soup base too.

Sweet and Sour Fish Soup (*Canh Chua Ca*)

In Vietnamese, *canh chua* literally means "sour soup." However, this refreshing soup has a lovely mélange of flavors comprising far more than just sour notes. The southern Vietnamese staple was served often when Huong C. Nguyen was growing up. A New York fashion designer who fuses her Vietnamese heritage with modern global influences, Huong was named for Song Huong ("Perfume River" in English), which runs through Hue, the former imperial capital of Vietnam and the birthplace of her father. The soup was the perfect palate cleanser for a meat dish like CARAMELIZED CHICKEN WITH LEMONGRASS AND CHILIES (page 179). A big bowl of the soup would be placed in the middle of the table and ladled into individual bowls to sip from throughout the meal.

Time: 1 hour
Makes: 6 to 8 first-course servings

> 12 ounces catfish fillets, cut into 1½-inch chunks (or any firm fish such as halibut and salmon, or peeled and deveined shrimp)
>
> ½ teaspoon salt
>
> Freshly ground black pepper
>
> 7 cups water
>
> 3 large ripe tomatoes, cored and chopped into large chunks (3 cups)
>
> 1 cup pineapple chunks (preferably fresh or frozen)
>
> ¼ cup plus 2 tablespoons tamarind paste (see page 25)
>
> 2 tablespoons vegetable oil
>
> 1 medium yellow onion, halved and cut into thin crescents
>
> 2 cloves garlic, chopped
>
> 1 fat 10-inch (4-ounce) taro stem (see Pat's Notes), peeled and cut crosswise into 1-inch diagonal slices
>
> 1½ tablespoons sugar
>
> 1 cup (3 ounces) fresh mung bean sprouts, tails snapped off
>
> 2 red Thai chilies, cut into rounds
>
> 2 tablespoons fish sauce

Garnishes:

> ½ cup loosely packed Thai basil leaves
>
> ½ cup loosely packed cilantro leaves, chopped

2 green onions, green parts only, cut into 1-inch diagonal slices

2 red Thai chilies, cut into rounds

Fish sauce for dipping

Garlic cloves, smashed with the flat part of a cleaver or large knife

✻ In a medium bowl, season the fish with the salt and pepper to taste. Set aside.

✻ In a large stockpot, bring the water, tomatoes, pineapple, and tamarind paste to a boil over high heat. Reduce the heat to medium. Cover and simmer for about 15 minutes, or until the tomatoes soften and their skins start to peel.

✻ Meanwhile, preheat a medium skillet over medium heat for about 1 minute. Swirl in the oil and heat until it becomes runny and starts to shimmer. Add the yellow onion and garlic and cook until fragrant, 30 to 45 seconds. Tip in the fish pieces and cook for 30 seconds on each side. (Don't worry if the fish is still pinkish.)

✻ Add the partially cooked fish and onion to the stockpot along with the taro stem and sugar. Raise the heat to high. Cook, skimming off any scum or foam that rises to the surface, until the fish turns opaque, about 2 minutes. Add the bean sprouts and chilies and give the soup a good stir. Sprinkle with fish sauce, then turn off the heat. Taste and adjust the hot, sour, salty, and sweet flavors, if desired.

✻ Ladle the soup into a large serving bowl. Arrange the basil, cilantro, green onions, and chilies on a plate. Pour fish sauce into small dishes and float a garlic clove in each. To eat, ladle the soup into individual bowls and garnish as desired. Dip the fish and vegetable pieces in fish sauce.

Pat's Notes: Taro stem is the English name for the vegetable known as *bac ha* in Vietnamese. They are crisp and slightly spongy, their porous structure enabling them to absorb the flavors of the stock. As they cook, the stalks become tender and soft. Buy taro stems that are crisp, without any sign of wilting, sliminess, or discoloration. They can be stored in the refrigerator for up to one week. To peel, use the tip of a small paring knife to lift the edge of the skin at the bottom of the stem and use your fingers to peel a strip down its length.

✂ Richer Soups ✂

Chicken Coconut Soup (*Tom Ka Kai*)

This soup is deceptively easy to make, but boasts all the wonderful flavors Thai cuisine is beloved for. Serve as a first course, or with a bowl of rice or rice noodles for a complete meal. Omit the coconut milk for a lighter-tasting soup.

Time: 45 minutes
Makes: 6 to 8 first-course servings or 4 main-course servings

13½-ounce can coconut milk

2 cups chicken stock (recipe on page 42)

2 plump stalks lemongrass, trimmed, bruised (see page 10), and halved

1-inch piece (1 ounce) young galangal, cut into 6 coins

5 kaffir lime leaves, torn in half

1 pound chicken breasts, cut into bite-sized pieces

½ cup fresh or canned mushrooms (button, straw, or shiitakes), sliced (optional)

¼ cup plus 2 tablespoons fish sauce

½ teaspoon sugar

6 red Thai chilies, smashed with the butt of a knife (if you don't like it too spicy, use less), plus more for garnish

¼ cup plus 2 tablespoons lime juice (from 3 large)

Cilantro leaves for garnish

✿ In a large pot, bring the coconut milk, stock, lemongrass, galangal, and lime leaves to a gentle boil over medium-high heat. Add the chicken, mushrooms, fish sauce, sugar, and chilies and return everything to a boil. Reduce the heat to medium and add the lime juice. Simmer until the chicken is fully cooked (cut into a piece to test), 3 to 4 minutes. Taste and adjust seasonings if desired.

✿ Fish out the herbs and discard. Ladle the soup into individual bowls and garnish with cilantro leaves and 1 chili per bowl.

Colonial Curried Chicken Soup
(Mulligatawny Soup)

This colonial adaptation of a South Indian vegetable curry literally means "pepper water." Brimming with chicken meat and piquant spices, it could be a substantial and delicious meal in itself.

Time: 1 hour
Makes: 8 first-course or 4 main-course servings

2 tablespoons vegetable oil

2 small yellow onions, very finely chopped (1½ cups), divided

3 cloves garlic, run through a garlic press or chopped very finely

3- to 4-pound chicken, skinned and cut into 18 pieces

2 quarts warm water

1½-inch piece fresh ginger, grated (1 tablespoon)

½ teaspoon ground paprika

½ teaspoon ground cumin

½ teaspoon ground turmeric

½ teaspoon freshly ground black pepper

2 tablespoons unsweetened desiccated coconut or coconut milk

10 curry leaves, or ½ teaspoon curry powder

1 tablespoon salt

½ cup cooked long-grain rice (preferably basmati)

1 large lemon

Chopped cilantro for garnish

❧ In a large pot, heat the oil over medium-high heat until it becomes runny and starts to shimmer. Add half the onions and the garlic and cook until the onions are light golden, 3 to 4 minutes. Add the chicken pieces and lightly brown them on all sides, 4 to 5 minutes.

❧ Add the remaining onions, the water, ginger, paprika, cumin, turmeric, and black pepper. Bring to a boil. Reduce the heat to medium. Cover and simmer for 10 to 15 minutes, or until the chicken is tender and cooked through.

✤ Remove the chicken pieces from the soup and scrape the meat from the bones. Skim off any fat and scum that has risen to the surface of the soup. Cut or shred the meat with your fingers and return to the soup. Add the coconut, curry leaves, and salt and return to a boil. Turn off the heat.

✤ Spoon 1 tablespoon rice each into 8 bowls. Ladle 1 cup of soup over the rice and squeeze about 1 teaspoon lemon juice into each bowl. Garnish with cilantro and serve hot.

Pat's Notes: Instead of cutting up a whole chicken, use bone-in chicken pieces instead.

Hearty Beef and Vegetable Soup

Beef and vegetable soup spells comfort food in any culture. Grandma Merla See (see page 100) cooked this Chinese-influenced version for her family using whatever vegetables were in her refrigerator. She'd add tomatoes if she wanted a thicker, spicier soup or leave it as a clear broth without. "It depended on my mood that day," she explains.

Time: 3 hours (30 minutes active)
Makes: 6 to 8 first-course servings or 4 main-course servings

> 2 pounds beef shanks or any meaty soup bones (or a combo of bones and stew beef)
>
> 4 quarts water
>
> 4 cloves garlic, smashed with the flat part of a cleaver or large knife
>
> 2 medium tomatoes, cut into eighths (1½ cups)
>
> 2 medium carrots, peeled and cut into 1-inch-thick rounds (1 cup)
>
> 1 large potato, peeled and cut into 1-inch cubes (2 cups)
>
> 1 large yellow onion, cut into eighths and separated
>
> 1 small daikon radish, peeled and cut into 1-inch-thick rounds (1½ cups)
>
> 2 tablespoons soy sauce
>
> 1 tablespoon salt
>
> ½ teaspoon freshly ground white or black pepper
>
> 2 stalks celery, cut into ½-inch-thick slices (1 cup)
>
> ¼ head small cabbage, cored and cut into 1½-inch squares (2 cups)
>
> Chopped green onions for garnish
>
> Chopped cilantro for garnish

❧ Rinse the shanks thoroughly in cold running water to remove all traces of blood and reduce the amount of residue in the soup.

❧ In a large stockpot, combine the bones and water and bring to a rolling boil over high heat. Skim off any scum or foam that rises to the surface. Toss in the garlic and reduce the heat to medium. Cover and simmer gently for 2½ to 3 hours, or until the meat is tender. Remove the shanks and scrape the meat from the bones. Discard the bones.

❄ Return the meat to the soup. Tumble in the tomatoes, carrots, potato, onion, and daikon. Cover and simmer for another 30 minutes, or until the vegetables are crisp tender. Add the soy sauce, salt, and pepper. Taste and adjust seasonings if desired. Add the celery and cabbage and simmer until they're tender but still crispy, 2 to 3 minutes.

❄ Serve immediately in soup bowls or ladle over rice for a complete meal. Garnish with green onions and cilantro.

Pat's Notes: If you prefer a meatier soup, substitute 1½ pounds lean stewing beef for the shanks. Trim any visible fat and silver skin from beef. Rinse thoroughly and proceed as above.

Grandma Says: Boil the beef bones a day ahead and refrigerate so you can skim the fat from the broth before making the soup.

Store the beef broth in the refrigerator for up to 3 days or freeze for up to 3 months.

Red and White Miso Soup (*Awase Miso Shiru*)

Hiroko Sugiyama, owner of Hiroko Sugiyama Culinary Atelier in Seattle, varies the amounts and types of miso she uses in her soup according to the seasons. Not everyone uses a combination of red and white misos, but Hiroko says it makes it more interesting. In the dead of winter, Hiroko likes a thick, sweet, predominantly white miso soup, while in summer she uses more red miso. Her winter recipe is 1 tablespoon of a rich, strong, dark red miso called *haccho* miso, and 10 tablespoons of *saikyo*, a special white miso. The proportion she gives in this recipe is suitable for year-round consumption. If you cannot find haccho or saikyo miso, explore different misos to find ones you like (see page 10). It takes time but it's worth the effort, she says.

Time: 30 minutes
Makes: 4 to 6 first-course servings

> Two 4½- by 2½-inch pieces deep-fried thin tofu (*usu age* or *abura age*) (see Pat's Notes)
> Boiling water
> ¼ cup red haccho miso
> 1½ teaspoons white saikyo miso
> 4 cups dashi (recipe on page 40) (preferably a mix of 3¼ cups Dashi I and ¾ cup Dashi II), divided
> 14-ounce package firm tofu, drained and cut into ½-inch cubes (2½ cups) (Hiroko uses *momen* tofu; see page 25)
> Chopped green onions for garnish

❧ Dip the fried tofu in boiling water for about 30 seconds, then rinse with cold running water. Press it between paper towels to soak up the oil. Cut into thin strips and set aside.

❧ In a small bowl, mix the red and white miso with 1 cup dashi with a wooden spoon, squishing the miso against the side of the bowl until smooth. Heat the remaining dashi in a large saucepan over medium-high heat. Strain the miso mixture into the saucepan and stir to mix well. Add the deep-fried tofu and firm tofu. Cook until heated through, 5 to 6 minutes. Do not let the soup boil; reduce the heat if it starts to a boil. Ladle the soup into individual bowls and shower with green onions.

Red and White Miso Soup

Variations: Add just about any ingredient of your choice to this soup—vegetables, fish, clams, or meat. Just cut into slivers or julienne pieces, cook in the dashi until tender, then add the miso and proceed as above.

Pat's Notes: Hiroko's preferred ratio of miso to dashi is 1 tablespoon miso to ¾ cup dashi. Adjust the proportions to suit your taste.

Usu age and abura age are different types of fried tofu and are widely available in Asian markets, either in cans or in cellophane packages.

Grandma Says: Don't allow the soup to boil once you add the miso. The miso will lose its aroma at high heat.

Healing Pork and Shrimp Rice Soup (*Kao Tom Moo*)

This rice soup, with the heady scent and flavor of garlic and ginger, is a perfect remedy for the common cold. It's ideal when family or friends need gentle, healing food, says Pranee Khruasanit Halvorsen, a native of Phuket, Thailand. As a little girl, Pranee's kitchen chores included grating coconut, pounding curry paste, and cooking rice. She now teaches Thai cooking classes in Seattle. In Thailand, *kao tom* (literally rice soup) is commonly eaten at breakfast, made using leftover cooked rice. The soup can be made with chicken or pork, but lots of garlic and ginger is a must.

Time: 45 minutes
Makes: 2 large main-course servings

2¼ cups chicken stock (recipe on page 42)

1 cup water, plus more as needed

2 cups cooked jasmine long-grain rice

2 tablespoons vegetable oil, divided

5 cloves garlic, chopped (1½ tablespoons)

2-inch piece fresh ginger, peeled and minced (2 tablespoons)

4 ounces ground pork

1 cup spinach leaves, chopped

1 tablespoon soy sauce

1 teaspoon salt

1 egg (optional)

1 teaspoon sesame oil (optional)

Garnishes:

8 cooked medium shrimp, peeled

Chopped green onions

Chopped cilantro leaves

Ground white or black pepper

❧ In a large saucepan, bring the stock, water, and rice to a boil over high heat. Reduce the heat to medium and simmer while you prepare the other ingredients.

In a small skillet, heat 1 tablespoon of the oil over medium heat until it becomes runny and starts to shimmer. Add the garlic and ginger and cook until golden and fragrant, 1 to 2 minutes. Don't burn them! Reserve half for garnish and add the rest to the soup.

In the same skillet, heat the remaining oil over medium-high heat. Add the pork and stir and cook until it just loses its blush, 1 to 2 minutes. Stir the partially cooked pork into the soup. Simmer until the rice grains have absorbed some of the stock and expanded about 1½ times their original size. The texture of the rice soup should not be as thin as a clear soup, nor as thick as congee or cooked oatmeal, another 2 to 3 minutes, or about 10 minutes total. The final dish should comprise about one-third liquid and two-thirds rice grains. Simmer for a few more minutes to reduce or add more water to reach the desired consistency.

Stir in the spinach, soy sauce, and salt. Return the soup to a boil and crack in the egg and drizzle with sesame oil. Give it one last stir, then ladle into individual bowls. Garnish with the reserved garlic and ginger, the shrimp, green onions, and cilantro. Sprinkle with pepper to taste.

Pat's Notes: Kao tom is thinner than the Chinese version of rice porridge (see LEFTOVER THANKSGIVING TURKEY–RICE PORRIDGE, page 274) and looks more like rice grains floating in soup. The grains are soft but are still whole. As the porridge sits, the texture will thicken. You can add more liquid or enjoy it as is.

Herb-Scented Chicken Soup (*S'ngao Chruok Moan*)

Just about every ingredient, from the culantro to the lemongrass, gives this refreshing Cambodian soup its sprightly flavor and delightful fragrance. For Phiroum Svy, a working mother of two teenagers, this soup is a simple-to-prepare meal when she's in a time crunch. Phiroum, whose name means "peacefulness" in Cambodian, likes to use bone-in chicken thighs in soups because they give the stock better flavor. Use breast meat if you prefer, but in my experience it tends to dry out and toughen after boiling. Try tilapia or salmon fillets instead of chicken.

Time: 1 hour
Makes: 2 main-course servings or 4 first-course servings

> 6 cups water
>
> 1 tablespoon uncooked jasmine rice
>
> 2½ pounds (4 small) bone-in chicken thighs
>
> 2 culantro leaves
>
> 1 clove garlic, smashed with the flat part of a cleaver or large knife
>
> ⅛-inch-thick coin galangal, peeled and smashed
>
> 1 plump stalk lemongrass, trimmed, bruised (see page 10), and cut into fourths on the diagonal
>
> 8 ounces button mushrooms, quartered (2 cups)
>
> 2 tablespoons fish sauce
>
> 1 teaspoon salt
>
> 2 kaffir lime leaves

Garnishes:

> ¼ cup chopped cilantro
>
> ¼ cup chopped culantro
>
> ¼ cup chopped green onions
>
> ¼ cup chopped Thai basil leaves
>
> 2 limes, cut into wedges
>
> Dipping Sauce (recipe follows)

In a large saucepan, bring the water and rice to a boil over high heat. Add the chicken, culantro, garlic, galangal, and lemongrass and return to a boil. Cover and simmer over medium heat for 15 minutes.

🌸 Remove the chicken from the soup and scrape the meat from the bones. Don't worry if the meat is not cooked through. Cut or shred the meat with your fingers into bite-sized pieces and return to the saucepan. Discard the bones. Add the mushrooms followed by the fish sauce and salt. Crumple the kaffir lime leaves to release their essential oils and flavor and toss into the soup. Simmer for another 3 to 4 minutes. The soup is ready when the mushrooms are cooked.

🌸 Fish out the large herbs, garlic, galangal, and lemongrass and discard. Ladle the soup into individual bowls. Arrange the cilantro, culantro, green onions, basil, and limes separately on a plate and put the dipping sauce into small bowls. Serve with the garnishes, dipping sauce, and jasmine rice. Pick and choose garnishes as you like and dip the chicken and mushroom pieces in the dipping sauce as you eat.

Dipping Sauce (*Tik Chror Louk*)

Makes: ½ cup

> 1 tablespoon lime juice (from ½ large)
> 1 tablespoon water
> 4 teaspoons fish sauce
> 1 clove garlic, minced
> 4 Thai basil leaves, finely chopped
> 2 Thai chilies, cut into rounds
> ¼ teaspoon sugar
> ¼ teaspoon salt

🌸 In a small bowl, combine the lime juice, water, fish sauce, garlic, basil, chilies, sugar, and salt.

Nepalese Nine-Bean Soup

Nepalese Nine-Bean Soup (*Kawatee*)

Healthful and simple, this nutritious soup is named for the nine different beans that go into it. In Nepal, *kawatee* is eaten during the harsh winters to "warm" and protect the body. Restaurant-owner Roshita Shrestha who hails from Kathmandu recommends it for women during confinement and while breastfeeding. Roshita ate kawatee often after the recent birth of her daughter in Seattle and says it also offers a taste of home. You can use any type of dried beans or legumes to make 2¼ cups total.

Time: 2 hours (20 minutes active) plus soaking
Makes: 4 main-course servings

¼ cup dried black beans

¼ cup dried kidney beans

¼ cup dried red or green lentils

¼ cup dried azuki beans

¼ cup dried black-eyed peas

¼ cup dried green mung beans

¼ cup dried lentils

¼ cup dried garbanzo beans

¼ cup dried soybeans

1 tablespoon vegetable oil

1 large clove garlic, minced

½-inch piece fresh ginger, grated (1 teaspoon), plus 1-inch piece ginger, cut into ¼-inch-thick coins

5 cups water, plus more as needed

2 tablespoons ghee, margarine, or butter

¼ teaspoon ajowan seeds (see Pat's Notes)

⅛ teaspoon asafetida powder (see Pat's Notes)

1½ teaspoons salt

❀ Rinse all of the beans and pick out any stones and grit. In a large bowl, soak them in enough water to cover by 2 inches for at least 8 hours. Drain and rinse.

❀ In a large heavy-bottomed pot or Dutch oven, heat the oil over medium-high heat until it becomes runny and starts to shimmer. Add the garlic and grated ginger and cook until fragrant, 15 to 30 seconds. Tip in the beans and stir and cook until lightly browned and well coated in oil, 4 to 5 minutes. Pour in the water and bring to a boil. Reduce the heat to medium. Cover and simmer for about 1¼ hours , or until the beans are tender and squish easily between your fingers.

❧ Toss in the ginger coins and simmer for another 15 minutes. The soup should not be too thick but have the consistency of a thin vegetable stew. Add more water if necessary.

❧ To make the tempering oil, heat the ghee in a small skillet over high heat until it melts and starts to bubble gently. Stir in the ajowan seeds and asafetida powder. The mixture will sizzle and sputter. Immediately stir the entire contents of the skillet into the soup. Add the salt and serve hot with basmati rice.

Pat's Notes: A tempering oil (called *channa* or *tarka*) adds extra richness and depth to a dish. Spices (usually whole) are mixed into hot ghee and allowed to "bloom" before the entire mixture is immediately poured into a dish at the end of cooking.

Ajowan seeds are small ridged seeds that look like celery seeds. They belong to the same family as coriander, cumin, celery, lovage, and fennel. When ground, ajowan tastes and smells like thyme, but is more intense with a peppery backnote. Ajowan seeds can be found in South Asian markets, but if necessary, thyme, cumin, or caraway may be used as a substitute.

Asafetida is a strong onion-garlic flavored powdered gum resin. After cooking, its flavor is like the mildest, mellowest garlic. It does wonders for the digestion, which is why it's often used in legume dishes. Buy it ground (Vandevi brand) and store in a very tightly sealed container. You can substitute the same amount of onion or garlic powder.

Watercress and Pork Rib Soup

Tender pork ribs add savory flavor to this light, nourishing soup, while sweet red dates balance the peppery bite of watercress. This dish is often served in Chinese households to restore balance in the body based on the Taoist concept of yin and yang (the idea of opposites in balance). Watercress is considered a predominantly yin, or cooling, food and ginger is a yang, or warming, food. You can substitute chicken for the pork ribs if preferred.

Time: 1½ hours (20 minutes active)
Makes: 6 first-course servings

> 4-ounce bunch watercress
>
> 1 pound pork spareribs, trimmed of excess fat and cut crosswise through the bone into 2-inch pieces
>
> 2 quarts water
>
> 6 pitted dried red dates
>
> ½-inch piece fresh ginger, cut into thin coins
>
> 2 teaspoons salt
>
> 1 teaspoon sugar

❧ Trim the watercress, discarding the tough, woody ends. Wash it thoroughly under cold running water and drain in a colander. Separate the leaves and stems and cut the stems into 1-inch lengths (using the stems is optional but why waste?).

❧ To parboil the ribs, bring a large saucepan of water to a rolling boil over high heat. Toss in the ribs and return to a rolling boil. Drain the ribs in a colander to get rid of fat and scum, and then return to the pot.

❧ Add the water, watercress stems, dates, and ginger. Bring to a boil over high heat, then reduce the heat to medium. Cover and simmer gently for 45 minutes to 1 hour, or until the ribs are tender. Skim off any scum or foam that rises to the surface.

❧ Toss in the watercress leaves and simmer until the leaves turn dark green, 2 to 3 minutes. Stir in the salt and sugar and serve immediately.

Profile of a Grandma: MERLA SEE

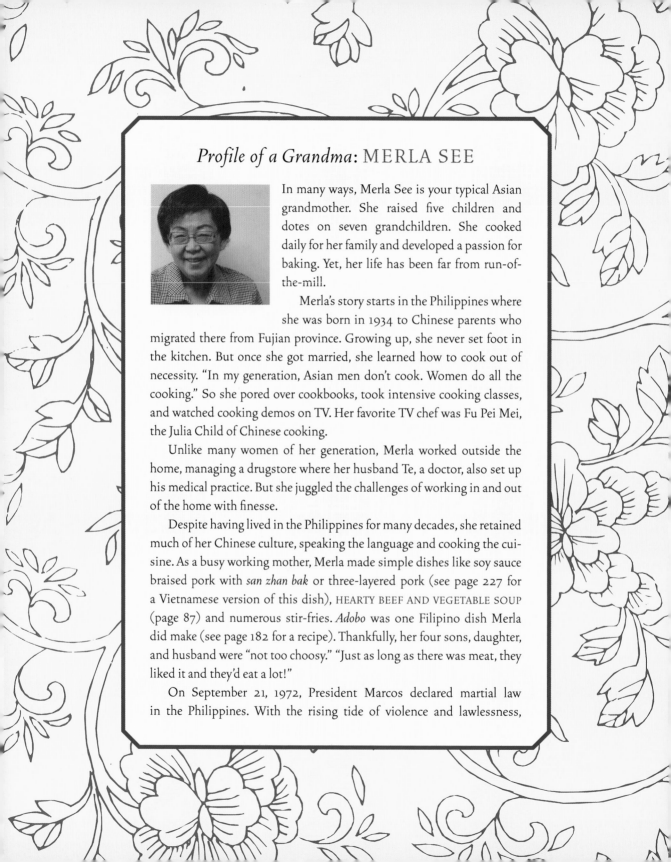

In many ways, Merla See is your typical Asian grandmother. She raised five children and dotes on seven grandchildren. She cooked daily for her family and developed a passion for baking. Yet, her life has been far from run-of-the-mill.

Merla's story starts in the Philippines where she was born in 1934 to Chinese parents who migrated there from Fujian province. Growing up, she never set foot in the kitchen. But once she got married, she learned how to cook out of necessity. "In my generation, Asian men don't cook. Women do all the cooking." So she pored over cookbooks, took intensive cooking classes, and watched cooking demos on TV. Her favorite TV chef was Fu Pei Mei, the Julia Child of Chinese cooking.

Unlike many women of her generation, Merla worked outside the home, managing a drugstore where her husband Te, a doctor, also set up his medical practice. But she juggled the challenges of working in and out of the home with finesse.

Despite having lived in the Philippines for many decades, she retained much of her Chinese culture, speaking the language and cooking the cuisine. As a busy working mother, Merla made simple dishes like soy sauce braised pork with *san zhan bak* or three-layered pork (see page 227 for a Vietnamese version of this dish), HEARTY BEEF AND VEGETABLE SOUP (page 87) and numerous stir-fries. *Adobo* was one Filipino dish Merla did make (see page 182 for a recipe). Thankfully, her four sons, daughter, and husband were "not too choosy." "Just as long as there was meat, they liked it and they'd eat a lot!"

On September 21, 1972, President Marcos declared martial law in the Philippines. With the rising tide of violence and lawlessness, thousands of Filipinos fled the country, Merla and her family among them.

It was trying times for Merla and Te. Uncertain of what lay ahead, they brought their two oldest children with them to Chicago, and left the three youngest ones in the care of their grandmother in the Philippines. Only after Te completed his residency and board exam, allowing him to practice medicine again, did they decide to settle permanently in the United States. Merla immediately returned to the Philippines to fetch their three young children.

In Chicago, Merla discovered her love for baking quite by accident. The birthday cakes she bought for her children were way too sweet for their taste. So she decided to try American cake recipes, but using less sugar. To her surprise, they came out perfect!

Over the years, Merla baked cakes for birthdays, holidays, and family gatherings and she earned a glowing reputation as master baker among her extended family. It came as no surprise when Merla's baking talent was recognized outside the family circle. She entered a neighborhood cooking and baking contest and won first prize. Her winning recipe? A chocolate chiffon cake recipe she found in an American cookbook that she tweaked to her liking.

Merla's most ambitious baking project was a gigantic multi-tiered cake to celebrate Te's parents' 60th anniversary. The cake required several dozen eggs and numerous sacks of flour and sugar. It comprised a staircase for each of the couple's six children; the staircases were lined with figurines representing the children, along with their spouses and their children. Merla collected the figures over one year, going from cake shop to cake shop meticulously comparing proportions. It took two days to make the cake—one day to bake and another to assemble and decorate. It was a lot of hard work, but all the relatives were talking about it for months after the celebration!

5

ON THE SIDE

Most people think of the main course first when planning a meal, but side dishes are just as important to an Asian family-style meal. Anxious to feed children and grandchildren a balanced diet, mothers and grandmothers will often prepare healthy side dishes of fresh vegetables, egg, tofu, and legumes. The dishes range from a quick stir-fry to a fragrant *dal* to a savory omelet. Some sides can also suffice as a simple, complete meal with rice. Refreshing and with a tangy bite, pickled and preserved vegetables serve as both side dishes and condiments, balancing the richness of meats and seafood in a main dish.

Cabbage Kimchi

Vegetables

Chinese Broccoli in Oyster Sauce

Eggplant Curry (*Bagaara Baingan*)

Eggy Stir-Fried Cabbage

Layered Vegetable Stew (*Pinakbet*)

Mixed Medley Stir-Fry

Spiced Chayote and Peas (*Safed Kaddu aur Matar ki Sabzi*)

Water Spinach with Shrimp Paste and Chilies (*Kangkung Belacan*)

Wok-Fried Pea Shoots

Tofu

Deep-Fried Tofu

Deep-Fried Tofu Simmered with Tomatoes

Pan-Fried Tofu Simmered in Sweet Miso Sauce (*Tofu no Misoni*)

Stir-Fried Mung Bean Sprouts with Tofu and Chives
(*Pad Tao Kua Tao Ngae*)

Tofu Omelet with Sweet Peanut Sauce (*Tahu Telur*)

Pulses and Legumes

Spiced Red Lentil Stew (*Palida*)

Yellow Split Pea Curry (*Matar Dal*)

Pickles and Salads

Cabbage Kimchi

Chinese Pickles (*Liang Ban Huang Gua*)

Green and Golden Zucchini Thread Salad (*Hobak Namul*)

Indian Cucumber and Tomato Relish (*Kachumber*)

Soybean Sprout Salad (*Kong Namul Sangchae*)

Spicy Korean Oyster Salad (*Kul Kimchi*)

✄ Vegetables ✁

Chinese Broccoli in Oyster Sauce

You've probably spied or tried Chinese broccoli (*gai lan* in Cantonese) in a restaurant, traditionally cloaked in oyster sauce which nicely complements the dark leafy green vegetable's slightly bittersweet taste. The good news is that it's super simple to make at home. Chinese broccoli is available at most Asian markets, but if you can't find it, try regular broccoli or broccoli rabe.

Time: 15 minutes (plus optional frying of the shallots)
Makes: 4 to 6 servings as part of a multicourse family-style meal

> 1 pound Chinese broccoli, trimmed
> ¼ cup oyster sauce
> Sesame oil for drizzling
> Fried shallots (see page 22) for garnish (optional)

✁ Cut the broccoli in half crosswise into leaf and stem sections and halve the thicker stems down the middle as they take longer to cook.

✁ Fill a large stockpot two-thirds full of water and bring to a rolling boil over high heat. Add the broccoli stems. Cook for 1 minute, then add the leafy portions. Cook until the leaves turn a bright jade green and the stalks are tender crisp, another 2 to 3 minutes. Don't overcook!

✁ Using a slotted spoon, scoop up the broccoli, shake off as much excess water as possible, and transfer to a serving platter. Drizzle with the oyster sauce and sesame oil to taste. Sprinkle with fried shallots and serve.

Variation—Cooking in the Microwave: On a rimmed plate, place the thicker stemmed ends in a shallow pool of water and microwave on high for 1 minute. Add the leafy sections and microwave for another 2 to 3 minutes. All microwaves are different, so some trial and error is required before you perfect this technique.

Variation—Cooking in an Asparagus Steamer: Arrange whole stalks of Chinese broccoli upright in the steamer basket and steam for 3 to 4 minutes. As with asparagus spears, the tender tops are cooked just right while the stems are tender-crisp.

Pat's Notes: Other green leafy vegetables such as watercress, water spinach, or Chinese flowering cabbage (*choy sum*) can be boiled or steamed and topped off with oyster sauce and sesame oil.

Eggplant Curry (*Bagaara Baingan*)

In India, this dish is made in large quantities and served as a pickle accompanying YELLOW SPLIT PEA CURRY (page 130) and rice. It's also good with AMMA'S RICE (page 225). It doesn't have to be refrigerated and is usually kept in an earthenware dish or jam jar and will last for a week (which explains why so much oil is used—it's a preservative!). The final dish is a delicious mix of sweet and sour; if you'd like to make it a little spicier, add a chopped jalapeño.

Time: 45 minutes, plus standing
Makes: 4 to 6 servings as a pickle or side dish

1 medium (1 pound) eggplant

1 teaspoon ground turmeric

2 teaspoons salt, divided

¾ cup vegetable oil, divided

1 large yellow onion, halved and cut into thin crescents (1½ cups)

3-inch piece (3 ounces) fresh ginger, peeled and cut into slivers

3 tablespoons toasted sesame seeds

2 teaspoons ground cumin

2 teaspoons ground coriander

2 teaspoons ground dried red chilies

½ cup finely grated unsweetened desiccated coconut (see Pat's Notes)

½ cup brown sugar

1 teaspoon tamarind paste (see page 25)

1 teaspoon sesame oil

❧ Trim the eggplant and halve lengthwise. Cut each half lengthwise into 3 slices and then each slice crosswise in half for a total of 12 pieces.

❧ Put the eggplant in a colander, sprinkle with the turmeric and 1 teaspoon salt, and toss to coat. Let the eggplant sit in the colander over the sink for 30 minutes.

❧ In a large nonstick skillet, heat ½ cup of the oil over medium heat until it becomes runny and starts to shimmer. Add the onion and stir and cook until soft and translucent, 3 to 4 minutes. Add the ginger and continue cooking until the onion turns golden brown, another 4 to 5 minutes. Add the sesame seeds, cumin, coriander, chili, and remaining salt and cook until the spices turn several shades darker and release their fragrance, 4 to 5 minutes. Remove the skillet from the heat.

❧ Pat the eggplant slices dry with paper towels and arrange in one layer in the skillet with the spices. Cover and cook over medium-low heat for 5 minutes. Uncover and stir and cook for another 4 to 5 minutes. Stir in the coconut and simmer for another 3 minutes. The coconut will soak up the oil so if it starts to scorch, add more oil. Raise the heat to medium and stir in the brown sugar and tamarind paste. Stir and cook until the sugar dissolves completely, 1½ to 2 minutes. Add the remaining oil and simmer for another 3 minutes. The eggplant should be soft and shiny with oil but not swimming in it.

❧ Dribble the sesame oil over the eggplant. Let it sit for at least 2 hours to allow the flavors to meld before serving. Serve at room temperature with freshly steamed basmati rice.

Pat's Notes: You can find unsweetened desiccated coconut in South Asian markets or health food stores. Don't buy the sweetened kind (used for baking) from the supermarket.

Eggplant soaks up a lot of oil. Use your discretion if you'd rather not add the last ¼ cup.

Eggy Stir-Fried Cabbage

Easy-to-make and very tasty, this is a busy weeknight go-to side dish, or pile it on freshly steamed rice for a simple one-dish meal. The sweet and crunchy cabbage ribbons are wonderfully paired with the briny shrimp and soft, custardy egg. The dish, probably Chinese-influenced, is common in Vietnamese and Indonesian households.

Time: 20 minutes
Makes: 4 side servings as part of a multicourse family-style meal or 2 servings as a one-dish meal

2 tablespoons vegetable oil

2 cloves garlic, minced

3 ounces (⅓ cup) tiny raw pink shrimp (optional)

½ medium head of cabbage, cored and cut into ¼-inch-wide ribbons (4 to 5 cups)

2 to 3 tablespoons water, divided

2 eggs

1 tablespoon fish sauce or soy sauce

Dash ground white pepper

Salt (optional)

In a large wok or skillet, heat the oil over medium heat until it becomes runny and starts to shimmer. Add the garlic and cook until fragrant, 15 to 30 seconds. Add the shrimp and cook until just pink, about 1 minute. Raise the heat to high. Throw in the cabbage and stir it swiftly around the wok until bright green and translucent, 4 to 5 minutes. Add a splash of water if the cabbage starts to brown too much. Reduce the heat to medium.

Make a well in the center of the wok by moving the cabbage up the sides. Crack the eggs into the well. Stir the eggs gently until the yolks break, keeping the cabbage out of the egg mixture for now. Let the eggs cook until almost set but still a little runny (think soggy scrambled eggs), about 2 minutes. Raise the heat to medium-high and mix everything together.

Add 2 tablespoons of water, the fish sauce, white pepper, and salt to taste. Toss with a couple more flourishes to ensure everything is evenly coated with seasonings. Serve immediately.

Layered Vegetable Stew (*Pinakbet*)

A popular Filipino dish, the basic components of *pinakbet* (also called *pakbet*) are tomatoes, squash, long beans, bitter melon, okra, eggplant, and fish sauce (*patis*) or fermented shrimp paste (*bagoong*). A version from California food blogger Marvin Gapultos uses only fish sauce. Don't pay too much attention to evenly chopping and measuring the vegetables; they don't have to be perfect. For the tomatoes, follow Marvin's mom's lead: she sticks her thumbs in the stem ends and rips them apart! Serve with a meat dish like CHICKEN ADOBO (page 182) and freshly steamed rice.

Time: 1¼ hours (45 minutes active)
Makes: 6 to 8 servings as part of a multicourse family-style meal

> 1½ pounds (about 5) very ripe large tomatoes, roughly chopped or ripped apart with your hands
>
> 1 pound (about ½ small) kabocha squash, peeled, seeded, and cut into ¾-inch cubes
>
> 1 small bitter melon, seeded and cut into ½-inch-thick crescents (1 cup)
>
> 1 small Japanese eggplant, halved lengthwise and cut into ½-inch-thick half moons (1 cup)
>
> 8 ounces (about 16) fresh young okra pods, stems trimmed and caps left intact
>
> 8 ounces long beans, trimmed and cut into 3-inch lengths (2 cups)
>
> 1 small sweet onion, cut into thin crescents (¾ cup)
>
> ¼ cup water
>
> 2 tablespoons fish sauce, plus more as needed
>
> 4 ounces deep-fried pork belly (*chicharron*) (see Pat's Notes), chopped into bite-sized pieces (1 cup) (optional)

❧ Place half of the tomatoes in the bottom of a 4- to 5-quart pot or Dutch oven (just big enough to fill to the top with vegetables). Layer the squash, melon, eggplant, okra, long beans, and onion on top, then top with the remaining tomatoes. Add the water and fish sauce.

❧ Bring the stew to a boil over medium-high heat. Reduce the heat to medium. Cover and simmer for 15 minutes, without strirring. Add the pork belly and simmer for another 10 minutes. The vegetables should be tender but not mushy and there should be just enough liquid for a light sauce. If the vegetables are not tender enough for your liking, simmer for another 5 minutes. Taste the sauce and add more fish sauce if necessary.

Pat's Notes: Tomatoes are an important ingredient here and determine how flavorful the final dish will be; use organic tomatoes in season, if possible. Ripe tomatoes will yield more juice.

Okra and bitter melon are definitely acquired tastes. You can omit them and increase the amount of the other vegetables if you so choose but according to Marvin, "without the bitter melon, it's not really a true pinakbet."

Chicharron, called *bagnet* in the Philippines, is sometimes available freshly fried at Asian or Latin markets. You can also make the fried bits at home—simply deep-fry slivers of pork belly, ensuring each piece has skin, fat, and meat, until they are golden-brown and crisp. Or buy fried pork rinds (available in bags) that are eaten as a snack. They'll render enough fat for an equally flavorful dish.

Mixed Medley Stir-Fry

A stir-fry is one of the simplest and most versatile dishes you can cook. Once you've cut up all the ingredients, the actual cooking is a breeze. Mix and match the meat and vegetables—just make sure all the ingredients are cut to similar size. The meat is cooked separately and then the vegetables are added in progressive order of cooking time; denser vegetables like broccoli and carrots take longer and go in first, while green leafy vegetables like spinach only require a brief fling in the wok. If you're not sure, just stir-fry them one by one and combine everything at the end. After a couple of tries you're bound to get the hang of it!

Time: 30 minutes plus marinating
Makes: 4 to 6 servings as part of a multicourse family-style meal

> 12 ounces pork loin
> 2 tablespoons Shaoxing rice wine or dry sherry
> 2 tablespoons soy sauce
> 1 teaspoon sesame oil (optional)
> 3 tablespoons vegetable oil, divided
> 2 cloves garlic, chopped
> ½-inch piece fresh ginger, minced (1 teaspoon)

8 ounces broccoli, cut into 1-inch florets (2 cups)

1 large carrot, peeled and cut into ¼-inch-thick diagonal slices (1 cup)

2 ounces snow peas, trimmed and strings removed (1 cup)

1 medium yellow onion, cut into wedges and separated (1 cup)

½ cup chicken stock or water

1 teaspoon sugar

Salt

Freshly ground black pepper

1 tablespoon cornstarch dissolved in 2 tablespoons water to form a slurry

❀ Handle the pork partially frozen so that it is easier to cut (if it's fresh, place in the freezer for about 30 minutes). Cut the pork along the grain into 1½-inch-thick strips. Then, with your knife at an angle almost parallel to the cutting surface, slice the pork diagonally against the grain into ⅛-inch-thick slices.

❀ Combine the pork, rice wine, soy sauce, and sesame oil in a medium bowl and toss to mix. Marinate for 20 minutes.

❀ Preheat a large wok or skillet over high heat for 1 minute. Swirl in 2 table-spoons of the vegetable oil and heat until it becomes runny and starts to shimmer. Spread the pork slices out in the wok with your spatula to get as much meat as possible in direct contact with the wok surface. Wait a few seconds to allow the pork to brown lightly, then toss. Stir and cook until the pork is nearly cooked through, 3 to 4 minutes. Remove and set aside.

❀ Reheat the wok over medium-high heat. Swirl in the remaining oil and add the garlic and ginger. Cook and stir until fragrant, 15 to 30 seconds. Throw in the broccoli and carrot and toss for about 2 minutes. Add the snow peas and onion and toss until the vegetables are evenly coated with oil. Add the stock, cover, and cook for 1 to 2 minutes, or until the broccoli turns bright green and all the vegetables are crisp.

❀ Return the pork to the wok. Sprinkle with the sugar and salt and pepper to taste. Stir everything swiftly around the wok to mix. Taste and adjust seasonings if desired. Give the cornstarch slurry a quick stir in the bowl and then pour into the wok, stirring until the sauce starts to bubble and thicken, about 30 seconds. Toss with a couple more flourishes to mix thoroughly. Serve immediately with freshly steamed rice.

Pat's Notes: Substitute flank steak, chicken breast, or tofu for the pork. The meats and tofu cook at different rates (chicken takes a little longer to cook and should be cooked through) so adjust cooking times accordingly.

Diversify your meat marinade—it can be as simple as oyster sauce (or any prepared sauce for that matter), and you can choose to add chili paste or broad bean sauce.

VEGETABLE CUTTING 101

You can stir-fry just about any vegetable. Here are some favorites and how to prep them:

Asparagus: Cut into ¼-inch diagonal pieces.

Bell Peppers (red or green): Seed and cut into 1-inch squares or ¼-inch-wide strips.

Bok Choy: Cut stems into ½-inch diagonal pieces and leaves into 2-inch pieces. Stir-fry the stems for about 1 minute before adding the leaves.

Broccoli: Cut into florets; if you choose to use the stalks, peel them and cut into thin slices or julienne pieces.

Eggplant: Peel, then cut into 1-inch cubes or finger-sized pieces.

Mushrooms (fresh): Cut through the stems into ¼-inch-thick slices.

Onions: Cut into small wedges.

Tomatoes: Cut into small wedges.

Zucchini (and other summer squash): Halve and cut into ¼-inch-thick diagonal slices.

Spiced Chayote and Peas
(*Safed Kaddu aur Matar ki Sabzi*)

The original version of this Bengali recipe uses white pumpkin (*Benincasa hispida*) that is cultivated extensively in India. It's hard to find in the United States so Grandma Niloufer Gupta (see page 140) uses chayote, a gourdlike fruit, instead. Niloufer insists that ground spices cannot take the place of whole spices in this recipe. Besides, whole spices are not hard to find, she says, and many specialty markets have fresh, good-quality spices that are superior even to those at South Asian markets here. In the end, this simple dish is a knockout—the lightly spiced chayote blooms with flavor, the peas add a touch of sweetness to every bite, and subtle notes of coriander hum in the background. Serve with ROTI (page 191) and YELLOW SPLIT PEA CURRY (page 130) or SPICED RED LENTIL STEW (page 128).

Time: 45 minutes
Makes: 4 to 6 servings as part of a multicourse family-style meal

> 1 pound (about 2) chayotes
>
> ¼ cup vegetable oil
>
> 1 teaspoon golden mustard seeds
>
> 1 teaspoon salt
>
> ½ teaspoon sugar
>
> ¼ cup (½ stick) butter
>
> 1 teaspoon coriander seeds
>
> ¼ teaspoon fenugreek seeds
>
> 2 small red bell peppers, diced (1½ cups)
>
> 1 ounce cilantro, leaves picked off (¼ cup) and stems chopped (2 tablespoons)
>
> 1 cup frozen peas, thawed

※ Peel the chayotes with a vegetable peeler and cut into quarters. Core and cut each quarter lengthwise in half. Chop crosswise into ½-inch-thick chunks.

※ In a large wok or skillet, heat the oil over medium-low heat until it becomes runny and starts to shimmer. Drop in a mustard seed; if it floats and starts to sputter, the oil is ready. Stir in the rest of the mustard seeds and cook until they are light brown and fragrant, 1 to 2 minutes. Toss in the chayote and stir constantly for 3 minutes. Add the salt and sugar and cook, stirring

Spiced Chayote and Peas

occasionally, for another 3 minutes. Add the butter, coriander, and fenugreek. Cover and simmer for 5 minutes, or until the chayote is almost cooked through. Add the bell peppers, cover, and cook until they release their juices, about 1 minute. Add the cilantro stems and peas and stir.

🌿 Simmer until the peas are heated through and the chayote is tender and cooked to your liking (bite into a piece to test), about 3 minutes. Don't simmer the peas for too long or they will overcook and turn dirty green. Taste and add more salt or sugar if desired. Transfer to a serving platter. Garnish with cilantro leaves and let the dish sit for at least 5 minutes to allow the flavors to meld before serving. Enjoy this dish with whole-wheat tortillas available at Latin markets or specialty markets.

Grandma Says: Cilantro changes its flavor when it comes into contact with steel, so pick the leaves off the stems, don't chop them.

If you can find black mustard seeds to use in this recipe, decrease the initial cooking time as they are often finer and burn quickly.

Water Spinach with Shrimp Paste and Chilies
(*Kangkung Belacan*)

Water spinach (also called morning glory or hollow spinach) is a long tubular leafy green. Easily found at Asian markets, it is called *kangkung* (also *kangkong*) in Malay, *rau muong* in Vietnamese and *ong choy* in Cantonese. This tasty dish recalls the earthy and aromatic flavors of Singapore and Malaysia.

Time: 30 minutes
Makes: 4 to 6 servings as part of a multicourse family-style meal

> 2 tablespoons dried shrimp, rinsed
>
> Boiling water for soaking
>
> 1 pound water spinach
>
> 5 Asian shallots or ½ small yellow onion, coarsely chopped (⅓ cup)
>
> 4 cloves garlic
>
> 3 long, fresh red chilies, stemmed, seeded if desired, and coarsely chopped; or 1 tablespoon prepared chili paste
>
> 2 teaspoons dried shrimp paste
>
> 3 tablespoons vegetable oil, or more if needed
>
> 2 teaspoons sugar
>
> Salt (optional; the shrimp paste is already salty, so add sparingly if at all)

❧ In a small bowl, soak the dried shrimp in enough boiling water to cover until softened, about 10 minutes. Drain, reserving 2 tablespoons of the liquid.

❧ Wash the water spinach in cold water and drain well. Trim off and discard the bottom 4 inches of the root ends which are usually very fibrous. Trim off and discard any tough, woody stems (the best way to find out is to bite into a stem—if it's chewy, discard). Cut into thirds, separating the stems and leaves.

❧ Combine the dried shrimp, shallots, garlic, chilies, and dried shrimp paste in the work bowl of a 3- to 4-cup food processor and whirl into a thick, clumpy paste resembling cooked oatmeal, about 1 minute. Scrape unground bits down toward the blade as you go. Do not overprocess; confetti-sized bits of chili are fine.

✽ In a large wok or skillet, heat the oil over medium heat until it becomes runny and starts to shimmer. Drop in a little shrimp-chili paste; if it starts to sizzle cheerfully, the oil is ready. Add the rest of the paste. Cook for 4 to 5 minutes, stirring and scraping the bottom of the wok continuously to cook the paste evenly and prevent scorching. (When frying chilies, the volatile oils will permeate the air so it's a good idea to have your vent on high and your windows open). If the paste absorbs all the oil and begins to stick to the wok, add more oil, 1 tablespoon at a time, until the paste starts moving easily around the wok again. If the paste starts to burn, pull the wok off the heat for a few seconds before continuing. Keep adjusting the heat as necessary. The paste is ready when its original pungent smell has mellowed to a pleasantly sweet fragrance with no trace of raw shallots or garlic. Visual clues to look out for: the cooked paste should be several shades darker than when raw, and should separate from the oil.

✽ Toss in the water spinach stems and stir to mix with the paste for about 30 seconds. Add the spinach leaves, sugar, and reserved dried shrimp liquid and raise the heat to medium-high. Stir the vegetables swiftly around the wok, sliding your spatula to the bottom of the wok and turning and tossing to coat with the seasonings, until the leaves are just wilted but still bright green and the stems are crisp, 2 to 3 minutes. Taste and add salt if desired. Transfer to a large platter and serve immediately with freshly steamed rice.

Variations: Try asparagus, okra, spinach, long beans, green beans, sweet potato/yam leaf, or broccolini in this recipe.

Wok-Fried Pea Shoots

Wok-Fried Pea Shoots

A brief fling in the wok is the perfect technique for cooking delicate pea shoots (sometimes called pea vines). Available at farmers markets and Asian markets (under the name *dou miao*), they should include a top pair of small leaves (the tip), delicate tendrils attached to the young stem, and a few larger leaves or blossoms. Select bright green, undamaged shoots.

Time: 10 minutes
Makes: 4 to 6 servings as part of a multicourse family-style meal

> 1 pound pea shoots, rinsed and drained well
> 2 tablespoons vegetable oil
> 3 cloves garlic, minced (1 tablespoon)
> ¼ cup chicken stock (recipe on page 42) or water
> 2 teaspoons soy sauce or fish sauce
> Sesame oil for drizzling (optional)

❧ Trim the pea shoots and remove any tough stems.

❧ Preheat a large wok or skillet over medium heat. Swirl in the oil and heat until it becomes runny and starts to shimmer. Add the garlic and cook until fragrant, 15 to 30 seconds. Raise the heat to high, throw in the pea shoots, and toss to coat evenly with the oil and garlic until the leaves are just wilted, 1 to 1½ minutes. Add the stock and soy sauce and toss until the liquid has reduced to a few tablespoons and the shoots are tender and bright green, another 1 to 2 minutes. Drizzle with sesame oil and serve immediately with a meat dish and freshly steamed rice.

Pat's Notes: Pea shoots are often confused with pea sprouts, the whole baby pea plant. However, shoots and sprouts can be used interchangeably.

This method can be used for many vegetables, from bok choy to *tatsoi* to Chinese flowering cabbage (*choy sum*). For vegetables with thicker stems or ribs, separate the leaves and stems and add the stems first as they require a longer cooking time.

✂ Tofu ✂

Deep-Fried Tofu

Many recipes, including this one, call for drained (or pressed) tofu. This simple process removes excess moisture, allowing more flavor to be absorbed in cooking. Deep-frying can be a messy job but nothing compares to just-fried tofu. One bite and you can tell the difference. Buy firm (also called regular) or extra-firm tofu for deep-frying. Serve with Thai sweet chili sauce or SWEET AND SOUR SAUCE (page 63). Or use in DEEP-FRIED TOFU SIMMERED WITH TOMATOES (see opposite page) or MIXED MEDLEY STIR-FRY (page 112).

Time: 15 minutes, plus draining the tofu
Makes: 4 to 6 servings part of a multicourse family-style meal or as a snack

> 14-ounce package firm or extra-firm tofu, drained (see page 26)
> 3 cups (or as needed) vegetable oil for deep-frying

✂ Cut the drained tofu into rectangular pieces 2 by 1 by ½ inch thick (or as close as you can get to these dimensions). Line a plate with paper towels.

✂ In a large wok, heavy skillet, or Dutch oven, heat the oil over high heat until it reaches 350 degrees F on a deep-fry thermometer (see page xiii for deep-frying tips). Reduce the heat to medium-high. Using a slotted spoon, gently lower the tofu into the oil one piece at a time and fry in a batch of 10 to 12 pieces until golden and crispy on both sides, 5 to 6 minutes. Remove the tofu with a slotted spoon, shaking off excess oil, and drain on paper towels.

✂ Bring the oil temperature back up to 350 degrees F before frying the next batch.

Pat's Notes: If using in another dish, you can fry the tofu ahead of time and keep covered at room temperature for a few hours.

Deep-Fried Tofu Simmered with Tomatoes

At Lan Tran's family restaurant, Minh's Restaurant, beef noodle soup (*bun bo hue*) and grilled catfish (*ca nuong*) are specialties on the menu. But at home, Lan prefers simpler fare like this super-easy dish concocted by her mother. It's basic enough to complicate—you can improvise by adding meat or other vegetables—or keep it simple as-is to serve with most any meat or seafood main dish. Many home cooks like to deep-fry their own tofu, but fried tofu is readily available in Asian markets and less messy.

Time: 20 minutes
Makes: 4 to 6 servings as part of a multicourse family-style meal

> 1 tablespoon vegetable oil
>
> Deep-Fried Tofu (see opposite page) or one 12-ounce package fried tofu (try to find a package with eighteen 1- by 2-inch rectangular pieces)
>
> 1½ pounds (about 4 medium) tomatoes, cut into 8 wedges each
>
> ¼ cup fish sauce
>
> 2 tablespoons sugar
>
> 2 green onions, green parts only, chopped

✳ Coat the bottom of a large nonstick skillet with the oil. Arrange the tofu pieces side-by-side in a single layer. Wedge the tomatoes in wherever you can around the tofu. If you have to pile the tomatoes on top of the tofu to form a second layer, that's okay.

✳ In a small bowl, mix the fish sauce and sugar together. Pour over the tofu and tomatoes in the skillet. Scatter the green onions over the top. Cover and bring to a simmer over medium heat. Cook until the tomatoes soften and their juices are released, 10 to 15 minutes. The skins will also start to peel away from the flesh. Serve hot with freshly steamed rice.

Pan-Fried Tofu Simmered in Sweet Miso Sauce
(*Tofu no Misoni*)

Tofu is the perfect canvas to absorb the layered flavors of an accompanying sweet and salty miso sauce. Be sure to spoon the thickened sauce over freshly steamed rice as you eat. Try the recipe with eggplant (see Variation) or feel free to substitute other vegetables in this simple and tasty braised Japanese dish.

Time: 30 minutes
Makes: 4 servings as part of a multicourse family-style meal

14-ounce package firm or extra-firm tofu

5 tablespoons vegetable oil, divided (or more if necessary)

3 tablespoons red or white miso

¾ cup dashi (recipe on page 40) or water

2 tablespoons sake

1 tablespoon sugar

½-inch piece ginger, minced (1 teaspoon)

❋ Cut the tofu into approximately 1-inch-thick slabs and drain to remove excess water (see page 26).

❋ In a large nonstick skillet, heat 2 tablespoons of the oil over medium heat until it becomes runny and starts to shimmer. Gently arrange half of the tofu slabs (or as many that can fit) in the skillet in one layer and pan-fry until the tofu is lightly browned with a crisp, outer skin, 4 to 5 minutes on each side. Use a splatter-guard to keep the oil from jumping up at you. Remove with a slotted spoon and drain on paper towels. Repeat with the remaining tofu, adding 2 more tablespoons of oil. When cool enough to handle, cut the tofu into 1-inch cubes.

❋ Whisk the miso, dashi, sake, and sugar together in a small bowl. Return the skillet to medium heat and add the remaining oil. Stir in the ginger and cook until fragrant, 30 to 45 seconds. Toss in the cubed tofu and pour the miso mixture over. Reduce the heat to low and cook until the tofu has absorbed the flavors of the sauce, 10 to 15 minutes. Stir occasionally to coat the tofu evenly and add more dashi or water if it starts to dry out. Serve with freshly steamed rice.

Variation: For Eggplant with Sweet Miso Sauce (*Nasu no Misoni*), use 1 pound
Japanese eggplants in place of the tofu. Simply cut unpeeled eggplant into ½-
inch-thick slices and soak in cold water for 20 minutes to remove the bitterness.
Pat dry. Fry in ¼ cup oil over medium heat for 8 to 10 minutes, then proceed
as above. Instead of ½ cup dashi, use ¼ cup. Sprinkle with 1 teaspoon toasted
sesame seeds just before serving.

Pat's Notes: Buy fried tofu at the Asian market and skip a step.

Stir-Fried Mung Bean Sprouts with Tofu and Chives (*Pad Tao Kua Tao Ngae*)

Together with pork and chives, the combination of soft and fried tofu plays a fun
game of textures in the mouth. Don't worry about cutting the tofu to the exact
measurements, they are only a guide. Just as long as the pieces are bite-sized and
manageable in the wok, you're good to go! Vegetarians can omit the pork for a tasty
and nutritious protein-rich dish. Serve with SHRIMP AND PINEAPPLE RED CURRY
(page 209).

Time: 15 minutes
Makes: 4 to 6 servings as part of a multicourse family-style meal

> 4 ounces pork loin
>
> 3 tablespoons vegetable oil
>
> 3 cloves garlic, minced (1 tablespoon)
>
> 6 ounces (about ½ package) soft tofu (not silken), cut into
>   1- by 1½-inch pieces
>
> 6 ounces (about ½ package) 1- by 1½-inch fried tofu pieces
>   (or see recipe on page 122 to fry your own tofu)
>
> 4 cups fresh mung bean sprouts, tails snapped off
>
> 3 tablespoons soy sauce or fish sauce
>
> 1 teaspoon sugar (optional)
>
> ¼ cup Chinese chives cut into 2-inch lengths
>
> Ground white pepper

✀ Handle the pork partially frozen so that it is easier to cut (if it's fresh, place
   in the freezer for about 30 minutes). Cut the pork along the grain into

1½-inch-thick strips. Then, with your knife at an angle almost parallel to the cutting surface, slice the meat diagonally across the grain into ⅛-inch-thick slices.

Preheat a large wok or skillet over medium heat for about 1 minute. Swirl in the oil and heat until it becomes runny and starts to shimmer. Add the garlic and cook until golden and fragrant, 15 to 30 seconds. Throw in the pork and stir and cook until the meat just loses its blush, about 2 minutes. Add both types of tofu, followed by the bean sprouts. Sprinkle with the soy sauce and sugar and toss gently for 1 minute, being careful not to break up the soft tofu. Add the chives and white pepper and stir everything swiftly, but gently, around the wok. Once the ingredients are heated through, about 1 minute, remove from the heat. Serve with freshly steamed rice

Tofu Omelet with Sweet Peanut Sauce (*Tahu Telur*)

This Indonesian dish is a favorite in many homes in East Java. Tofu and eggs are fried together, forming an omelet which crisps up at the edge, and then topped with a sweet and spicy sauce tinged with black shrimp paste (*petis udang* in Indonesian). This thick, black paste has a fairly pungent smell, but adds a wonderful depth of flavor to many dishes. It tastes much better than it smells, honest!

Time: 30 minutes
Makes: 4 to 6 servings as part of a multicourse family-style meal

Sauce:

> 2 tablespoons vegetable oil
>
> 2 cloves garlic, thinly sliced lengthwise
>
> 2 teaspoons smooth peanut butter
>
> 1 teaspoon black shrimp paste (optional)
>
> 3 tablespoons hot water
>
> 3 tablespoons Indonesian sweet soy sauce (see page 24)
>
> 2 teaspoons lime juice (from 1 small lime)
>
> 1 red Thai chili, cut into rounds (optional)

Omelet:

> 4 eggs
>
> Pinch of salt

14-ounce package firm tofu, drained (see page 26) and cut into
2- by 2- by ½-inch squares

1 tablespoon vegetable oil

Chopped celery leaves or shredded cucumber for garnish

❧ To make the sauce, in a large nonstick skillet, heat the oil over medium-high heat until it becomes runny and starts to shimmer. Add the garlic and cook, stirring constantly, until golden brown and crispy, 1 to 2 minutes. Watch carefully as the garlic can burn easily. Scoop up the garlic with a slotted spoon and drain on paper towels. When the garlic is cool enough to handle, crush with your fingers or a fork.

❧ Combine the peanut butter and shrimp paste in a small bowl. Pour in the hot water and mix into a smooth paste by squishing the peanut butter and paste against the side of the bowl with a spoon. When well-blended, add the crushed garlic, soy sauce, lime juice, and chili and mix thoroughly.

❧ To make the omelet, beat the eggs with the salt in a medium bowl. Gently fold in the tofu so that it doesn't break up. Return the skillet to medium-high heat (don't bother wiping away any leftover oil). Swirl in the oil and heat until it becomes runny and starts to shimmer. Pour in the tofu-egg mixture and spread the tofu out as evenly as possible. Cook the eggs until the underside is golden brown and the edge is starting to crisp up, 5 to 6 minutes. Flip the omelet (here's a trick: slide the omelet onto a plate first and then flip it back into the skillet uncooked side down). Cook for another 2 to 3 minutes, or until the underside is golden brown and the egg cooked to your liking. Try to keep the omelet in one piece, but if it breaks up don't worry about it. Slide onto a serving platter. Pour the sauce over the omelet and garnish with celery leaves.

Pat's Notes: Instead of frying your own garlic, you can buy ready-fried garlic in round plastic containers in Asian markets. Use about 1 tablespoon for this dish and the rest to flavor soups and stir-fries.

If you prefer, you can cook the tofu-egg mixture in 2 batches in a small (6-inch) skillet—you'll have a better chance of keeping the omelet in one piece.

Spiced Red Lentil Stew (*Palida*)

Palida is very similar to *dal*—the ubiquitous side dish at many an Indian meal. The key difference is the aromatic garam masala that's added toward the end of cooking. While the original recipe from Grandma Niloufer Gupta (see page 140) calls for chana dal, this legume isn't readily available in the West. She suggests using red lentils instead, a salmon-colored pulse that will turn a dull yellow when cooked. Brown lentils or yellow split peas are also worthy stand-ins. Serve warm with INDIAN CUCUMBER AND TOMATO RELISH (page 137) and ROTI (page 191) or store-bought whole-wheat tortillas.

Time: 1 hour (30 minutes active) plus soaking
Makes: 4 to 6 servings as part of a multicourse family-style meal

> 4 cups water
>
> 8 ounces (1 cup) red lentils, picked over, rinsed, and soaked for at least 4 hours
>
> 2 medium onions, finely chopped (2 cups)
>
> ½-inch piece fresh ginger, grated (1 teaspoon)
>
> 2 teaspoons ground coriander
>
> 1 teaspoon ground cumin
>
> 1 teaspoon ground paprika
>
> ¼ teaspoon ground turmeric
>
> 1 tablespoon butter
>
> Garam masala (see page 8): 3 green cardamom pods, two ½-inch sticks cinnamon, 4 cloves, 2 bay leaves
>
> 1 teaspoon sugar
>
> Salt

❧ Combine the water, lentils, onions, ginger, coriander, cumin, paprika, and turmeric in a medium pot and bring to a boil over high heat. Reduce the heat to medium. Cover and simmer for 15 to 20 minutes, or until the lentils split and are a little mushy but not yet cooked through. Skim off any foam or scum that rises to the surface.

- In a small skillet, melt the butter over low heat. Add the garam masala and cook until the cardamom has plumped up and the spices have released their fragrance, 4 to 5 minutes. Turn off the heat. Stir in the sugar, 1 teaspoon salt, and ¼ cup of the cooked lentils. Once blended, stir the entire contents of the skillet into the pot with the lentils.

- Simmer the stew over low heat until the lentils are tender and cooked through, another 10 to 15 minutes. The lentils should be mushy and soft and have the texture of a thick, pouring custard sauce.

- Fish out the whole spices. Taste and add salt as needed.

Pat's Notes: Chana dal, also called *Bengal gram dal,* is very similar to the yellow split peas that are sold in supermarkets, only the grains are smaller and sweeter. They are more closely related to garbanzo beans. You may be able to find them at South Asian markets in the United States. If you do, follow the same procedure as above.

The flavor of this dish improves with time so it's a great make-ahead dish. Let it cool completely before refrigerating for up to 5 days or freezing for up to 3 months. Reheat over low heat, adding water if necessary to thin it to a pouring consistency.

Yellow Split Pea Curry (*Matar Dal*)

Pulses like split peas are a rich source of daily protein for many families in India who rarely eat meat or are vegetarian. Though they are incomplete proteins, when combined with a starch (rice or bread) they make a complete protein. This simple curry, while rather bland on its own, is a perfect complement to richer meat curries. Serve with RICK'S CHICKEN CURRY (page 188) and freshly steamed rice or ROTI (page 191).

Time: 1 hour (10 minutes active)
Makes: 4 to 6 servings as part of a multicourse family-style meal

4 cups water, or more if needed

8 ounces (1 cup) yellow split peas, picked over, rinsed, and drained

1 red Thai chili, smashed with the butt of a knife, a glass mug, or a meat tenderizer

1 clove garlic, sliced paper-thin

1 teaspoon cumin seeds

1 teaspoon salt

❀ In a large saucepan, bring the water and split peas to a boil over high heat. Skim off any scum or foam that rises to the surface and watch carefully so that it doesn't boil over. Reduce the heat to medium and simmer until the peas are tender and resemble a coarse purée, 50 minutes to 1 hour. Add water as needed to prevent the mixture from drying out. If the final consistency is too thin or too thick for your liking, raise the heat and reduce it further or add more water. Throw in the Thai chili and continue to simmer while you cook the garlic and cumin.

❀ Heat a small dry, nonstick skillet over medium heat until hot. Add the garlic and cook until golden brown and fragrant, 15 to 30 seconds. Stir in the cumin seeds. The seeds will release their aroma almost instantly. As soon as you smell their fragrance, pull the skillet from the heat. (Be careful not to overcook the seeds or they'll turn bitter. If this happens, throw them out and start again.) Pour the garlic-cumin mixture into the pot with the peas. Stir in the salt and the curry is done.

Grandma Says: Don't add salt until the last few minutes of cooking or it will make the split pea skins tough.

Cabbage Kimchi

Sour-sweet and spicy with nutty overtones, *kimchi* is a delightful explosion of tastes and textures in the mouth. The methods of making kimchi are just as varied as the ingredients that go into it, but Chinese cabbage is the most common. Kimchi isn't all that difficult to make, as demonstrated by this recipe from Yangja Cho Im, a seventy-something grandma who is both an artist and avid home cook. In fact, the active Floridian makes it almost every week. Yangja calls it a "not so traditional" kimchi recipe, but to non-connoisseurs (like me), it tastes pretty authentic. If you're up for an extra challenge—both in terms of prep and palate—tack on some of the optional ingredients to make it a more traditional kimchi. Serve well-chilled as a side dish or in BIBIMBAP (page 259).

Time: 30 minutes plus fermenting
Makes: ½ gallon (12 to 16 servings as part of a multicourse family-style meal)

> 1 large head (about 3 pounds) firm Chinese cabbage
>
> 3 Kirby cucumbers, or 2 lean Korean cucumbers, trimmed and quartered lengthwise (or cut into bite-sized pieces, if you prefer)
>
> 1 small daikon radish, peeled and cut into bite-sized pieces (half moons are fine) (2 cups)
>
> 2 tablespoons coarse sea or kosher salt
>
> 2 Korean green chilies, cut diagonally into ¼-inch-thick rings
>
> 1-inch piece fresh ginger, grated (1 tablespoon)
>
> 1 clove garlic, minced
>
> 1 green onion, white and green parts, cut into ½-inch lengths
>
> 2 tablespoons Korean red pepper powder
>
> 1 tablespoon sugar

❧ Rinse the cabbage and halve it lengthwise. Cut the core out with a V-notch and discard. Cut the leaves into 1- by 1½-inch pieces.

❧ In the largest nonreactive bowl you have, mix the cabbage, cucumbers, and radish together and sprinkle evenly with the salt. Let the salted vegetables sit for 3 hours, tossing every half hour. The salt will draw out water from the vegetables.

❧ Add the chilies, ginger, garlic, green onion, red pepper powder, and sugar, to the salted vegetables. (For the more traditional version, see variation below). Mix well with your hands (be sure to wear rubber gloves to avoid chili burn).

❧ Transfer the pickled vegetables to a ½-gallon jar or divide among several smaller quart or other jars, pressing down firmly to remove any air bubbles and cover the vegetables with as much liquid as possible. Leave about 2 inches at the top to give the vegetables room to breathe.

❧ Wrap the mouth of the jar with plastic wrap before screwing on the lid to prevent odors from escaping. Keep at room temperature overnight, then refrigerate for up to 1 week.

Variation: For the more traditional version, add

> 1 large red bell pepper, coarsely chopped (1½ cups)
>
> 1 small yellow onion, coarsely chopped (¾ cup)
>
> 1 teaspoon Korean salted shrimp (*saeujeot*) (see Pat's Notes)
>   or fish sauce
>
> 2 tablespoons water

> Combine the chilies, ginger, garlic, green onion, red pepper powder, and sugar with the bell pepper, onion, salted shrimp, and water in the jug of an electric blender. Whirl to a thick liquid. Pour over the salted vegetables and proceed as above.

Pat's Notes: Korean salted shrimp is available in 1- or 2-quart jars in the refrigerated sections of Korean markets.

When making kimchi, use nonreactive materials (glass, stainless steel, or ceramic) for all cooking utensils, measuring spoons, bowls, and containers. Do not use plastic as it picks up colors. For storage, use sterilized wide-mouth glass or ceramic jars with screw-top lids.

This kimchi recipe lends itself well to personal taste preferences. Add or take away the hot chilies and red pepper powder, or add more garlic if you desire. Feel free to experiment with the spicing to please the family palate.

Chinese Pickles (*Liang Ban Huang Gua*)

Traditionally, prepared ginger syrup is used to sweeten the pickling brine, but because it's not commercially available in the United States, maple syrup is the next best thing. While the diagonal cuts in the cucumber are mostly for aesthetics, they also allow the vegetable to soak up flavor from the brine; skip this step if you're in a rush. Serve it as a palate cleanser for any meat dish or with SPECIAL INDONESIAN FRIED RICE (page 279).

Time: 15 minutes plus standing and brining
Makes: 4 to 6 servings as a condiment

> 2 large (10- to 12-inch-long) cucumbers
> 1 small carrot, peeled and thinly sliced
> 1 teaspoon salt
> 1 cup distilled white vinegar
> ½ cup water
> 3 tablespoons pure maple syrup
> 2 tablespoons sugar
> 1 thin coin fresh ginger
> Pinch of cayenne pepper (optional)

❧ Using a vegetable peeler or sharp paring knife, peel the cucumbers, leaving alternate strips of green. Cut each cucumber lengthwise into four spears and remove the seeds using a teaspoon.

❧ Lay each spear skin-side up on a chopping board horizontal to your body. Feather the edge closest to you by making diagonal cuts no more than halfway across the width of the spear from left to right on one side. Repeat with the remaining spears. Cut the cucumber crosswise into ½-inch diagonal slices.

❧ Place the cucumber and carrot in a colander over the sink and sprinkle with the salt. Let sit for 30 minutes.

❧ In a small bowl, mix the together the vinegar, water, maple syrup, sugar, ginger, and cayenne. Microwave on medium-high for 1 minute. Stir the brine, making sure all the sugar has dissolved. Alternatively, heat the brine in a small pot over low heat on the stove until the sugar dissolves. Taste and adjust the seasonings if desired. Cool completely.

Green and Golden Zucchini Thread Salad

Rinse the cucumbers and carrot and drain. Place in a nonreactive container with a tight-fitting lid and pour the cooled brine over. Cover and refrigerate for at least 2 hours, or preferably 12 hours. Drain, reserving the brine, and serve.

Variation: If you don't have maple syrup, just use more sugar.

Pat's Notes: The pickles will keep for up to 1 week in the refrigerator.
    Add chopped red bell pepper for more color, or red Thai chilies for heat.

Grandma Says: The brine can be reused once for another batch of pickles.

Green and Golden Zucchini Thread Salad (*Hobak Namul*)

Tasty and colorful, this dish is one of hundreds of small side dishes (*banchan* or *pan-chan*—an assortment of fresh, pickled and sautéed vegetables, tofu, fish, and fish cakes) that accompany a Korean meal. An everyday dish with a mild flavor, it is especially calming with spicy food. If you can't find yellow zucchini, any yellow squash will do. The threads make this salad attractive, but you can cut the zucchini into ribbons or half-moons if you prefer. It keeps in the refrigerator for a day. Serve with KOREAN BARBECUED BEEF SHORT RIBS (page 154).

Time: 45 minutes plus standing
Makes: 4 to 6 servings as part of a multicourse family-style meal

2 green and 2 yellow medium (8- to 10-inch) zucchini

1 large carrot, peeled

1 Korean green chili or jalapeño (optional)

Salt

2 teaspoons sugar

Ground white pepper

Juice from ½ large lemon (2 tablespoons)

1 teaspoon grated fresh ginger (from a ½-inch piece)

1 tablespoon sesame oil

Toasted sesame seeds for sprinkling

- Trim the zucchini and halve them lengthwise. Remove the seeds with a teaspoon and discard. Using a box shredder or mandolin, separately cut the zucchini and carrot into threads. Thinly slice the hot green chili to the same thickness as the zucchini. Don't worry if the pieces are not the same length.

- Place the zucchini in a colander over the sink, sprinkle with 1 teaspoon salt, and let stand for 15 minutes. Working in batches, wrap the zucchini in a non-terry dish cloth and gently wring out excess moisture. Do this 2 or 3 times to extract as much water as possible, but don't completely crush the zucchini. Repeat with the carrot.

- Combine the zucchini, carrot, and chili in a medium bowl and fluff them up. Sprinkle with the sugar and white pepper. Stir in salt to taste and toss to mix well. Add the lemon juice, ginger, and sesame oil. Sprinkle with sesame seeds, toss, and serve.

Pat's Notes: If you'd like to peel fresh ginger before grating (it's not really necessary), scrape off the papery skin with a spoon. It will come off very easily and reduces waste because you will remove very little flesh.

  If you don't have a box shredder or mandolin, use a vegetable peeler or a very sharp knife to slice the zucchini lengthwise into thin horizontal sheets. Then stack 2 to 3 sheets at a time and slice them into threads.

Grandma Says: If preparing this dish in advance, add the sesame oil right before serving to keep the colors bright and the flavor fresh.

Indian Cucumber and Tomato Relish (*Kachumber*)

A quick and easy relish, *kachumber* is an excellent complement to the fiery flavors of Indian food.

Time: 15 minutes
Makes: 4 to 6 servings as a condiment

> 2 medium yellow onions, finely chopped (2 cups)
> 1 large lemon
> ¼ teaspoon salt
> 4 medium tomatoes, seeded (reserve the seeds) and chopped (4 cups)
> 2 teaspoons sugar
> 1 medium cucumber, peeled and chopped (2 cups)
> Mint leaves for garnish

❧ Place the onions in a large bowl. Squeeze the juice from the lemon (about 3 tablespoons) over them. Sprinkle with the salt and mix well.

❧ In a separate bowl, mix the tomato seeds with the sugar. Tumble the tomatoes and cucumber into the bowl with the onions and toss well to combine. Right before serving, add the tomato seeds and toss again. Garnish with a handful of mint leaves.

Soybean Sprout Salad (*Kong Namul Sangchae*)

A crisp, refreshing Korean side dish (*banchan* or *panchan*), this dish involves hardly any actual cooking. Most of your time will be spent on the first task, which is to take each soybean sprout and snap off its stringy tail (the lower 1 to 2 inches). It takes 20 to 25 minutes for 1 pound of sprouts. There's no skill involved and it's worth the effort as the appearance and texture of the salad will be far superior. Serve with freshly steamed short-grain rice and a main dish, or in BIBIMBAP (page 259).

Time: 30 minutes plus chilling
Makes: 4 to 6 servings as part of a multicourse family-style meal

> 1 pound fresh soybean sprouts, tails snapped off
>
> 1 green onion, white and green parts, finely chopped
>
> 1 large clove garlic, minced
>
> 2 tablespoons sugar
>
> 1 tablespoon sesame oil
>
> 2 teaspoons Japanese soy sauce
>
> 1 teaspoon toasted sesame seeds
>
> ¼ teaspoon Korean red pepper powder (optional)

❀ In a medium pot, bring 6 cups of water to boil over high heat. As soon as the water starts to boil, turn off the heat. Add the soybean sprouts and soak until they're pliable but still crisp, about 1 minute. Drain in a colander and rinse under cold running water.

❀ In a large bowl, combine the green onion, garlic, sugar, sesame oil, soy sauce, sesame seeds, and red pepper powder. Add the sprouts and toss gently. Chill in the refrigerator for at least 1 hour before serving.

Pat's Notes: Soybean sprouts can often be found prewashed in cellophane bags in Asian markets. They shouldn't be confused with mung bean sprouts, which look similar but are skinnier and have smaller "heads." Though they are different, mung bean sprouts can be used in this recipe in place of soybean sprouts.

Spicy Korean Oyster Salad (*Kul Kimchi*)

A *kimchi* dish is probably being invented as we speak. Yes, they are that prolific and every Korean cook has her own version. This rendition from Jean Lee has fresh oysters, lots of red pepper flakes, and romaine lettuce and is a palate-inspiring blend of sweet, spicy, and briny. Buy freshly shucked oysters from your favorite fishmonger or in quart jars at the supermarket. This dish will keep for 2 to 3 days, depending on the freshness of the oysters, but it should be refrigerated any time it's not being immediately served. Serve with freshly steamed short-grain rice and a main dish like KOREAN BARBECUED BEEF SHORT RIBS (page 154) or in BIBIMBAP (page 259).

Time: 20 minutes plus marinating
Makes: 4 to 6 servings as part of a multicourse family-style meal

¼ cup plus 1 tablespoon brown sugar

¼ cup plus 1 tablespoon fish sauce

¼ cup Korean red pepper flakes

5 to 6 cloves garlic, minced (2 tablespoons)

1 tablespoon rice vinegar

1 tablespoon toasted sesame seeds

4 romaine lettuce hearts (1 pound), halved lengthwise

5 green onions, white and green parts, chopped

1 red Thai chili, cut into rounds

3 cups raw oysters, rinsed in salt water to remove any grit and drained (about ⅔ quart)

In a large nonreactive bowl, mix together the brown sugar, fish sauce, pepper flakes, garlic, and vinegar. Sprinkle in the toasted sesame seeds and mix to form a coarse paste. Add the lettuce, green onions, and chili and toss until the leaves are well-coated. Add the oysters and mix gently. Let the kimchi sit in the refrigerator for at least 3 hours, or preferably 12 hours. Just before serving, stir the kimchi again.

Pat's Notes: If you don't have a bowl big enough to contain all the ingredients, divide them equally among two of your biggest bowls. As the lettuce shrinks, mix everything together in one bowl.

If you use whole heads of romaine, cut larger leaves crosswise as well. The leaves may seem large at first but they will wilt and shrink to 4 to 5 inches.

Profile of a Grandma: NILOUFER GUPTA

 Born in Bombay (now Mumbai) and raised in Calcutta (now Kolkata) in a conservative Shia Khoja Muslim family, Niloufer Gupta led a different life from many women of her generation.

When Niloufer lost her father at age twelve, she and her mother moved back in with her mother's family where she was "indulged" she says. Greatly influenced by the British, her uncles and aunts were entrepreneurs as well as professionals. They spoke both English and Hindustani at home and while most Muslim children started learning to read Arabic at age seven to recite the Koran, Niloufer only started at thirteen.

In a society where girls are trained to be good housewives, Niloufer's upbringing was just the opposite. "I wasn't allowed to go into the kitchen or to do anything that involved fire." (In those days, cooking was done over coal fires.) Nonetheless, nothing could stop the culinary instincts her late father had instilled in her. "I have fond memories of my father making a tomato soup and putting sherry into it," she remembers. A teenaged Niloufer decided she wanted to be a typical Indian girl and began taking domestic science classes in high school.

After attending Saint Xavier's College in Bombay, Niloufer enrolled at the Inner Temple (one of the four Inns of Court) to become a barrister-at-law and also joined the London School of Economics and Political Science at the University of London to study international relations and economics. During the long summer vacations, she augmented her culinary education by taking classes at the London branch of the famous Le Cordon Bleu. "I wanted to prove to my family I could be a professional earning a living on my own and also hold my own in the world of Western cuisine," she says.

London was also where Niloufer met her husband-to-be, Abhijit. However, sparks didn't fly until they returned to Bombay.

Niloufer defied convention yet again. She was twenty-seven when she married, considered fairly late for an Indian woman. Not only was Abhijit the same age as she was (brides were normally paired with men who were at least seven years older), it was also a love match. To take things even further, she was Muslim and he was Hindu. Without a doubt, the religious difference caused quite an uproar among their families, but both sides eventually came around.

Over the next ten years, Niloufer and Abhijit had three children. As a working mother, Niloufer often came home at nine o'clock on weekday evenings, so she left meal preparations to their cook. When weekends and special occasions rolled around, Niloufer took over the kitchen. With her diverse culinary background, Niloufer drew inspiration from a multi-cultural pantry, cooking everything from French, to Bengali, to Eurasian and Muslim dishes. Her young daughters, Aaliyah and Rabia, took on the roles of sous chefs, chopping, stirring, and adding ingredients to the pot.

Aaliyah remembers these occasions fondly and often recreates her favorite dishes including SPICY LAMB CASSEROLE (page 157). Cooking this dish brings back memories of family dinners and the love that goes into food preparation, she says. "I have an intuitive sense of how it should taste, so in some sense, making this recipe is a nostalgic and evocative process."

Now, at seventy-two, Niloufer divides her time between their home in Bangalore; Delhi, where their son and his family live; Mumbai, where their second daughter lives; and Seattle, where Aaliyah lives with her husband and twin sons. Whenever Niloufer visits her children and grandchildren, her cooking skills are very much in demand. Her grandchildren have their standard orders—prawns with potatoes, beef with coconut sauce, and Spicy Lamb Casserole are top items on the menu. And Niloufer is always happy to oblige.

6

THE CENTERPIECE

A meat, poultry, or seafood dish always takes pride of place at the center of the Asian table.

Asians, especially the Chinese, have been dedicated hog lovers throughout history. Pork is popular because pigs are easy to raise and mature quickly. Pork fat, more commonly known as lard, adds unsurpassed flavor to many dishes, and pork belly is a favorite cut that's gaining popularity in American kitchens. When it comes to poultry, dark meat is generally favored over white. Whole chicken or duck is poached, steamed, or braised, and bone-in chicken parts are preferred. In Asia, beef is a luxury reserved for special occasions because it costs more and is harder to find. When beef is served, economy cuts are often used. Lamb and goat show up too, most frequently in South Asian curries and casseroles.

Seafood also plays a starring role. Fish is the primary protein in many coastal communities and they aren't sourced just from the ocean: freshwater marine life thrives in rice paddy fields, rivers, lakes, and streams. There are no qualms about heads or tails, and whole fish are enjoyed more than fillets. Larger varieties of shrimp, as well as lobster, are expensive and eaten sparingly.

Today, lower prices and Western influences have made meat and seafood more accessible, especially in the United States. Steak is eaten widely; shrimp can be a weekly affair. But there is one constant—mothers and grandmothers count on easy-to-make dishes that can be prepared in large quantities to feed their families.

Chinese Barbecued Pork

Beef and Lamb

Beef, Tomato, and Pepper Stir-Fry

Gingered Oxtail Stew

Grilled Beef Kebabs, Filipino Style (*Inasal*)

Japanese-Style Hamburgers (*Wafu* Hamburgers)

Korean Barbecued Beef Short Ribs (*Kalbi*)

Spicy Lamb Casserole (*Gosht Ka Saalan*)

Steamed Meatballs with Tangerine Peel (*Niu Rou Yuan*)

Stir-Fried Beef with Mustard Greens

Pork

Aged Chinese Marinade (*Lao Shui*) with Pork

Burmese Pork Curry (*Whethar Sebyan*)

Chinese Barbecued Pork (*Char Siu*)

Crispy Fried Meatballs (*Bakso Goreng*)

Lao Sausage (*Sai Oua*)

1-2-3-4-5 Sticky Spareribs (*Tang Chu Pai Gu*)

Roasted Pork Tenderloin with Mustard Sauce (*Kao Zhu Li Ji*)

Sweet and Sour Pork (*Gu Lao Rou*)

Thai Basil Pork (*Pad Gkaprow Mu*)

Poultry

Brandied Chicken and Mushrooms in Oyster Sauce

Caramelized Chicken with Lemongrass and Chilies
(*Ga Xao Sa Ot Cay*)

Chicken Adobo (Vinegar-Braised Chicken)

Chicken and Eggs in a Golden Curry (*Kuku Paka*)

Lao Chicken and Herb Salad (*Larb Gai*)

Mochiko Fried Chicken

Rick's Chicken Curry

Sichuan Chili Chicken (*Gung Bao Ji Ding*)

Teochew Braised Duck (*Lo Ack*)

Vietnamese Chicken Curry (*Ca Ri Ga*)

Seafood

Black Bean–Steamed Fish

Clay Pot Lemongrass-Steamed Fish (*Pla Nueng Morh Din*)

Miso-Smothered Salmon

Shrimp and Mung Bean Sprout Omelets

Shrimp and Pineapple Red Curry (*Kaeng Kue Sapparod*)

Shrimp with Homemade Black Bean Sauce

Stuffed Egg-Crepe Rolls (*Yu Gun*)

Tangy Tomato Shrimp

Teriyaki Squid

✂ Beef and Lamb ✄

Beef, Tomato, and Pepper Stir-Fry

Don't let the various steps in this popular Cantonese dish fool you; it's fairly easy to make and the results are delicious. As with all stir-fries, the dish is very versatile. Instead of tomatoes, bell pepper, and Chinese salted black beans, try using broccoli, green beans, or bok choy with fresh ginger (or any other combo that strikes your fancy). Served with a bowl of freshly steamed rice, it makes a no-fuss complete meal.

Time: 45 minutes
Makes: 4 to 6 servings as part of a multicourse family-style meal

> 1 pound round steak
>
> 1 tablespoon Shaoxing rice wine or dry sherry
>
> 1 tablespoon oyster sauce
>
> ½ teaspoon sugar
>
> 1 tablespoon plus 1 teaspoon soy sauce, divided
>
> 2 tablespoons vegetable oil, divided
>
> 1 clove garlic, smashed with the flat part of a cleaver or a large knife
>
> 2 teaspoons Chinese salted black beans (see page 4), rinsed and drained
>
> 1 medium yellow onion, cut into 8 to 10 wedges and separated
>
> 1 medium green bell pepper, cut into 10 to 12 strips
>
> 2 stalks celery, trimmed and sliced on the diagonal
>
> 2 teaspoons cornstarch dissolved in 3 tablespoons water to form a slurry
>
> 2 ripe medium tomatoes, each cut into 8 wedges

✄ Handle the beef partially frozen so that it is easier to cut (if it's fresh, place in the freezer for about 30 minutes). Cut the beef along the grain into 1½-inch-thick strips. Then, with your knife at an angle almost parallel to the cutting surface, slice the meat diagonally across the grain into ⅛-inch-thick slices.

Beef, Tomato, and Pepper Stir-Fry

In a medium bowl, toss the beef with the rice wine, oyster sauce, sugar, and 1 tablespoon soy sauce. Cover the bowl and let the meat marinate in the refrigerator for 10 minutes, or up to 12 hours.

Preheat a large wok or skillet over high heat for 1 minute. Swirl in 1 tablespoon of the oil and heat until it becomes runny and starts to shimmer. Add the garlic and cook until fragrant, 15 to 30 seconds; discard the garlic (you just want to flavor the oil). Add the salted black beans and onion and stir for 1 minute. Add the bell pepper and celery and stir-fry until crisp-tender, 2 minutes. Set aside in a bowl.

In the same wok, swirl in the remaining oil and heat over high heat. Divide the marinated meat into 4 batches. Stir-fry one batch for about 2 minutes (don't worry if the meat is still a little pink), and set aside on a plate. Repeat with the remaining batches of meat.

Return the cooked vegetables to the wok over high heat. Add the cooked meat and stir everything swiftly around the wok until heated through, about 1 minute. Stir the cornstarch slurry and add to the wok. Toss to coat the meat and vegetables evenly. Cook until the mixture thickens and the meat and vegetables look glossy, about 1 minute. Add the tomatoes and 1 teaspoon soy sauce. Continue tossing until heated through, about another minute. Taste and adjust seasonings if desired. Serve immediately with freshly steamed rice.

Gingered Oxtail Stew

Oxtail may be made up of mostly bone and cartilage, but it is one tasty cut. The bones and marrow also produce a very rich, flavorful, thick stock, thanks to the collagen released during cooking. Oxtail turns tender only after a long simmer on the stove, so if you don't really want to hang out in your kitchen for 4 hours, a slow cooker or pressure cooker is your best friend (see Pat's Notes). The amount of ginger may seem over- or under-powering, depending on your taste; use as much as you so desire.

Time: 4¼ hours (15 minutes active)
Makes: 4 to 6 servings as part of a multicourse family-style meal

About 3 quarts water

2½ to 3 pounds oxtails, trimmed of fat and joints separated

2-inch piece fresh ginger, peeled and cut into coins

2 tablespoons dark soy sauce

2 tablespoons oyster sauce

2 tablespoons broad bean sauce (see page 3)

2 tablespoons Shaoxing rice wine or dry sherry

1 tablespoon sugar

Freshly ground black pepper

Chopped green onions for garnish

Chopped cilantro for garnish

To parboil the oxtails, bring the water to a boil in a large heavy-bottomed pot or Dutch oven. Toss in the oxtails and return to a rolling boil. Drain the oxtails in a colander to get rid of fat and scum and then return to the pot.

Fill the pot with just enough water to cover. Add the ginger, soy sauce, oyster sauce, bean sauce, rice wine, sugar, and pepper and stir to mix. Cover and simmer over medium-low heat until the meat is fall-off-the-bone tender, 3½ to 4 hours.

Transfer to a serving plate and scatter with green onions and cilantro. Serve with freshly steamed rice or wheat noodles.

Pat's Notes: To cook in a slow cooker, place the oxtails and remaining ingredients in a large electric slow cooker after parboiling. Cover and cook on low for 8 hours.

To cook in a pressure cooker, add the oxtails and remaining ingredients to a pressure cooker after parboiling. Cover and bring to high pressure over high heat (about 5 minutes). Reduce to medium heat or the lowest setting required to maintain high pressure; cook for 40 to 45 minutes.

Grilled Beef Kebabs, Filipino Style (*Inasal*)

Inasal is an Ilonggo (a dialect spoken in the Philippines' Visayas region) word meaning "to grill." Traditional inasal uses chicken, pork, or fish, rather than beef. However, Tisa Escobar favors beef because her mom, Victoria, always grilled beef kebabs in their California home. Top sirloin or top blade steak (known sometimes as blade or flatiron steak) are the preferred cuts for kebabs.

Time: 45 minutes plus marinating and soaking
Makes: 4 to 6 servings as part of a multicourse family-style meal

> 1 cup Japanese soy sauce
> 1 cup lemon-lime soda or beer
> ¼ cup kalamansi (see page 9), lime, or lemon juice
> 1 head garlic (8 to 10 cloves), minced
> 1 medium yellow onion, chopped (1 cup)
> ¼ cup brown sugar
> 1 teaspoon freshly ground black pepper
> 2 pounds boneless top sirloin steak, cut into 1-inch cubes
> Vegetable oil for brushing
> Chili Dipping Sauce (recipe follows)

✤ In a large nonreactive bowl, mix together the soy sauce, soda, juice, garlic, onion, brown sugar, and pepper. Add the beef and mix well to coat. Cover with plastic wrap and marinate in the refrigerator for 1 to 3 hours.

✤ Soak 16 wooden skewers in water for at least 1 hour.

✤ To grill the kebabs, prepare a medium charcoal fire (you can hold your hand over the rack for no more than 3 or 4 seconds) with the rack 4 to 6 inches from the coals, or preheat a gas grill to medium. To broil the kebabs, position a rack about 4 inches from the heat source and preheat the broiler.

✻ While the grill or broiler is heating, thread 4 to 5 steak pieces onto each skewer. Set aside to let the excess marinade drip off. Reserve a small portion of the marinade for basting.

✻ If you are grilling, brush the grilling rack with vegetable oil and place the kebabs on top. Grill for 8 to 10 minutes in total for medium, or until the beef is cooked to desired doneness. Turn the kebabs 2 or 3 times to cook all surfaces and baste frequently with reserved marinade in the first 5 minutes of cooking.

✻ If you are broiling, brush the broiler pan with vegetable oil and place the kebabs in one layer (you may have to broil them in batches). Broil for 3 to 4 minutes on each side for medium, or until the beef is cooked to desired doneness. Baste once or twice with the reserved marinade in the first 5 minutes of cooking.

✻ Place the kebabs on a serving platter and tent loosely with foil. Let the meat rest for 5 minutes. Serve with the dipping sauce.

Variation: Throw in 1 tablespoon finely chopped lemongrass and/or 1 teaspoon grated fresh ginger to the marinade to add more layers of flavor.

Use the flavorful marinade for grilling a whole chicken, chicken thighs, or cubed pork shoulder.

Pat's Notes: Soda or beer tenderizes the meat and adds flavor too.

Chili Dipping Sauce

Makes: About ⅔ cup

> ½ cup cane vinegar or rice vinegar
> 5 cloves garlic, minced (1½ tablespoons)
> Pinch of salt
> 4 red Thai chilies, chopped

✻ In a medium bowl, mix together the vinegar, garlic, salt, and chilies. Let sit for at least 30 minutes before serving.

Japanese-Style Hamburgers (*Wafu* Hamburgers)

A popular meal eaten at home, these hamburgers sans buns are similar to Salisbury steaks. In this recipe from Yuki Morishima, seasoned beef patties are cooked, doused in sauce, and then served with broccoli and carrots. For a healthy twist, Yuki, a Tokyo native who has lived in the United States for about twenty years, learned from her mother to add tofu to the patties to cut down on the amount of meat. You can also make the burgers with ground pork.

Time: 45 minutes
Makes: 4 servings as part of a multicourse family-style meal

14-ounce package firm or medium-firm tofu

½ cup panko bread crumbs (see Pat's Notes)

¼ cup milk

8 ounces ground beef

2 green onions, white and green parts, finely chopped
  (2 tablespoons)

1-inch piece fresh ginger, peeled and minced (1 tablespoon)

2 teaspoons Japanese soy sauce

Freshly ground black pepper

2 tablespoons vegetable oil

3 tablespoons Japanese soy sauce

2 tablespoons mirin

1 tablespoon sugar

Grated daikon radish for garnish

☙ Wrap the tofu in cheesecloth or a non-terry kitchen towel and squeeze out as much water as possible. You want the tofu crumbled.

☙ In a large bowl, mix the panko and milk together. Add the crumbled tofu, beef, green onions, ginger, soy sauce, and pepper and mash everything together. Divide the mixture into 4 balls and flatten to form patties about ½ inch thick and 4 inches in diameter. They will be very soft.

☙ In a large nonstick skillet, heat the oil over medium-high heat until it becomes runny and starts to shimmer. Place the patties in the skillet and cook until the undersides are brown, 5 to 6 minutes. Flip and cook until cooked through, another 5 to 6 minutes.

❧ Meanwhile, to make the sauce, combine the soy sauce, mirin, and sugar in a small bowl.

❧ When the burgers are done, reduce the heat to low and add the sauce to the burgers in the skillet and simmer for 1 minute. Slide the burgers onto 4 individual plates. Drizzle the sauce over the tops and garnish with grated daikon.

Pat's Notes: Panko, Japanese bread crumbs with a coarser texture than regular bread crumbs, is used as a coating for deep-fried food, especially seafood. It is available in the Asian section of larger supermarkets. Unopened packages last indefinitely, but once opened, panko should be frozen.

Korean Barbecued Beef Short Ribs (*Kalbi*)

All Korean grandmothers have their own little secrets for making and tenderizing *kalbi*. Soda, sugar, and Asian pears are all common tenderizing agents. Grandma Sang Jung Choi (see page 252) massages kiwis into Korean-style short ribs—beef ribs cut about ¼ inch thick across the bone (instead of between bones) with three bones per slice—they are often available in Asian markets. Your butcher may also have the similarly cut flanken-style or cross-cut beef chuck short ribs; just ask if the slices can be cut a little thinner.

Time: 30 minutes plus marinating
Makes: 6 to 8 servings as part of a multicourse family-style meal

4 pounds Korean-style beef short ribs

2 kiwis, peeled and puréed in a blender

2 tablespoons light brown sugar

½ cup soy sauce

6 cloves garlic, finely chopped (2 tablespoons)

1-inch piece fresh ginger, grated (1 tablespoon)

2 tablespoons toasted sesame seeds

2 tablespoons toasted sesame oil

1 tablespoon honey

1 tablespoon Korean red pepper powder

¼ teaspoon ground black pepper

Korean Barbecued Beef Short Ribs

20-ounce bottle lemon-lime soda
Vegetable oil for brushing

❧ Using your hands, massage the short ribs with the kiwi purée. Sprinkle each piece evenly with sugar and let sit while you make the marinade.

❧ In a medium bowl, mix together the soy sauce, garlic, ginger, sesame seeds, sesame oil, honey, red pepper powder, pepper, and soda. Place the ribs in a single layer in a wide shallow pan and pour the marinade over, turning to coat. Cover with plastic wrap and marinate in the refrigerator, turning occasionally, for at least 1 hour, or preferably 12 hours.

❧ Prepare a medium charcoal fire (you can hold your hand over the rack for no more than 3 or 4 seconds) with the rack 4 to 6 inches from the coals, or preheat a gas grill to medium. While the grill is heating up, drain the ribs from the marinade. Reserve the marinade for basting, if desired.

❧ Brush the grill rack with oil and grill the ribs in batches until they turn caramel brown and develop slightly charred edges, 6 to 8 minutes on each side. Baste with the reserved marinade during the first 10 minutes of grilling if you like.

❧ Serve with freshly steamed short-grain rice and CABBAGE KIMCHI (page 131).

Pat's Notes: If you prefer, omit the soda and add more sugar or honey for a little extra sweetness.

Spicy Lamb Casserole (*Gosht Ka Saalan*)

This vibrant Indian casserole from Hyderabad was handed down to Aaliyah Gupta from her mother Niloufer (see page 140), a lawyer and culinary school graduate. So much more than the sum of its parts, it is Aaliyah's go-to dish when expecting company. Grind whole spices yourself in a coffee grinder or buy them in powdered form in the bulk section of most supermarkets.

Time: 1½ hours (45 minutes active), plus marinating
Makes: 6 to 8 servings as part of a multicourse family-style meal

⅓ cup distilled white vinegar

6 large cloves garlic, smashed with the flat part of a cleaver or a chef's knife blade

1 tablespoon ground ginger

1 tablespoon ground cumin

1 tablespoon ground coriander seeds

2 teaspoons ground mustard seeds

2 teaspoons ground cayenne

2 teaspoons salt, divided

2 pounds boneless lamb shoulder, trimmed of fat and cut into 1½- to 2-inch cubes

½ cup vegetable oil

Whole spices: 8 cloves, 8 black peppercorns, 4 bay leaves, 2 black cardamom pods, 2 one-inch sticks cinnamon, 1 star anise pod

2 medium yellow onions, finely chopped (2 cups)

2 pounds (2 large) russet potatoes, peeled and cut into 2-inch cubes

3 cups warm water

14-ounce can crushed tomatoes

4 teaspoons tomato paste

❀ In a large bowl, combine the vinegar, garlic, ginger, cumin, coriander, mustard, cayenne, and 1 teaspoon salt. Add the lamb and toss to coat evenly. Cover with plastic wrap and marinate in the refrigerator for 1 hour.

❀ In a large heavy-bottomed pot or Dutch oven, heat the oil over medium heat until it becomes runny and starts to shimmer. Add the whole spices and cook and stir until they release their fragrance, 2 to 3 minutes. Stir in the onions and cook until golden brown, 8 to 10 minutes.

❧ Add the seasoned lamb and stir and cook until the meat releases its juices, 2 to 3 minutes. Tumble in the potatoes and add the remaining salt. Cook and stir for another 5 minutes, then add the warm water, crushed tomatoes, and tomato paste. Bring to a boil. Reduce the heat to low. Cover and simmer for 30 minutes, stirring occasionally. Uncover and simmer until the sauce is the consistency of ketchup, another 10 minutes. Taste and adjust the salt if desired. Fish out the whole spices and discard. Serve with freshly steamed basmati rice and INDIAN CUCUMBER AND TOMATO RELISH (page 137).

Steamed Meatballs with Tangerine Peel
(*Niu Rou Yuan*)

Denver-based nutritionist Mary Lee Chin and her mother Bow Yee Lee Chin have always made their own dried tangerine peel, a common ingredient in Chinese dishes. Just save the skins after peeling a tangerine (or orange, mandarin, or tangelo), place them in a covered basket to dry for a week and then store in an airtight container. The peels can also be dried out in a very slow oven or in a dehydrator. Mary says it's important to scrape the pith (the white inner part of the peel) before drying to remove the bitterness.

Time: 45 minutes
Makes: 4 to 6 servings as part of a multicourse family-style meal

2 green onions, green parts only, finely chopped

1½-inch-square piece dried tangerine peel, soaked in water until soft, pith removed, and very finely chopped

1-inch piece fresh ginger, peeled and grated (1 tablespoon)

2 tablespoons cornstarch

1 teaspoon salt

½ teaspoon sugar

¼ teaspoon freshly ground black pepper

1 pound lean ground beef (preferably sirloin)

- In a large bowl, mix together the green onions, tangerine peel, ginger, cornstarch, salt, sugar, and pepper. Add the ground beef and mix gently with your hands. Set aside for 15 minutes to allow the flavors to blend.

- Set up your steamer (see page xv for other steaming options). Fill the steamer pan half full with water and bring to a rolling boil over high heat. Reduce the heat to medium until you are ready to steam.

- Shape the beef mixture into about 16 one-inch balls. Arrange the meatballs in a single layer on a greased pie plate (or rimmed platter) that will fit inside a steamer without touching the sides. The size of your steamer will determine how many meatballs you can steam at a time.

- Return the water in the steamer to a rolling boil. Place the plate of meatballs in the steamer basket or rack. Cover and steam the balls over high heat for 7 to 8 minutes, or until they are firm to the touch and cooked through. Turn off the heat and wait for the steam to subside before lifting the lid. Lift it away from you to prevent scalding yourself and to keep condensation from dripping onto the meatballs. Carefully remove the meatballs and set aside to cool. Repeat as many times as necessary. When the meatballs are cool enough to handle, transfer to a serving platter and serve.

Pat's Notes: Tangerine peel is used to flavor meat and poultry dishes. Large pieces are added to braised dishes, but the peel is usually ground or minced for stir-fries. Dried tangerine peel can be found in plastic packages where seasonings are shelved.

Stir-Fried Beef with Mustard Greens

For this recipe, Yi Thao buys chuck steak with bits of muscle and chops it up into a coarse mince with a cleaver. I find it easier to use slivered flank steak instead. Health-conscious Yi doesn't use any oil to cook the beef, as the meat releases juices that prevent it from sticking to the pan. If you're skeptical, a little oil won't hurt.

Time: 30 minutes
Makes: 4 to 6 servings as part of a multicourse family-style meal

> 1 pound flank steak or top sirloin
>
> 1 plump stalk lemongrass trimmed, bruised (see page 10), and halved crosswise
>
> 2 cloves garlic, minced
>
> 1½-inch piece fresh ginger, peeled and cut lengthwise into 6 slices
>
> 1½ teaspoons salt
>
> 8 ounces Asian mustard greens (see page 12), trimmed and cut into 1-inch pieces (6 to 7 cups)
>
> 1 teaspoon sugar

✻ Handle the beef partially frozen so that it is easier to cut (if it's fresh, place in the freezer for about 30 minutes). Cut the beef along the grain into 1½-inch-thick strips. With your knife at an angle almost parallel to the cutting surface, slice the meat diagonally across the grain into ⅛-inch-thick slices. Then cut into about ¼-inch slivers.

✻ Preheat a large wok or skillet over high heat for about 1 minute. Add the beef, lemongrass, garlic, ginger, and salt. Stir-fry until the beef just loses its blush, 1 to 2 minutes. The beef will release its own juices that prevent it from sticking to the pan.

✻ Add the mustard green stems and the sugar. Stir-fry for about 30 seconds, then add the leaves and stir-fry until the vegetables are tender and bright green, another minute. Taste and adjust seasonings if desired. Discard the lemongrass and ginger and serve with freshly steamed rice.

❧ Pork ❧

Aged Chinese Marinade (*Lao Shui*) with Pork

This recipe was handed down to Ivy Chan from her father, Kwok Sing Chan. Ivy grew up in Hong Kong and is now a Seattle-based chocolatier, drawing from her Asian background to create unique confections. When Ivy was growing up, there was always aged marinade (lao shui, which literally means "old water") in the freezer ready-to-use. The older the marinade is, the more flavorful it becomes. You can flavor everything from beef tendon or brisket, to chicken wings, to a hunk of pork tenderloin with this marinade. And it can take many forms: some may caramelize the sugar first, some like to add a stick of cinnamon, and some toss in dried chilies to spice things up a bit. Of course, you don't have to reuse the marinade if you don't want to—it's still delicious made from scratch each time. This method is very similar to red-cooking (*hong shao*)—simmering in dark soy sauce that gives meat a reddish tint—but with leftover sauce to keep.

Time: 2 hours (10 minutes active) plus standing
Makes: 4 to 6 servings as part of a multicourse family-style meal

> 2½ to 3 pounds skin-on pork belly or shoulder, cut into 2-inch chunks
>
> 2 cups water
>
> ½ cup soy sauce
>
> ¼ cup sugar
>
> 2 tablespoons Shaoxing rice wine or dry sherry
>
> 5 star anise pods
>
> ¼-inch-thick coin fresh ginger (optional)
>
> 4 or 5 Sichuan peppercorns

❧ Blanch the pork belly to remove the excess fat: Bring a large pot of water to a boil. Add the pork belly and simmer for 3 to 4 minutes. Drain in a colander and rinse with cold running water.

❧ In a large heavy-bottomed pot or Dutch oven, bring the water, soy sauce, sugar, rice wine, star anise, ginger, and peppercorns to a boil over high heat. Carefully lower the pork into the liquid and return to a boil. Reduce the heat to medium-low. Cover and simmer for 2 to 2½ hours, or until the meat is melt-in-your-mouth tender. Flip the meat halfway through cooking to flavor and color it evenly.

❧ Turn off the heat and let the meat sit in the marinade partially covered for 6 to 8 hours. (If you prefer, let it cool to room temperature, then cover and store in the refrigerator).

❧ Before serving, set the pot on the stove and simmer over medium heat until the meat is heated through, 5 to 10 minutes. Transfer the meat to a rimmed platter, drizzle some marinade over, and serve immediately. The pork can also be served cold.

❧ Pour the remaining sauce into a freezer-safe container and freeze until the next use. This is what Ivy calls the "mother sauce." To reuse, thaw it in the refrigerator and then bring it to a boil on the stove. Add more sugar, soy sauce, or wine to taste and proceed as above. Every time you cook something new in the marinade, its flavor will deepen and become richer. After five or six uses, the sauce will have matured.

Grandpa Says: It's important to skim off the scum and excess oils from the surface of the marinade every time you cook a new batch of meat to "refresh" it.

Burmese Pork Curry (*Whethar Sebyan*)

Burmese curries, the mildest, mellowest of curries, don't call for the myriad of spices that Indian curries normally do. Paprika is added more for color than heat, so if you'd like to turn up the heat, substitute ground chilies for up to half of the paprika. Instead of pork, try the recipe with your choice of protein—beef, chicken, or even shrimp. For a one-wok meal, throw in bite-sized vegetable pieces such as squash (an optional ingredient below), cauliflower, or potatoes.

Time: 1 hour 20 minutes (20 minutes active)
Makes: 4 to 6 servings as part of a multicourse family-style meal

4 cloves garlic, chopped (1 tablespoon)

1 tablespoon fish sauce

1 tablespoon soy sauce

2 teaspoons ground turmeric

1½-inch piece fresh ginger, peeled and grated (1½ tablespoons)

2 pounds boneless pork shoulder or loin, trimmed and
     cut into 1-inch cubes

¼ cup vegetable oil

2 medium yellow onions, chopped (2 cups)

1 tablespoon ground paprika

1 pound winter squash (such as kabocha or hubbard)
     cut into 1-inch cubes (2 to 3 cups) (optional)

Salt (optional)

Cilantro leaves for garnish

❧ In a large bowl, combine the garlic, fish sauce, soy sauce, turmeric, and ginger. Add the pork and mix well to coat.

❧ Preheat a large heavy skillet over medium heat for about 1 minute. Swirl in the oil and heat until it becomes runny and starts to shimmer. Add the onions and stir and cook until translucent and ruffled with brown edges, 3 to 4 minutes. Add the paprika and mix until the onions are evenly coated.

❧ Add the pork and raise the heat to medium-high. Stir and cook to brown the pork for about 1 minute. Cover and simmer over medium-low heat for about 40 minutes. Add the squash and cook for another 20 to 25 minutes, or until the meat and squash are tender. Adjust the heat if necessary, you don't want the meat to burn.

🥄 Taste and add salt if desired. Transfer to a serving platter and garnish with cilantro leaves. Serve with freshly steamed rice and a vegetable side dish.

Pat's Notes: Pork shoulder is a favored cut of meat for Asian cooks. Inexpensive and relatively fatty, it's perfect for braising or roasting. The upper portion of the shoulder is called pork butt (or Boston butt) and is sold boneless. The lower arm portion, or picnic shoulder, is sold whole, usually bone-in, as either the meatier upper arm portion or the lower foreleg portion; picnic shoulders usually have some skin attached. If you prefer a leaner (albeit drier) cut, use pork loin.

Grandma Says: You don't need to add water to the curry as the pork will release its own juices. Add some tomatoes with the squash if you'd like to thicken the sauce.

Chinese Barbecued Pork (*Char Siu*)

The words *char siu* literally mean "fork burnt or roasted," a nod to the traditional preparation method of skewering strips of pork with long forks or hooks and cooking them over a fire or in a hot oven. These tender, juicy morsels of pork go with just about everything and transcend many Asian cultures (look for them in Japanese SOMEN SALAD, page 242). It may be a fixture at Chinese deli counters but it is fairly simple to make. Red food coloring is often added to give the meat its signature deep red sheen, but this can be omitted when making at home.

Time: 1 hour (15 minutes active) plus marinating
Makes: 4 to 6 servings as part of a multicourse family-style meal

> 2½ to 3 pounds boneless pork shoulder (measuring about 8 by 6 by 3 inches)
>
> ⅔ cup sugar
>
> ½ cup soy sauce
>
> 2 green onions, smashed with the flat part of a cleaver or a large knife
>
> 2 cilantro stems (preferably with their roots attached; see page 5), smashed with the flat part of a cleaver or a chef's knife blade
>
> 1 star anise pod
>
> 1 tablespoon Shaoxing rice wine or dry sherry (optional)
>
> ½ teaspoon sesame oil
>
> ½ teaspoon 5-spice powder

❧ Cut the pork lengthwise into four long strips. Lay each strip flat on the cutting board and cut in half lengthwise. You will end up with 8 strips about 1½ inches wide, and 7 to 8 inches long. Place in a dish large enough to hold all the pieces in one layer.

❧ In a small bowl, mix the together the sugar, soy sauce, green onions, cilantro, star anise, rice wine, sesame oil, and 5-spice powder. Pour the marinade over the pork. Cover with plastic wrap and marinate in the refrigerator for at least 2 hours, or preferably a day and a half.

❧ Preheat the oven to 400 degrees F.

❧ Remove the pork from the marinade and place on a broiling rack set on top of a foil-lined roasting pan to catch the drippings. Reserve the marinade. Bake for 40 to 45 minutes, flipping halfway, or until the pork starts caramelizing and is just beginning to char at the edges. Baste at least once on each side during the first 30 minutes of cooking.

❧ Transfer the pork to a chopping board and let rest for about 10 minutes before cutting crosswise into ¼-inch-thick slices. Meanwhile, simmer the reserved marinade over medium heat for at least 10 minutes, skimming off any scum that rises to the surface.

❧ Serve with freshly steamed rice or noodles topped with the marinade sauce.

Pat's Notes: The traditional method of hanging pork strips to cook has its benefits— it allows the meat to cook evenly from all sides. If you'd like to try this, hang pork strips from metal S-hooks on a high rack in your oven over a foil-lined pan on the lowest rack to catch the drippings.

Crispy Fried Meatballs (*Bakso Goreng*)

Bakso goreng is a Chinese dish modified by Chinese immigrants in Indonesia. Linawati Hioe, a Hakka born and raised in Jakarta, furnished this recipe. Her daughter Luwei, a self-proclaimed picky eater, remembers loving the crispy, savory meatballs even as a child. Now that Luwei has her own family, she recreates her mom's recipe often. There are many variations: you can add chopped green onions or dried cuttlefish (soaked first to soften). Of course, Halal versions use chicken or beef instead of pork. The meatballs are delicious eaten with rice and a vegetable side dish and also make great party poppers (appetizers you can easily pop into your mouth) for entertaining!

Time: 1¼ hours
Makes: 40 to 45 meatballs (8 to 10 servings as part of a multicourse family meal)

2 pounds ground pork
1 pound peeled and deveined shrimp, chopped to a fine mince with a cleaver or large chef's knife, or in a food processor
2 green onions, white and green parts, finely chopped
2 eggs

¼ cup cornstarch

1 tablespoon fish sauce

1 tablespoon sugar

1 tablespoon salt

1 teaspoon ground white pepper

2 cups (or as needed) vegetable oil for deep-frying

Chili sauce for serving

❧ In a large bowl, mix together the pork, shrimp, green onions, eggs, cornstarch, fish sauce, sugar, salt, and white pepper with your hands. The resulting mixture should be moist and clump well into balls.

❧ Line a plate with paper towels. In a large wok, heavy skillet, or Dutch oven, heat the oil over high heat until it reaches 350 degrees F on a deep-fry thermometer (see page xiii for deep-frying tips). Fry a small piece of the pork mixture and taste. Adjust seasonings if desired. Reduce the heat to medium-high.

❧ Grab a handful of the pork mixture and shape into a golf ball-size ball (about 1-inch in diameter) by squeezing it out of the hole at the top of your fist. Place the meatball in an oiled tablespoon and carefully drop into the oil. Fry in a batch of 8 to 10 meatballs until golden brown and crispy, 4 to 5 minutes. Remove meatballs with a slotted spoon, shaking off excess oil, and drain on paper towels.

❧ Use a slotted spoon or a wire mesh strainer to remove any debris from the oil and return to 350 degrees F before frying the next batch. Repeat with remaining meat mixture.

❧ Serve with chili sauce and/or freshly steamed rice.

Pat's Notes: This recipe makes a lot of meatballs. Use some of the meat mixture to stuff peppers, eggplant, or tofu for steaming or frying. Or throw leftover meatballs into a soup. Using HOMEMADE CHICKEN STOCK (page 42) as a base, add anything from julienne carrots, snow peas, and wood ear mushrooms to dried lily buds.

Grandma Says: For perfectly shaped meatballs, shape with a mini ice cream scoop or cookie scoop.

Lao Sausage (*Sai Oua*)

Before Grandma Keo Choulaphan (see page 176) bought her sausage-stuffing machine, she stuffed sausages into their casings by hand with a spoon—a very long and arduous process. With the modern appliance and her son's help, the process is much swifter now. A food grinder or stand mixer with the right attachment does the trick as well. Keo recommends buying pork with a medium-coarse grind, including the skin too, for good texture. If you don't fancy making sausages, form the meat into hamburger-style patties or meatballs. You can deep-fry, steam, or broil the patties or meatballs and add them to a soup with cellophane noodles and vegetables.

Time: 1½ to 2 hours (depending on your sausage-stuffing prowess) plus soaking
Makes: 10 to 12 four-inch sausages (8 servings as part of a multicourse family-style meal)

> 5 feet of 38- to 42-millimeter (1½- to 1¾-inch) diameter hog casing (see Pat's Notes), unraveled
>
> ½ cup frozen ground lemongrass (see page 10), thawed and soaked in ½ cup water
>
> ¼ cup water, plus more as needed
>
> 2 cloves garlic
>
> 1 kaffir lime leaf
>
> ¼-inch piece galangal (1½ inches in diameter), peeled
>
> 2 teaspoons crushed dried chili flakes, or 4 whole dried chilies
>
> Pinch of crushed Sichuan peppercorns
>
> 2 pounds ground pork
>
> ¾ cup (about 1 ounce) finely chopped cilantro leaves and stalks
>
> ¾ cup (about 1 ounce) finely chopped culantro
>
> ½ cup (about 3 fat stalks) finely chopped green onions, white and green parts
>
> 1 small yellow onion, very finely chopped, preferably with a food processor (½ cup)
>
> 1 tablespoon fish sauce
>
> 1 tablespoon sugar
>
> 1½ teaspoons salt

Soak the hog casing overnight in cold water. Place in a bowl in the sink and open one end of the casing and flush the inside with warm water from the faucet. Place in fresh warm water at your work station.

- Place the soaked lemongrass, water, garlic, lime leaf, galangal, chili flakes, and peppercorns in the jug of an electric blender. Cover and blend on high speed for about 1 minute, or until a coarse watery paste forms. Scrape unground bits down toward the blade with a rubber spatula as you go. Add water, 1 to 2 tablespoons at a time, if necessary for the ingredients to come together.

- In a large bowl, mix together the lemongrass mixture, pork, cilantro, culantro, green and yellow onions, fish sauce, sugar, and salt with your hands. Microwave a small portion of the sausage mixture and taste. Adjust seasonings if desired.

- To make the sausage, use a food grinder (or a stand mixer) with a sausage stuffing attachment and horn. Pull the entire length of casing over the tip of the sausage horn, squeezing it together like the folds of an accordion. Leave a few inches extra and tie a double knot at the end. Fill the mouth of the grinder with the meat mixture and crank the meat through the grinder to fill the casing until the sausage is packed tightly, but not to the point of bursting. As you fill it, the casing will inflate and gradually ease away from the horn. When all the meat is used, slip the casing from the horn.

- For a coil, tie the open end with a double knot. For individual links, pinch the sausage every 4 inches, twist the links and tie with kitchen twine. Prick all over with a clean pin to remove any air bubbles.

- Cook the sausage as desired (broil, barbecue, or boil) until it reaches an internal temperature of 160 degrees F, or the meat shows no trace of pink when pierced with the tip of a knife. Freeze uncooked sausage for up to 1 month.

Pat's Notes: If you can't find frozen ground lemongrass, prepare 3 stalks (see page 10) and chop in a food processor until very fine.

It is difficult to estimate how much casing you will require but one pound of meat will stuff approximately 2 feet of 35- to 42-millimeter casing. Casings are usually sold in hanks or bundles (a traditional hank is 100 yards). One hank will stuff approximately 100 to 125 pounds. The good news is if you're planning on making sausages on a regular basis, salted casings keep indefinitely when stored properly (rinse, pack in salt, and refrigerate). Asian markets and some vendors sell them in "home size" packs with enough casing to stuff 25 pounds of sausage. If not, just make patties or meatballs.

1-2-3-4-5 Sticky Spareribs (*Tang Chu Pai Gu*)

If you're one to think that Chinese recipes are complicated, this dish dispels all preconceptions. Not only is it easy to remember the amounts of the ingredients (1, 2, 3, 4, and 5 tablespoons), it's almost effortless to prepare. To put it simply, this dish has an excellent ease-of-preparation to tastiness ratio. For a tangier taste, switch the proportions of vinegar and sugar.

Time: 45 minutes (5 minutes active)
Makes: 4 to 6 servings as part of a multicourse family-style meal

> 1 tablespoon Shaoxing rice wine or dry sherry
>
> 2 tablespoons vinegar
>
> 3 tablespoons sugar
>
> 4 tablespoons soy sauce
>
> 5 tablespoons water, plus more as needed
>
> 2 pounds meaty pork spareribs, trimmed of excess fat, cut crosswise in half through the bone, and cut between the bone into individual riblets (have your butcher do this)

In a large wide-mouthed heavy-bottomed pot or Dutch oven, combine the rice wine, vinegar, sugar, soy sauce, and water. Add the spareribs and bring to a boil over high heat. Reduce the heat to medium and simmer for 40 to 45 minutes, stirring occasionally. If the meat dries out and starts to burn, add water, 1 tablespoon at a time. The ribs are ready when the meat is tender and glossed with a sticky, reddish-brown glaze and the liquid has been absorbed. Serve with freshly steamed rice and a vegetable side dish.

Variations: Instead of Shaoxing rice wine, experiment with other forms of alcohol, like beer or brandy.

Roasted Pork Tenderloin with Mustard Sauce
(*Kao Zhu Li Ji*)

This dish sounds very much like an all-American roast, but it comes from Lynn Chang's Cantonese maternal grandmother whom she calls *popo*. The original recipe uses Chinese rice wine but Lynn's mother, Li, suggests using more readily available bourbon. It can be served as a main course with rice and a vegetable side dish like CHINESE BROCCOLI IN OYSTER SAUCE (page 107).

Time: 1 hour 10 minutes (10 minutes active) plus marinating
Makes: 4 to 6 servings as part of a multicourse family-style meal

> ¼ cup soy sauce
>
> ¼ cup bourbon
>
> 3 tablespoons brown sugar
>
> 3-pound extra-lean pork tenderloin
>
> Mustard Sauce (recipe follows)

❀ Combine the soy sauce, bourbon, and brown sugar in a large zip-top plastic bag. Add the pork, seal the bag, and shake to coat the pork evenly. Marinate in the refrigerator for at least 3 hours, or up to 12 hours.

❀ Preheat the oven to 350 degrees F. Line a small roasting pan with foil.

❀ Place the marinated pork in the prepared pan. Roast uncovered for about 1 hour, or until the internal temperature reaches 155 degrees F. Do not overcook.

❀ Transfer the pork to a chopping board and let rest for 5 minutes. Slice into 1-inch medallions and serve with the mustard sauce.

Mustard Sauce

> ⅓ cup sour cream
>
> ⅓ cup mayonnaise
>
> 1 tablespoon dry mustard
>
> 3 green onions, white and green parts, finely chopped

❀ In a small bowl, mix together the sour cream, mayonnaise, mustard, and green onions to form a smooth, creamy sauce.

Sweet and Sour Pork (*Gu Lao Rou*)

There are endless variations of this quintessential Chinese dish, but it always tastes best homemade. The pork cut of choice is pork shoulder—not too lean, not too fatty (see Pat's Notes on page 164). Other cuts may be leaner, and healthier, but they often turn tough and chewy when fried. So trim the fat if you must, or substitute chicken breast.

Time: 1 hour plus marinating
Makes: 4 to 6 servings as part of a multicourse family-style meal

1 egg, lightly beaten

3 tablespoons self-rising flour

1 teaspoon Shaoxing rice wine or dry sherry

½ teaspoon salt

¼ teaspoon freshly ground black pepper

1 pound pork shoulder, cut into 1-inch cubes

2 cups plus 2 tablespoons vegetable oil, divided

1 clove garlic, minced

1 medium carrot, peeled and cut thinly on the diagonal

1 medium yellow onion, cut into 8 wedges and separated

1 green or red bell pepper, cut into 1-inch squares

8-ounce can pineapple chunks, well drained (1 cup)

Sauce:

⅔ cup water

3 tablespoons ketchup

2 tablespoons sugar

1 tablespoon cornstarch

1 teaspoon soy sauce

3 tablespoons distilled white vinegar

❧ In a medium bowl, combine the egg, flour, rice wine, salt, and pepper. Add the pork and toss with your hands, making sure to coat each piece. Marinate in the refrigerator for at least 2 hours, or preferably 12 hours.

❧ Bring the pork to room temperature before cooking.

❧ Line a plate with paper towels. Preheat the oven to 300 degrees F.

❧ In a large wok, heavy skillet, or Dutch oven, heat the 2 cups oil over high heat until it reaches 350 degrees F on a deep-fry thermometer (see page xiii for deep-frying tips).

❧ Reduce the heat to medium-high. Using tongs, drop the pork a few pieces at a time into the hot oil, ensuring that the pieces don't stick together. Fry in a batch of 7 to 8 pieces until golden brown and crispy, 5 to 6 minutes. Remove the pork with a slotted spoon, shaking off excess oil, and drain on paper towels. Keep warm in the oven.

❧ Use a slotted spoon or a wire mesh strainer to remove any debris from the oil and return the oil to 350 degrees F before frying the next batch. Repeat with remaining pork.

❧ Discard the oil and wipe the wok with a paper towel.

❧ Heat the 2 tablespoons fresh oil over medium-high heat until it becomes runny and starts to shimmer. Add the garlic and cook until fragrant, about 30 seconds. Toss in the carrot and onion and stir-fry for about a minute. Add the pepper and stir-fry until tender-crisp, about 2 minutes. (If you prefer softer carrots, cook ahead by microwaving or steaming.) Add the pineapple, give everything a quick stir and turn off the heat, leaving the vegetables in the wok.

❧ To make the sauce, in a small saucepan, combine the water, ketchup, sugar, cornstarch, and soy sauce. Cook over medium-high heat, stirring continuously, until the sauce starts to bubble and thicken, 1 to 2 minutes. Reduce the heat to low and stir in the vinegar.

❧ Tumble the cooked pork nuggets into the wok with the vegetables and pour the sauce over. Toss to coat and transfer to a large rimmed platter or bowl. Serve immediately with freshly steamed rice.

Grandma Says: You can deep-fry the pork nuggets ahead of time. Refrigerate or freeze until needed. Then reheat with a quick dip in hot oil or in the oven. Don't forget to bring the meat to room temperature first.

Thai Basil Pork (*Pad Gkaprow Mu*)

This versatile recipe is a Thai favorite that often appears at breakfast or on the dinner table as part of a family-style meal. Ground pork is usually paired with the jagged leaves of holy basil (*bai gkaprow*). However, Thai sweet basil (*bai horapa*) is much easier to find in Asian markets in the United States and makes a worthy stand-in. If all else fails, substitute any basil or a mixture of basil and mint for a bright, refreshing flavor. Ground chicken or turkey also works well in this dish, as well as fresh seafood: shrimp, scallops, mussels, and firm-flesh fish like salmon or halibut.

Time: 20 minutes
Makes: 4 to 6 servings as part of a multicourse family-style meal

2 tablespoons vegetable oil

6 cloves garlic, minced (2 tablespoons)

5 Asian shallots or ½ small onion, cut into thin slices (⅓ cup)

1½ pounds ground pork

6 red Thai chilies, cut into rounds

2 tablespoons oyster sauce

2 tablespoons fish sauce

1 teaspoon soy sauce

1 teaspoon brown sugar

1½ cups packed fresh holy basil or Thai basil leaves

Pinch of freshly ground black pepper (optional)

❧ Preheat a large wok or skillet over high heat for 1 minute. Swirl in the oil and heat until it becomes runny and starts to shimmer. Reduce the heat to medium. Add the garlic and shallots and cook until the garlic is light golden and fragrant, 15 to 30 seconds. Raise the heat to high and stir in the pork, breaking up clumps with the edge of your spatula. Stir and cook until the meat has just lost its blush, 1 to 2 minutes.

❧ Reduce the heat to medium and throw in the chilies. Add the oyster sauce, fish sauce, soy sauce, and sugar and stir to coat the meat evenly. Stir in the basil and cook until the basil is wilted and the pork is cooked through, another 30 seconds to 1 minute. Transfer to a serving dish and sprinkle with pepper. Serve hot with freshly steamed rice.

Thai Basil Pork

Profile of a Grandma: KEO CHOULAPHAN

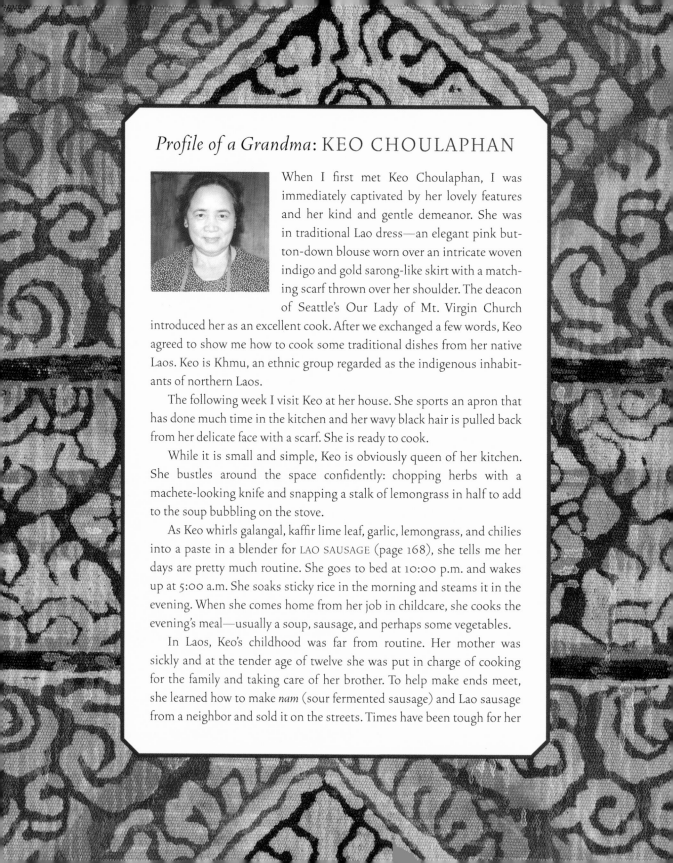

When I first met Keo Choulaphan, I was immediately captivated by her lovely features and her kind and gentle demeanor. She was in traditional Lao dress—an elegant pink button-down blouse worn over an intricate woven indigo and gold sarong-like skirt with a matching scarf thrown over her shoulder. The deacon of Seattle's Our Lady of Mt. Virgin Church introduced her as an excellent cook. After we exchanged a few words, Keo agreed to show me how to cook some traditional dishes from her native Laos. Keo is Khmu, an ethnic group regarded as the indigenous inhabitants of northern Laos.

The following week I visit Keo at her house. She sports an apron that has done much time in the kitchen and her wavy black hair is pulled back from her delicate face with a scarf. She is ready to cook.

While it is small and simple, Keo is obviously queen of her kitchen. She bustles around the space confidently: chopping herbs with a machete-looking knife and snapping a stalk of lemongrass in half to add to the soup bubbling on the stove.

As Keo whirls galangal, kaffir lime leaf, garlic, lemongrass, and chilies into a paste in a blender for LAO SAUSAGE (page 168), she tells me her days are pretty much routine. She goes to bed at 10:00 p.m. and wakes up at 5:00 a.m. She soaks sticky rice in the morning and steams it in the evening. When she comes home from her job in childcare, she cooks the evening's meal—usually a soup, sausage, and perhaps some vegetables.

In Laos, Keo's childhood was far from routine. Her mother was sickly and at the tender age of twelve she was put in charge of cooking for the family and taking care of her brother. To help make ends meet, she learned how to make *nam* (sour fermented sausage) and Lao sausage from a neighbor and sold it on the streets. Times have been tough for her but through sheer hard work and determination, Keo has survived on her own terms. "I do and I learn my own way," she insists.

Rightly so, Keo's pride and determination rule in her kitchen. During the weekends, she makes sausages, nam, beef jerky, spring rolls, and egg rolls to sell to friends and acquaintances. And she makes them the way she likes it. "If people don't like it, I'll eat it," she says.

Keo may not have much formal education, but she more than makes up for it with resolve and resilience. Her strong character was obviously attractive to her husband, Bountha. "He came five times to my father to say he loved me," relates Keo, not without a hint of glee. The fifth time was a charm and they married in 1969 when Keo was seventeen. Although the marriage was arranged, Keo grew to love him dearly.

In the late 1970s, Keo and Bountha decided to flee the communist regime in Laos. To pave a safe passage for Keo and their two children, Bountha wanted to set off first. Keo, who was three months pregnant, refused. She didn't want to be left behind, nor did she want to face any uncertainty about his well-being. Keo told him simply, "I see you die. You see me die."

Eventually, the family crossed the Mekong River together in a canoe and escaped to Thailand. They stayed in a refugee camp on the Thai-Lao border for 11 months where her second son was born. After a long wait, Keo and her family were finally given safe passage to the United States. She still remembers the exact day she arrived in Seattle. It was February 26, 1981.

Today, at 54, Keo and Bountha have four children and are grandparents to two beautiful little girls. Keo worries that her grandchildren are not learning the Khmu language and culture and tries to visit them as often as possible. Back home in Khmu villages, Khmu culture is traditionally passed down through evening storytelling sessions. As the next best thing, Keo hopes to record the many folktales that she holds as treasures in her head—not just for her grandchildren but also future generations of Khmu children who might otherwise not know their culture.

❦ Poultry ❧

Brandied Chicken and Mushrooms in Oyster Sauce

In this dish created by Juliana Suparman, chicken, mushrooms, and onion are tossed together in a wok and enhanced by the nuanced flavors of spicy ginger and a splash (or two) of brandy. Swift and tasty, it is a perfect weeknight dinner dish. Juliana, an Indonesian Chinese grandmother of two boisterous boys, often cobbles a meal together using whatever ingredients are available on hand, and this dish is one example that became a family favorite. When her children were growing up, Juliana often sneaked in slivers of chicken liver to give them their daily dose of iron.

Time: 30 minutes
Makes: 4 to 6 servings as part of a multicourse family-style meal

2 tablespoons vegetable oil

3 cloves garlic, minced (1 tablespoon)

One 1-inch piece fresh ginger, peeled and slivered

1 large yellow onion, halved and cut into thin crescents

1½ pounds boneless chicken thighs, cut into bite-sized pieces

8 ounces fresh button or cremini mushrooms, stemmed and sliced (2 cups)

¼ cup oyster sauce

1 tablespoon sweet soy sauce (see page 24)

½ teaspoon salt

½ teaspoon ground white pepper

2 tablespoons brandy

Chopped green onions for garnish

❧ Preheat a large wok or skillet over medium-high heat for 1 minute. Swirl in the oil and heat until it becomes runny and starts to shimmer. Add the garlic and ginger and cook until fragrant, about 30 seconds. Add the onion and stir and cook until it is soft and translucent, 3 to 4 minutes.

❧ Raise the heat to high. Add the chicken and stir and cook until no longer pink, 2 to 3 minutes. Add the mushrooms followed by the oyster sauce, soy sauce, salt, and pepper. Stir everything swiftly around the wok until well mixed. Stir in the brandy and simmer over medium-low heat until the chicken is cooked through, 2 to 3 minutes. Sprinkle with green onions and serve with freshly steamed rice and a vegetable side dish.

Caramelized Chicken with Lemongrass and Chilies
(*Ga Xao Sa Ot Cay*)

The subtle, citrusy scent of lemongrass, the bittersweet flavor of caramel, and the heat of red chilies marry very well in this popular Vietnamese chicken dish. Every Vietnamese cook has his or her own recipe—this version comes from Huong Thu Nguyen, who ran a Vietnamese restaurant in Denville, New Jersey, in the 1980s. Even now that she has retired to Hawaii's Big Island, this is still a core dish in her kitchen. "It takes awhile to make good caramel sauce without burning it," she notes. So keep practicing! You may be tempted to use chicken breasts instead of thighs as well as remove the skin. Please don't. Thigh meat is juicier and more succulent and the skin has tons of flavor, all of which add to this delightful dish. Serve with freshly steamed rice and SWEET AND SOUR FISH SOUP (page 82).

Time: 45 minutes
Makes: 4 servings as part of a multicourse family-style meal

> 1 pound boneless chicken thighs with skin, cut into ½-inch chunks
> 1 teaspoon salt
> Freshly ground black pepper
> 4 plump stalks lemongrass, trimmed, bruised (see page 10), and minced (¾ cup), divided
> 2 tablespoons vegetable oil
> 2 tablespoons sugar
> 1 large yellow onion, halved and cut into thin crescents
> 1½ tablespoons minced garlic, divided (4 to 5 cloves)
> 3 red Thai chilies, cut into rounds
> 2 teaspoons fish sauce
> Chopped cilantro leaves for garnish
> Chopped green onions for garnish

Caramelized Chicken with Lemongrass and Chilies

❧ In a medium bowl, season the chicken with the salt and ¼ teaspoon black pepper. Add 3 tablespoons of the lemongrass, toss, and set aside.

❧ In a large skillet (if possible, use a pan with a light interior such as stainless steel so you can monitor changes in color), heat the oil over medium-high heat until it becomes runny and starts to shimmer. Add the sugar and cook and stir continuously. After 1 to 2 minutes, the sugar will start to clump together then melt into a syrup. Cook and stir for another 2 to 3 minutes, or until the clear syrup thickens into a gooey caramel-brown liquid suspended in the oil. You will also smell a pleasant burnt sugar aroma. Watch the caramel closely during this process as it can burn very quickly. If the caramel starts to turn black and smell acrid, pull the skillet off the stove for a few seconds before continuing.

❧ Stir in the remaining lemongrass, the onion, and 1 tablespoon of the garlic and cook and stir until the ingredients turn golden brown and fragrant, 1 to 2 minutes. Add the chicken and raise the heat to high. Cook, tossing the chicken in the caramel sauce, for about 1½ minutes. If there isn't enough sauce to evenly coat the chicken, carefully add water, 1 tablespoon at a time. If the mixture starts to sputter and seize, pull the skillet off the stove until it ceases. Throw in the chilies and cook and stir until the chicken is no longer pink, 2 to 3 minutes. Add the fish sauce and the remaining garlic. Stir with a couple more flourishes to mix well. When the chicken is just cooked through (cut into a piece to check), taste and adjust seasonings if desired. Remove from the heat and transfer to a serving platter. Sprinkle with black pepper to taste and garnish with cilantro leaves and green onions.

Grandma Says: Add the fish sauce at the last minute and it won't stink up your kitchen or your clothes.

Chicken Adobo (Vinegar-Braised Chicken)

You could call *adobo* the Philippines' unofficial national dish, even though it's more often eaten in homes than in restaurants. There are many types of adobo—chicken (traditionally the legs are used but you can use breasts too), pork (pork loin), beef (stew beef or chuck), liver, vegetables, and even squid! No two adobo recipes are alike. Improvise and experiment to get just the right balance of flavors—especially sour to salt—that dances to the right tune on your tongue. The frying adds a crispy finish to the meat but you can skip this step if you are ravenous . . . or just lazy! Adobo keeps well and like most braises, tastes even better the next day. Serve hot with GARLIC FRIED RICE (page 33).

Time: 1¼ hours
Makes: 8 servings as part of a multicourse family-style meal

> 1½ cups cane vinegar or distilled white vinegar
>
> 1 cup water
>
> 6 cloves garlic, smashed with the flat part of a cleaver or large knife
>
> 2 bay leaves
>
> 1½ teaspoons black peppercorns, crushed
>
> 8 whole chicken leg quarters (4 to 5 pounds), cut into drumstick and thigh sections
>
> ¾ cup soy sauce
>
> 3 tablespoons vegetable oil
>
> Chopped green onions for garnish

❧ In a large nonreactive pot or Dutch oven, mix together the vinegar, water, garlic, bay leaves, and black peppercorns. Add the chicken. Bring to a boil over high heat. Reduce the heat to medium. Cover and simmer for 20 minutes.

❧ Add the soy sauce and stir to coat the chicken evenly. Cover and simmer for another 20 minutes, or until the chicken is cooked through. Using tongs, transfer the chicken to a plate, shaking off as much excess liquid as possible. Pat the pieces dry with paper towels. Discard the bay leaves. Skim the fat from the sauce and set aside.

❧ In a large skillet, heat the oil over high heat until very hot but just before smoking. In batches, add the chicken and pan-fry until crisp and browned evenly on both sides, 2 to 3 minutes on each side. Add the reserved sauce and stir for a few minutes while scraping up the brown bits at the bottom of the pan. Simmer over low heat until reduced slightly, about 10 minutes.

Transfer the chicken to a rimmed platter, pour the sauce over, and scatter with green onions.

Variations: Add coconut milk to the adobo, either right at the beginning, or at the end when the cooking is done.

Instead of bay leaves, try throwing in some oregano (fresh or dried) and/or some fresh chilies.

Add ½ cup pineapple cubes, ½ cup halved cherry tomatoes, and 1 tablespoon butter after the sauce has reduced. Cover tightly and simmer until the butter has melted and tomatoes have wilted, 3 to 4 minutes. Serve hot with freshly steamed rice.

Try making this dish with pork and apple cider vinegar (we all know apples and pork go super together!) or experiment with more nontraditional French sherry or Japanese rice vinegars for an adobo with your name on it.

Pat's Notes: Made from sugar cane syrup, cane vinegar is one of the most commonly used vinegars in Filipino cooking. With a mellow flavor, it ranges in color from dark yellow to golden brown. Contrary to what you might think, it is not sweeter than other vinegars.

Grandma Says: To easily remove garlic skins, rinse the cloves in hot water first.

Chicken and Eggs in a Golden Curry (*Kuku Paka*)

This recipe from Mumtaz Rahemtulla, a fourth-generation Kenyan of Indian (Gujarati) descent, is widely known by its Swahili name, *kuku paka*. It shows up on Indian menus as well—not surprising considering the Swahili culture combines African, Arab, and Indian influences. Rich and savory, kuku paka is easy to prepare for a family meal or a casual dinner with friends. The sauce also tastes great with boiled corn—on the cob or just the kernels—which is called corn paka.

Time: 1¼ hours (45 minutes active) plus marinating
Makes: 6 servings as part of a multicourse family-style meal

Two 13½-ounce cans coconut milk, divided

2 teaspoons minced garlic (2 cloves), divided

2 teaspoons grated fresh ginger (from a 1-inch piece), divided

1½ teaspoons salt, divided

3- to 4-pound broiler-fryer chicken, skinned and cut into 12 to 14 pieces; or 3 pounds chicken parts (a combination of bone-in thighs and drumsticks works well here)

¼ cup loosely packed cilantro leaves, chopped

½ teaspoon ground turmeric

3 red or green Thai chilies, cut into thin rounds

6 hard-boiled eggs

❀ In a large bowl, mix 1 can of coconut milk, 1 teaspoon of the garlic, 1 teaspoon of the ginger, and 1 teaspoon of the salt. Add the chicken and use your hands to coat each piece evenly with the marinade. Cover and marinate in the refrigerator for at least 6 hours, or preferably 12.

❀ Position a rack 4 to 6 inches from the heat source and preheat the broiler. Using tongs, pick up each piece of chicken and allow excess marinade to drip off. Place the chicken pieces on a broiler rack set on top of a baking pan lined with foil to catch the drippings. Reserve the leftover marinade.

❀ Broil the chicken for 8 to 10 minutes on each side, or until nicely browned. The pieces will not cook at the same rate so remove them as they are done to avoid overbrowning. (The chicken does not have to be cooked through because it will simmer for another 30 minutes.)

In a large and wide heavy-bottomed pot or Dutch oven, mix together the leftover marinade, the remaining coconut milk, garlic, ginger, and salt, along with the cilantro, turmeric, and chilies. Bring to a boil over medium heat. Add the chicken and eggs and simmer over low heat, turning once or twice during cooking to coat evenly, until the chicken and eggs have turned golden yellow and absorbed most of the sauce, about 30 minutes. Serve immediately with freshly steamed basmati rice.

Lao Chicken and Herb Salad (*Larb Gai*)

Larb (also spelled *laap*, *larp*, *laab*) is the unofficial national dish of Laos, and is also very popular in Thailand judging by its oft-seen appearance at Thai restaurants. Yi Thao prefers to buy lean chicken breast meat and cut out all the fat before mincing it with a cleaver. You can use ground chicken from the supermarket, or grind chicken chunks in your food processor. I find breast meat a little dry and prefer dark meat, which has more moisture and flavor. Yi's version of larb uses more herbs than most; each brings a unique flavor to the dish. I must caution first-timers that the raw kaffir lime leaves, galangal, and lemongrass add a strong, herbal flavor to the dish, so start with a little and adjust according to your taste.

Time: 40 minutes
Makes: 4 to 6 servings as part of a multicourse family-style meal

> 1½ pounds ground chicken thighs or breasts
>
> Salt
>
> ⅓ cup roasted rice powder (see Pat's Notes)
>
> 1 cup loosely packed cilantro stems and leaves, half the sprigs reserved for garnish and the remaining stems and leaves finely chopped
>
> ½ cup loosely packed spearmint leaves, torn into small pieces
>
> ½ cup loosely packed Vietnamese coriander, chopped
>
> 5 stalks culantro, chopped (½ cup)
>
> 4 green onions, green parts thinly sliced and white and pale green parts (the bottom 2 inches) thinly cut lengthwise for garnish
>
> Juice of 1 large lime (2 tablespoons)
>
> 1 tablespoon fish sauce

1 teaspoon crushed dried red chilies

3 red or green Thai chilies, cut into rounds

3 kaffir lime leaves, finely chopped

½-inch piece fresh galangal (¾ ounce), minced

1 plump stalk lemongrass, trimmed, bruised (see page 10), and minced

❧ Heat a medium nonstick wok or skillet over high heat for 1 minute. Add the chicken and sprinkle with a pinch of salt. (Yi doesn't add any oil but you can if you want to.) The chicken will stick to the pan at first, but once its juices are released, the meat will loosen. Cook and stir until the chicken is fully cooked but not too brown, 6 to 7 minutes. Transfer the meat to a large bowl and let cool for about 5 minutes.

❧ Add the rice powder, chopped cilantro, spearmint, coriander, culantro, sliced green onions, lime juice, fish sauce, dried chilies, and 1 teaspoon salt. Mix well. Add the Thai chilies, lime leaves, galangal, and lemongrass (all amounts more or less to taste). Mix well. Taste the salad; it should be a nice balance of heat (fresh and dried chilies), salt (fish sauce), and tart (lime juice). Don't be afraid to add more of anything for a flavor balance that's to your taste. Garnish with the reserved cilantro sprigs and green onions and serve at room temperature with WHITE GLUTINOUS RICE (page 38).

Pat's Notes: Ground roasted rice is available in Asian markets or you can make your own by roasting uncooked sticky rice in a dry skillet over the stove until brown. Then grind to a fine powder in a coffee grinder or with a mortar and pestle.

If you can't find all the herbs that Yi uses, the dish will still taste delicious with only cilantro, spearmint, and green onions.

Mochiko Fried Chicken

When raising three rowdy boys, Daisy Kushino (see page 200) often made this classic Japanese American dish: it was a cinch to make and an easy dish to feed them while they were sitting in a highchair or at a picnic. Mochiko chicken is probably adapted from *tatsuta age*, Japanese marinated fried chicken, and is very versatile: serve small pieces as finger food or cut the chicken into bigger pieces for a main course. Flour made from Japanese sweet rice (which is similar to glutinous rice) is called mochiko flour or sweet rice flour and can be found in the Asian aisle of most supermarkets. Look for Koda Farms Blue Star Brand which comes in a white box.

Time: 45 minutes plus marinating
Makes: 4 to 6 servings as part of a multicourse family-style meal

> 2 pounds boneless, skinless chicken thighs or breasts
> 2 eggs, lightly beaten
> ¼ cup soy sauce
> ¼ cup plus 2 tablespoons mochiko flour
> ¼ cup plus 2 tablespoons cornstarch
> ¼ cup sugar
> 4 green onions, white and green parts, chopped (¼ cup)
> 2 cloves garlic, minced
> Vegetable oil for shallow frying

❧ Using a meat pounder, pound the chicken gently to flatten it without tearing it. This tenderizes the meat and allows it to cook evenly. Cut into 2- to 3-inch chunks.

❧ In a large bowl, mix together the eggs, soy sauce, mochiko flour, cornstarch, sugar, green onions, and garlic. Tumble in the chicken and toss to coat evenly. Cover and marinate in the refrigerator for at least 4 hours, or preferably 12 hours.

❧ Bring the chicken to room temperature before frying.

❧ Line a plate with paper towels. In a large heavy skillet, heat about 1 inch of oil over high heat until it becomes runny and starts to shimmer. Reduce the heat to medium. Using tongs or cooking chopsticks, carefully lower thickly coated chicken pieces one at a time into the oil. You are shallow-frying, so the pieces will only be half submerged. Fry in a batch of 7 to 8 pieces (don't overcrowd the pan) until both sides are crispy and evenly golden brown, 2½ to 3 minutes on each side. Remove the chicken with a slotted spoon, shaking off excess oil, and drain on paper towels.

🥄 Use a slotted spoon or a wire mesh strainer to remove any debris from the oil and repeat until all the chicken is cooked. Serve hot with freshly steamed short-grain rice, or cold as an appetizer or picnic food.

Pat's Notes: Add 1 teaspoon grated ginger to the marinade for a little kick.

Grandma Says: When expecting company, you can undercook the chicken and when ready to serve, finish it off in a 375 degree F oven for 5 to 6 minutes so it will crisp up and be nice and warm.

Rick's Chicken Curry

A. Rick Rupan's family hails from India by way of Guyana and his curry recipe is a riff on a traditional Indian curry. During family get-togethers in New York and Long Island where Rick grew up, males were not allowed in the kitchen, traditionally considered a woman's domain. However, Rick was able to weasel his way in when his mom and aunts were cooking. This curry is one of the dishes he picked up. Rick insists on using bone-in chicken parts because they impart a rich, full flavor to the curry. The marrow in the leg bones, especially, adds immense flavor. If you must, use boneless thigh meat cut into big chunks. Serve hot with ROTI (page 191) or freshly steamed basmati rice and YELLOW SPLIT PEA CURRY (page 130).

Time: 2¾ hours (1 hour active)
Makes: 6 to 8 servings as part of a multicourse family-style meal

> 5 to 6 pounds bone-in chicken parts, skin removed from thighs and breasts (about 2 small whole chickens cut into 8 parts each—2 breasts, 2 thighs, 2 legs, and 2 wings, or buy individual chicken parts)
>
> 1 large lime, halved
>
> Salt
>
> 3 tablespoons vegetable oil
>
> 1 large yellow onion, chopped (1½ cups)

4 cloves garlic, minced (1¼ tablespoons)

3 tablespoons tomato paste

2 tablespoons curry powder

2 tablespoons Aunty Kaisrie's Spice Blend (recipe follows) or store-bought garam masala (see page 8)

1 tablespoon ground paprika

3 large Roma tomatoes, chopped (1½ cups)

1½ cups water

2 pounds (2 large) russet potatoes, peeled and cut into eighths

2 red Thai chilies, smashed to reveal the seeds

Roti (recipe follows)

❧ Using a cleaver or large knife, cut the chicken parts through the bone into stew bits: cut breasts and thighs into 4 to 6 sections each; cut drumsticks into 3 sections each; and separate the wings into drumettes and wingettes.

❧ In a large bowl, squeeze the lime juice all over the chicken and sprinkle with 2 teaspoons salt. Toss in the lime halves and mix everything with your hands. Discard the lime halves. Rinse the chicken with cold running water and drain in a colander.

❧ In a large heavy-bottomed pot or Dutch oven, heat the oil over medium heat until it becomes runny and starts to shimmer. Add the onion and garlic; cook and stir until the onion is soft and translucent, 3 to 4 minutes. Raise the heat to medium-high and add the tomato paste, curry powder, spice blend, paprika, and 1½ teaspoons salt. Stir until the tomato paste is fully incorporated into the mixture. Reduce the heat to medium and cook until the spices release their fragrance, about 10 minutes. Toss in the tomatoes and cook, stirring occasionally, until they release their juices and start turning to mush, 6 to 7 minutes.

❧ Add the chicken to the pot and raise the heat to high. Stir to coat the meat evenly with the tomato-spice mixture for 3 to 4 minutes. When steam starts rising from the pot, reduce the heat to medium-low and cover. Simmer for 45 minutes.

❧ Uncover and let the curry bubble over medium heat to reduce and concentrate the flavors for another 45 minutes, until the meat starts to look a little dry and flaky. Add the water, potatoes, and chilies. Mix well and taste the curry; add more salt if desired. Cook until you can easily pierce a potato with the tip of a knife, another 15 to 20 minutes.

❀ Serve hot with the roti.

Aunty Kaisrie's Spice Blend (*Masala*)

Masala—the Hindi word for a blend of spices—is at the heart of Indian cooking. Rick's Aunty Kaisrie is the family *masalchi*, or spice-blender. A masala can comprise just two or three spices or up to a dozen or more and it may be added whole or ground and at different stages of cooking. The popular garam masala (see page 8) is a blend of savory aromatic spices added near the end, or at the end, of cooking when making curries. The following spices are available at South Asian markets and in the bulk section of gourmet markets. To make a larger or lesser amount of this blend, increase or decrease the ingredients in proportion to one another.

Time: 45 minutes
Makes: ¾ cup

> 2-inch stick cinnamon, broken up
> 1 tablespoon black onion seeds
> 1 tablespoon black peppercorns
> 2 tablespoons cardamom seeds
> ¼ cup aniseed
> ¼ cup black mustard seeds
> ¼ cup fenugreek seeds
> ¼ cup cumin seeds

❀ In a medium cast-iron skillet, dry roast the spices one at a time over medium heat, stirring until they turn a few shades darker and release a musky aroma. Transfer to separate plates as they are roasted and let cool. Each spice takes varying lengths of time to roast so pay careful attention not to burn them. Grind the spices separately in a clean coffee or spice grinder until ground. Combine and sift all the spices together. Store the masala in an airtight jar for 2 to 3 months.

Roti (Indian Flatbread)

Roti is an unleavened flatbread that's usually eaten with curries. In the Caribbean, a variation known as *buss up shut* is common. The name comes from "busted-up shirt" because the flatbread is basically "busted up" or torn into shreds before serving. As Rick showed me, all you have to do is scrunch it over the sink with both hands and voilà. So if you want to bust up *this* roti, you'll have buss up shut.

Time: 1½ hours
Makes: 8 roti (4 servings)

> About 2½ cups all-purpose flour, plus more for dusting
> Pinch of salt
> 1½ cups water
> About ¾ cup vegetable oil for drizzling and pan-frying

* Place 1½ cups flour and the salt in a large mixing bowl. Pour the water in gradually and mix into a smooth paste, squishing out any lumps against the side of the bowl with a wooden spoon. Tip the remaining flour (or more or less as needed) in a little at a time and mix the dough with your hands until it is smooth and pliable and starts to pull away from the side of the bowl. Don't worry if it still sticks to your fingers.

* Sprinkle flour liberally on a dry work surface and glove your hands in flour. Knead the dough until it comes together into a ball. Don't overknead or the dough will be tough and rubbery. Cover with a damp cloth and set aside for 30 minutes.

* After the dough has rested, divide it into 8 equal portions and roll each portion between your palms into a ball. Dust each ball with flour until it doesn't stick to your fingers. Set them aside and cover with a damp cloth as you work.

* Dust a rolling pin with flour and roll a ball into a circle 4 to 5 inches in diameter. Drizzle with about 1 tablespoon of oil and smear it all over the circle. Take the right and left edges and fold them toward the center, with the edges overlapping, to form a long rectangle. Fold the rectangle into thirds to form a bundle. Place the bundle on a plate dusted with flour. Repeat with the remaining balls of dough. Keep track of the order you make the bundles.

* Roll each bundle of dough into a circle again, starting with the first one you made, and repeat the entire process. Don't be afraid to dust liberally with flour when necessary.

* When finished, roll out each bundle into a circle 5 to 6 inches in diameter and as thick as a single cheese slice. As you roll the dough, flip it with every quarter turn to get a perfect circle that's evenly thick all over. If the dough gets stuck to the rolling pin while rolling, dust with more flour. Gently slap the circle from one hand to the other to flatten it.

* Heat a greased 8-inch cast-iron or nonstick skillet over medium heat. Carefully place a roti in it. After about 1 minute, it will start to puff up. Drizzle with about 1 teaspoon oil and smear it all over using a spatula. Press down on the roti to ensure even browning. Flip and cook for 30 seconds. Keep flipping and pressing down on the roti every 30 seconds or so until both sides are spotted with lovely golden brown patches, about 3 times on each side and about 4 minutes total.

Pat's Notes: Rolling the dough into a perfect circle takes practice. Don't be disheartened if your roti is shaped like "The Blob" rather than a perfectly round pancake.

Sichuan Chili Chicken (*Gung Bao Ji Ding*)

This dish, known widely in the United States as kung pao chicken, is a glorious medley of chicken, red chilies, and peanuts. The just-cooked chicken is succulent, the chilies add just the right amount of heat, and the nuts are thrown in at the very last minute to add crunch. The same dish can be made with pork or shrimp, and while peanuts are more traditional, cashew nuts are a grander substitute if you're expecting special guests.

Time: 30 minutes
Makes: 4 to 6 servings as part of a multicourse family-style meal

> 1½ to 2 pounds boneless chicken thighs, cut into ½-inch cubes
>
> 2 tablespoons Shaoxing rice wine or dry sherry
>
> 1 tablespoon cornstarch
>
> 3 tablespoons oyster sauce
>
> 2 tablespoons soy sauce
>
> 2 teaspoons sugar
>
> 3 tablespoons vegetable oil
>
> 3 cloves garlic, minced (1 tablespoon)
>
> 1-inch piece fresh ginger, peeled and minced (1 tablespoon)
>
> 8 whole dried red chilies
>
> 1 medium yellow onion, halved, cut into thin crescents, and separated
>
> 3 green onions, white and green parts, cut into thin rings
>
> ½ cup dry-roasted peanuts
>
> Ground chili flakes (optional)

❧ In a medium bowl, toss the chicken with the rice wine and cornstarch. Set aside.

❧ In a small bowl, mix together the oyster sauce, soy sauce, and sugar. Set aside.

❧ Preheat a large wok or skillet over medium-high heat for 1 minute. Swirl in the oil and heat until it becomes runny and starts to shimmer. Add the garlic, ginger, and chilies and cook briefly until the garlic is golden and the oil is fragrant and tinged with red, 30 seconds to 1 minute. Don't burn them! Pull the wok off the stove if necessary to prevent overheating. Add the chicken and stir and cook until no longer pink, 3 to 4 minutes. Add the onion and cook for 1 minute.

🍴 Add the oyster sauce mixture to the wok. Stir everything swiftly around the wok, cooking until the sauce is thick and shiny and the chicken is cooked through (cut into a piece to test), another 3 to 4 minutes. Taste and adjust seasonings if desired.

🍴 Add the green onions and peanuts, toss with a couple more flourishes, and transfer to a serving platter. Sprinkle with chili flakes for more heat and serve hot with freshly steamed rice and a vegetable side dish.

Teochew Braised Duck (*Lo Ack*)

As a newlywed, Rosalind Yeo learned how to make this dish from her mother-in-law using a Chinese rice bowl as a measuring implement. The recipe is now a family favorite, often served at Chinese New Year as well as for everyday meals. While this is essentially a Teochew (also Chow Chiu or Chaozhou) dish, the addition of lemongrass and galangal is very Southeast Asian. The sweetness of the duck contrasts sharply with the tart dipping sauce, resulting in a tingly sweet-sour sensation in your mouth.

Time: 1½ to 2 hours (30 minutes active)
Makes: 4 to 6 servings as part of a multicourse family-style meal

2 tablespoons sea or kosher salt, divided

4- to 5-pound duck, rinsed and patted dry with paper towels

2 cups water, plus more as needed

½ cup dark soy sauce

2 plump stalks lemongrass, trimmed, bruised (see page 10), and halved

1-inch piece fresh galangal, smashed

1 tablespoon sugar

4 whole cloves

4 star anise pods

Two 2-inch sticks cinnamon

1 teaspoon black peppercorns

Chili-Lime Dipping Sauce (recipe follows)

❧ Rub 1½ tablespoons of the salt evenly all over the duck, including inside the cavity.

❧ In a large wok or Dutch oven (or any vessel large enough to hold the whole duck), mix together the water, soy sauce, lemongrass, galangal, sugar, cloves, star anise, cinnamon, peppercorns, and remaining salt. Bring to a boil. Reduce the heat to medium-low. Gently lower the duck into the wok. The liquid should reach halfway up the duck. Top it off with additional water if necessary. Cook, basting the duck every 5 minutes or so, for 20 minutes so that it colors evenly. Cover and simmer for another 40 to 60 minutes, or until the duck is tender and the meat is fall-off-the-bone tender, flipping the duck halfway through cooking. If the sauce looks like it's drying up, add more water, ¼ cup at a time.

✻ Total cooking time should be 1 to 1½ hours. To check for doneness, poke the duck in the thigh with a chopstick. If the juices run clear, the duck is cooked. Or, use a meat thermometer to check if the internal temperature has reached 165 degrees F.

✻ Turn off the heat and leave the duck immersed in the sauce for another hour if desired.

✻ Cut the duck into serving pieces and arrange on a serving platter. Skim the fat from the surface of the sauce, then drizzle the sauce over the duck. Serve with freshly steamed rice and the dipping sauce.

Variations: Add fried tofu or hard-boiled eggs 20 minutes before the duck is done. Or jazz up the dish with a medley of intestines, duck liver, and gizzards.

Chili-Lime Dipping Sauce

Time: 15 minutes
Makes: About ½ cup

> 4 cloves garlic
> 2 long, fresh red chilies (such as Holland or Fresno),
>   or 2 tablespoons prepared chili paste
> 8 tablespoons key lime juice (from 8 small limes)
> Salt

✻ Pound the garlic and chilies in a mortar and pestle, or whirl in a small food processor, until a coarse paste forms. Add the lime juice and salt and mix well.

Teochew Braised Duck

Vietnamese Chicken Curry (*Ca Ri Ga*)

This mild adaptation of an Indian curry has a Vietnamese twist added—sweet potatoes. Cathy Danh's grandmother cuts up her chicken into various parts. But Cathy likes to make it with just drumsticks since they're a hot commodity in her family. She also uses a combo of white and sweet potatoes. If possible, allow the curry to sit overnight so that the chicken really absorbs the flavors from the spice-rich gravy.

Time: 2½ hours (30 minutes active)
Makes: 4 to 6 servings as part of a multicourse family-style meal

1 tablespoon vegetable oil

1 large yellow onion, chopped (1½ cups)

2 tablespoons Vietnamese or Madras curry powder

2¼ teaspoons salt

3- to 4-pound chicken, cut into 8 serving pieces; or 3 pounds bone-in chicken parts of your choice (drumsticks, wings, breasts, etc.)

20-ounce can (2⅓ cups) coconut milk

1 cup water, plus more as needed

2½ pounds sweet potatoes and/or russet potatoes, peeled and cut into 2-inch chunks

❧ In a large pot, heat the oil over medium heat until it becomes runny and starts to shimmer. Add the onion and stir and cook until slightly softened, about 2 minutes. Add the curry powder and ¼ teaspoon salt and stir until fragrant, about 15 seconds.

❧ Add the chicken and brown for 3 to 4 minutes on each side. Don't worry about completely cooking the chicken at this point, you just want to sear the meat so that it retains its juices and doesn't fall apart during cooking.

❧ Add the coconut milk and water followed by the potatoes. Make sure the chicken pieces and potatoes are completely submerged in the liquid. If necessary, add more water. Raise the heat to high and bring to a boil. Reduce the heat to medium-low and cover. Simmer for at least 1 hour, preferably 2. When the dish is done, the chicken will be fall-apart tender and the gravy will be thick from the starch of the potatoes. Add the remaining salt. Serve hot with freshly steamed rice or French bread.

Variations: When frying the onion, throw in chopped lemongrass or crumpled kaffir lime leaves for a very Southeast Asian flavor.

Add red chili flakes or ground red dried chilies to give the curry a little more kick.

For a lighter curry, decrease the amount of coconut milk and top off the difference with water.

Pat's Notes: For a true Viet flavor, buy Vietnamese curry powder from an Asian market. This golden curry mixture is very similar to a Madras curry powder and is made of curry leaves, turmeric, chili, coriander, cumin seeds, cinnamon, cloves, bay leaves, allspice, and salt. Cathy's grandmother prefers the Con Voy brand but D&D Gold Madras curry powder is also recommended.

Grandma Says: Cut the potatoes into big chunks so they won't disintegrate during the long cooking time.

Profile of a Grandma: DAISY KUSHINO

Daisy Kushino's life has been a web of serendipitous moments. Whether it was her move from Hawaii to Chicago, her placement on a bowling team, or the adoption of her first two sons, she sums it up as such: "It's just the people you meet in your life."

Born in 1929 in Halawa, Hawaii, Daisy led a carefree, country life. Chickens clucked in the front yard and fresh shrimp and fish were waiting to be caught almost at their doorstep. Like many of the Japanese on the island, her father worked in the sugar industry. Her mother lovingly tended a garden brimming with assorted vegetables that found their way onto the dinner table daily. Carrots, broccoli, daikon radish, kabocha squash, cauliflower, peas, taro, cabbages, eggplant... "You name it, we had the vegetable," she says.

While Daisy's mom was a great cook and baker, Daisy didn't learn how to cook from her. Her parents emphasized schoolwork more than "learning to do things in the kitchen." However, Daisy and her siblings did have one task—grating potatoes for her mom to make yeast. "That was our job," says Daisy. "No one makes their own yeast anymore!" Daisy did, however, inherit her green thumb from her mother. Gardening is now her passion.

At eighteen, Daisy packed up her things and moved to Chicago. A teacher had helped her secure a spot at Gregg Business College. Daisy considers this time her formative years. Her roommates at the Evangeline Residence (a residence for single working women run by the Salvation Army) became good friends and she goes so far as to say, "I am the person I am today because they watched over me."

Then, a chance encounter with a member of the Japanese American Citizens League in Chicago led Daisy to her husband, Thomas. She was invited to a bowling event and when she showed up on the specific night, they were divided into teams. And as fate would have it, she and Thomas were on the same team. They married soon after.

As a new wife, Daisy picked up cooking, first from Tom's mom and then by taking cooking classes. One was offered by the local gas company (who knew?) and another was taught by a chef at the neighborhood Chinese restaurant they patronized regularly. She also learned to cook many family favorites from a cookbook published in 1972 by the Women's Fellowship of Christ Church of Chicago.

Daisy and Tom must have seemed the perfect set of parents. Twice, a friend or acquaintance approached them to ask if they'd be interested in adopting. Twice they said "yes" and ended up adopting two boys. Then at the age of forty-five, Daisy found herself pregnant—with another son.

Daisy's three children were all somewhat fussy eaters when they were little. They weren't too fond of seafood—shrimp was just about the only thing they liked—and her oldest, Scott, "loved his McDonald's," says Daisy. "In spite of what we were going to have for dinner, my husband would bring McDonald's home for him." She can laugh about it now, but you can just imagine how annoyed she must have been at the time.

Despite the children's affinity for burgers and spaghetti, they would get their fill of Japanese food at numerous family potluck gatherings. The spread of many traditional Japanese dishes included Daisy's specialties such as SOMEN SALAD (page 242) and MOCHIKO FRIED CHICKEN (page 187).

Generous, warm, and full of kindness, Daisy is eager to share her love with the next generation. She does not have any grandchildren—yet. But she is hopeful. "I have my fingers crossed that someday it'll happen while I'm still here," she says wistfully. This time, however, she has to rely on the hope of a serendipitous meeting for one of her sons.

❧ Seafood ❧

Black Bean–Steamed Fish

Steaming is a favored Chinese method of cooking fish. This recipe pairs salty black beans with your choice of fish steaks (try cod, striped bass, halibut, or salmon) or fillets (flounder, sole, black cod, or bass) for a simple heart-healthy dish. Ask your fishmonger for fish pieces of similar weight and shape so they cook at the same rate.

Time: 20 minutes (10 minutes active)
Makes: 4 servings as part of a multicourse family-style meal

> 1 tablespoon Chinese salted black beans (see page 4), rinsed, drained, and dried
>
> 1 teaspoon minced garlic (1 large clove)
>
> 1 teaspoon minced peeled fresh ginger (from a ½-inch piece)
>
> 1 teaspoon cornstarch
>
> 1 teaspoon soy sauce
>
> Four 1-inch-thick fish steaks or fillets (about 6 ounces each)
>
> Chopped green onions for garnish
>
> Cilantro sprigs for garnish

❧ Crush the beans in a small bowl with the back of a spoon. Add the garlic, ginger, cornstarch, and soy sauce and mix well to form a thick paste.

❧ Set up your steamer (see page xv for other steaming options). Fill the steamer pan half full of water and bring to a rolling boil over high heat. Reduce the heat to medium until you are ready to steam.

❧ Place the fish on a greased pie plate (or rimmed platter) that will fit inside the steamer without touching the sides. The size of your steamer will determine how many pieces of fish you can steam at a time. Spread the paste evenly over one side of each piece of fish. Set the plate of fish in the steamer basket or rack. Return the water in the steamer to a rolling boil. Set the steamer basket or rack on top of the steamer pan. Cover and steam for 6 to 10 minutes, or until the flesh turns opaque and flakes easily with a fork.

🌼 Turn off the heat and wait for the steam to subside before lifting the lid. Lift it away from you to prevent scalding yourself and to keep condensation from dripping onto the fish. Carefully remove the fish and garnish with green onions and cilantro sprigs. Serve immediately with freshly steamed rice and a vegetable side dish.

Pat's Notes: Steaming time depends on the thickness and texture of the fish. Thicker steaks and denser varieties will take longer. I prefer to err on the side of undercooking. Check for doneness early and continue steaming if the fish isn't cooked enough to your taste. You can always cook it a little longer, but once fish is overcooked, you'll be eating cardboard.

Clay Pot Lemongrass-Steamed Fish

Clay Pot Lemongrass-Steamed Fish
(*Pla Nueng Morh Din*)

Steaming whole fish on a lattice of lemongrass in a clay pot leaves it silky, tender, and imbued with a subtle citrusy scent. Any white fish with natural fat, such as trout, Pacific cod, and striped bass, would work well in this simple Thai dish from Pranee Khruasanit Halvorsen, who learned to make it from her grandmother, Kimsua. Pranee remembers her grandma's frugal nature: she would only use the discarded outer layers of the lemongrass to line the clay pot for this dish, saving the tender white core for others. Clay pots are relatively inexpensive and are available in many Asian markets (see page 335). You will need a 12- to 14-inch clay pot for this recipe, or you can use a steamer.

Time: 30 minutes (20 minutes active)
Makes: 2 servings as part of a multicourse family-style meal

> ¾- to 1-pound whole trout, head and tail intact, scaled, gutted, and cleaned
>
> 4 plump stalks lemongrass, trimmed and bruised (see page 10)
>
> 1 tablespoon sea or kosher salt
>
> ½ cup water, or more as needed

※ Lay the fish flat on a cutting board. To ensure the fish cooks evenly, use a sharp knife to make 3 or 4 diagonal bone-deep cuts in the fish perpendicular to the backbone about 1 inch apart. Turn the fish over and repeat.

※ Fold one lemongrass stalk in half and rub it all over the fish, inside and out. Discard. Gently rub the salt into the skin of the fish and inside its cavity.

※ Tear each of the 3 remaining lemongrass stalks into 4 strips. Lay the lemongrass strips in a grid-like pattern on the bottom of the clay pot in 3 layers. Trim the stalks if they don't fit. Place the fish on top of the lattice, tucking in the tail if necessary. Add enough water to reach the bottom layer of lemongrass without touching the fish.

※ Cover and bring the water to a boil over medium heat. Once steam starts to appear from the hole in the lid, about 5 minutes, check the water level and add more water if necessary. Steam for another 8 to 10 minutes, or until the flesh is opaque and flakes easily when tested with a fork at its thickest part. Check on the water level at least once more during steaming.

- Serve the fish from the clay pot, or carefully transfer onto a serving plate using two spatulas. Spoon the liquid over the fish before serving.

Pat's Notes: If you'd like to steam two whole fish at the same time (I wouldn't put more than this in the steamer at one time), you can use the same amount of lemongrass.

Miso-Smothered Salmon

This recipe comes from Gary Kiyonaga's Uncle Tosh who passed on both his love of fishing and this easy miso salmon recipe to his nephews. Preparing the flavoring paste is a cinch. Then all it takes is a few days of marinating and a few minutes in the oven or on the grill. Cooking time varies with the thickness of the fish and cooking method, but whatever you do, don't overcook it!

Time: 30 minutes plus marinating
Makes: 4 to 6 servings as part of a multicourse family-style meal

2 pounds center-cut, skin-on salmon fillets about 1-inch thick
Salt
½ cup white miso
¼ cup sake
1 tablespoon Japanese soy sauce
1 tablespoon sugar
1 green onion, white and green parts, finely chopped

- Sprinkle the salmon with salt then rinse with cold running water.

- In a medium bowl, mix the miso, sake, soy sauce, sugar, and green onion together into a paste. Spread the paste over both sides of the salmon, ensuring all surfaces are covered. Place the salmon in a container with a tight-fitting lid or in zip-top bags and marinate in the refrigerator for at least 3 days.

- When ready to cook, scrape off the excess miso paste. Bake, broil, or grill the salmon as desired.

- To bake the salmon, preheat the oven to 400 degrees F. Place the salmon skin-side down on a baking pan coated with cooking spray and bake for 10 to 15 minutes, or until the flesh is opaque and flakes easily when tested with a fork at its thickest part, or until desired doneness.

- To broil the salmon, position a rack about 4 inches from the heat source and preheat the broiler. Place the salmon skin-side down on a broiler pan coated with cooking spray and broil for 8 to 10 minutes, or until the flesh is opaque and flakes easily when tested with a fork at its thickest part, or until desired doneness.

- To grill the salmon, prepare a medium charcoal fire (you can hold your hand over the rack for no more than 3 or 4 seconds) with the rack 4 to 6 inches from the coals, or preheat a gas grill to medium-high. Place the salmon skin-side down on a grill rack coated with cooking spray. Grill for 3½ to 4 minutes, closing the lid on a gas grill. With a wide spatula, carefully turn the pieces over, and grill for another 5 to 6 minutes, or until the flesh flakes easily when tested with a fork at its thickest part, or until desired doneness.

Pat's Notes: This recipe can be easily multiplied for larger amounts of salmon.
After the salmon is refrigerated for at least 3 days, it can be frozen for up to 1 week.

Shrimp and Mung Bean Sprout Omelets

Shards of spicy ginger and sweet shrimp are neatly bundled into omelets for an easy supper with rice, or on its own at breakfast for a morning jumpstart. While this recipe comes from Tony Lew's Malaysian Chinese grandmother, it transcends many cultures.

Time: 40 minutes
Makes: 6 (8-inch) omelets (6 servings as part of a multicourse family-style meal)

> 6 ounces (2 cups) mung bean sprouts, tails snapped off
> Boiling water
> About 5 tablespoons vegetable oil, divided
> 8 ounces medium (36/40 count) shrimp, peeled and deveined
> 1 small white onion, chopped (¾ cup)

1-inch piece fresh ginger, peeled and cut into fine shreds
  (1 tablespoon)

6 eggs

2 tablespoons water

2 teaspoons soy sauce

Dash salt

Dash ground white or black pepper

In a heatproof bowl, soak the mung bean sprouts in boiling water for 1 minute until soft. Rinse under cold running water, drain, and set aside.

In a medium skillet, heat 1 tablespoon of the oil over medium-high heat until it becomes runny and starts to shimmer. Add the shrimp and stir and cook until they just turn pink, 45 seconds to 1 minute. Transfer to a plate and set aside.

In the same pan, heat 1 tablespoon oil over medium heat. Add the onion and ginger and stir and cook until the onion is soft and translucent, 3 to 4 minutes. Toss in the mung bean sprouts and stir with a couple of flourishes to mix well and heat through, no more than 10 seconds. Turn off the heat.

In a medium bowl, beat the eggs with the water, soy sauce, salt, and pepper. Lightly brush the bottom of an 8-inch nonstick skillet or omelet pan with 1½ tablespoons of the oil and heat over medium for 1 minute. Swirl in about ½ cup of the egg mixture to coat the bottom of the skillet in a thin, even layer. Cook until the bottom is light golden but the surface is still a little soggy, 45 seconds to 1 minute. Lift the edge of the omelet to check. Scoop 4 or 5 shrimp (or whatever looks like one-sixth the amount of shrimp) onto the left half of the omelet followed by about ¼ cup of the bean sprout mixture. Fold the omelet over to form a half moon. If you'd like to ensure that the omelet is fully cooked through, cover the skillet for 15 to 30 seconds. Slide the omelet onto a plate and cover to keep warm while you make the remaining omelets. Serve with freshly steamed rice and a vegetable side dish.

Pat's Notes: To shred ginger, use a very sharp knife to cut the ginger into paper thin coins. Stack the coins a few at a time and cut into fine, delicate shreds.

Shrimp and Pineapple Red Curry
(*Kaeng Kue Sapparod*)

Succulent ruby crescents of shrimp pair wonderfully with the sweetness of pineapple in this Thai curry that is sumptuous and easy-going (both in flavor and ease of cooking). Pranee Khruasanit Halvorsen, a Thai culinary instructor, prefers using homemade curry paste, but making it is a rather time consuming process and the ingredient list lengthy. In lieu, Pranee recommends Mae Ploy brand curry paste. Try this same recipe with duck breasts and lychee fruits.

Time: 30 minutes
Makes: 4 to 6 servings as part of a multicourse family-style meal

> 1 cup coconut milk, divided
>
> 2 tablespoons red curry paste
>
> ½ cup water
>
> ⅔ cup canned pineapple chunks, drained, plus ¼ cup of the juice
>
> 8 ounces medium (36/40 count) shrimp, peeled and deveined, tail-on
>
> 3 kaffir lime leaves
>
> 1 plump stalk lemongrass, trimmed (see page 10) and cut on the diagonal into thin ovals
>
> Roasted ground peanuts for garnish (optional)

❧ In a medium saucepan, heat 3 tablespoons of the coconut milk and the curry paste over medium-high heat. Stir until well combined. Add 2 more tablespoons of coconut milk. Bring to a boil and cook until the coconut oil separates from the mixture and rises to the surface, about 3 minutes. Stir in another 3 tablespoons of coconut milk and the water.

❧ Add the pineapple chunks and juice, and the remaining coconut milk. Raise the heat to high and bring to a boil again. Reduce the heat to medium and add the shrimp. Stir and cook until they just turn pink, 1 to 2 minutes.

❧ Crumple the kaffir lime leaves to release the essential oils and throw them into the pan along with the lemongrass. Give everything one thorough mix before removing from the heat. Garnish with peanuts and serve immediately with freshly steamed rice.

Shrimp with Homemade Black Bean Sauce

Smoky and aromatic, prepared black bean sauce is ubiquitous in the aisles of Asian markets. But as with just about any food, from-scratch really does taste better. Furthermore, when you make your own, you can control the amount of sodium. Feel free to adjust the amount of high-sodium ingredients (i.e., soy sauce and store-bought stock) to compensate for the salty black beans. Cathy Chun learned to make this tasty recipe, and many others, from her late father, David, who was the cook in the house.

Time: 25 minutes
Makes: 4 to 6 servings as part of a multicourse family-style meal

⅔ cup chicken stock (recipe on page 42)

2 tablespoons Chinese salted black beans (see page 4), rinsed, dried, and mashed

1 tablespoon soy sauce

2 cloves garlic, minced

2 teaspoons cornstarch

1 teaspoon oyster sauce

1 teaspoon sugar

2 tablespoons vegetable oil, divided

2 green and/or red bell peppers, cut into 1-inch squares

8 ounces (10 to 12 stalks) asparagus, trimmed and cut into 1-inch lengths

1½ pounds medium shrimp (36/40 count), peeled and deveined

2 tablespoons water

※ In a small bowl, mix together the stock, black beans, soy sauce, garlic, cornstarch, oyster sauce, and sugar. Set aside.

※ Preheat a large wok or skillet over high heat for 1 minute. Swirl in 1 tablespoon of the oil and heat until it becomes runny and starts to shimmer. Reduce the heat to medium and throw in the bell peppers and asparagus. Stir and cook until just tender, about 2 minutes. Transfer the vegetables to a plate.

In the same wok, swirl in the remaining oil and heat until it becomes runny and starts to shimmer. Add the shrimp and stir and cook until they just turn pink, 1 to 2 minutes. Add the black bean mixture and stir to coat the shrimp. Add the cooked vegetables and stir everything swiftly around the wok. Add the water and stir with a couple more flourishes until all the ingredients are cooked to your liking. Serve immediately with freshly steamed rice.

Variations: Instead of shrimp, use 2 to 3 pounds littleneck or cherry-stone clams. Try this basic sauce with chicken or pork, and mix and match with different vegetables—broccoli, snow peas, or carrots are suitable additions.

Stuffed Egg-Crepe Rolls (*Yu Gun*)

When Grandma Nellie Wong (see page 218) was growing up in New Zealand, she made fish paste from scratch for this dish. She'd scrape the fish flesh off the bones and mix it with egg white. Today, fish paste is readily available in frozen tubs in Asian markets. Look for a light grey emulsion—the color of fresh fish meat. Don't buy a product that's light brown or darker grey, a sign that it's been frozen too long. When Nellie moved to South Bend, Indiana, she couldn't find fish that was fresh enough to make the paste so she substituted ground pork. Now she prefers a combination of pork and fish. You can also stuff vegetables like bell peppers and eggplant with the paste.

Time: 1 hour
Makes: 4 to 6 servings as part of a multicourse family-style meal

Filling:

8 ounces ground pork

8 ounces fish paste

4 water chestnuts, finely chopped

2 medium dried black mushrooms, rehydrated (see page 11) and finely chopped

2 green onions, white and green parts, cut into thin rings

1 egg, lightly beaten

1 tablespoon soy sauce

2 teaspoons Shaoxing rice wine or dry sherry

2 teaspoons water

2 teaspoons cornstarch

1 teaspoon sugar

1 teaspoon salt

½ teaspoon minced peeled fresh ginger (from a ¼-inch piece)

Ground white pepper

Egg Crepes:

4 large eggs

Vegetable oil

Salt

Soy sauce

Sesame oil or Light Sauce (recipe follows)

To make the filling, in a large bowl, mix together the pork, fish paste, water chestnuts, mushrooms, green onions, egg, soy sauce, rice wine, water, cornstarch, sugar, salt, ginger, and pepper to taste to form a thick paste. Set aside.

To make the egg crepes, prepare them one at a time: Beat 1 egg lightly with a pinch of salt in a small bowl using a pair of chopsticks or a fork. You don't want the egg to become frothy so don't introduce too much air. Lightly brush the bottom of an 8-inch nonstick skillet with oil and heat over medium for 1 minute. Swirl in the egg mixture to coat the bottom of the skillet in a thin, even layer. Cook until the omelet surface is nearly dry and the underside is light golden, 1½ to 2 minutes. Lift the edge of the omelet to check. Flip and cook for another minute or so. Slide onto a plate. Repeat with the remaining eggs. Set the crepes aside to cool.

Set up a steamer (see page xv for other steaming options). Fill the steamer pan half full of water and bring to a rolling boil over high heat. Reduce the heat to medium until you are ready to steam.

When the crepes are cool enough to handle, spread one quarter of the filling (about ½ cup) evenly over each crepe, leaving about a ½-inch border all around the edge. Roll into a fat cigar and seal the edge with a little filling. Place the roll seam-side down on a greased pie plate (or rimmed platter) that will fit inside the steamer without touching the sides. Repeat with the remaining crepes, arranging them in a single layer on the plate. The size of your steamer will determine how many rolls you can steam at a time.

❧ Return the water in the steamer to a rolling boil. Set the plate of rolls in the steamer basket or rack. Cover and steam over high heat for 20 minutes, or until the filling is firm and no longer pink.

❧ When done, turn off the heat and wait for the steam to subside before lifting the lid. Lift it away from you to prevent scalding yourself and to keep condensation from dripping onto the rolls. Carefully remove the rolls and set aside to cool. Repeat as many times as necessary.

❧ When the rolls are cool enough to handle, transfer them to a serving platter and cut into 1-inch diagonal pieces. (Reserve the "drippings," the juices left at the bottom of the plate, to make the sauce.) Drizzle, to taste, with soy sauce and sesame oil or light sauce.

Pat's Notes: If you don't have a brush to lightly grease the bottom of your skillet, wrap a 5-inch square of paper towel around the tip of a chopstick with an elastic band to form a "sponge."

Grandma Says: Adding ginger and sherry to the filling neutralizes the "fishy" smell. Nellie prefers dry sherry to Shaoxing rice wine since she is guaranteed there are no additives.

Light Sauce

Makes ½ cup

> ½ cup drippings (make up the difference with chicken stock if necessary)
> 1 teaspoon cornstarch mixed with 2 tablespoons water to make a slurry

❧ Heat the drippings in a small saucepan over medium heat until bubbling. Stir in the cornstarch slurry and mix until the sauce thickens, 2 to 3 minutes.

Tangy Tomato Shrimp

Tangy Tomato Shrimp

By cooking the shrimp in their shells, all the moisture is preserved and the shrimp meat remains nice and plump. For Hong Kong-born May Leong and her family, the fun part of eating this dish is licking the sauce off each shrimp before peeling. This way you taste the sweet juice of the shrimp mingled with the tangy sauce. When May was growing up, her Cantonese mother, Oi Yee Leong, cooked a variety of dishes and May couldn't tell the Chinese dishes apart from the others. She thought corned beef and cabbage was a Chinese dish until she met her Irish husband! Only then did she realize her mom must have gotten the recipe from one of their former Irish neighbors. This dish is one of the few Chinese-influenced dishes May remembers learning from her mom before she passed away in 1984 at the tender age of forty-four.

Time: 30 minutes
Makes: 6 to 8 servings as part of a multicourse family-style meal

> 3 tablespoons vegetable oil, divided
>
> 1 large yellow onion, sliced into 8 wedges and separated
>
> 4 medium ripe tomatoes, each cut into 8 wedges
>
> 3 cloves garlic, minced (1 tablespoon)
>
> 2 to 2½ pounds unpeeled medium (36/40 count) shrimp, deveined
>
> 1½ teaspoons salt
>
> ¼ cup ketchup
>
> 2 tablespoons sugar
>
> ½ cup rice vinegar

❧ Preheat a large wok or skillet over high heat for 1 minute. Swirl in 1 tablespoon of the oil and heat until it becomes runny and starts to shimmer. Add the onion and tomatoes and stir and cook until the tomato skins start to slip off and the flesh softens, 3 to 4 minutes. Add the garlic and cook and stir until the tomatoes are slightly mushy and the juices are released, another 2 to 3 minutes. Transfer the tomato mixture to a plate and set aside.

❧ In the same wok, swirl in the remaining oil and heat over high until it becomes runny and starts to shimmer. Toss in the shrimp and sprinkle with the salt. Stir and cook for about 2 minutes. Don't worry if not all the shrimp have turned pink yet.

❧ Return the tomato mixture to the wok. Add the ketchup and sugar and stir everything swiftly around the wok. Splash in the vinegar and stir to mix. Simmer over medium heat until all the shrimp have turned pink and opaque, 2 to 3 minutes. Shrimp cooks really fast so don't step away from the stove. You don't want to overcook the shrimp as they will be rubbery. Remove from the heat and serve immediately with freshly steamed rice and a vegetable side dish.

Pat's Notes: Buy unpeeled medium shrimp no more than 3 inches long and, of course, the fresher the better. Previously frozen shrimp are okay (and usually what's available) as long as they haven't been sitting around too long. If in doubt, do the sniff test for ammonia or other "fishy" off odors.

Estimate about ¼ to ½ pound shrimp per person, depending on appetites!

If you'd like to adjust the seasonings, remove the shrimp first so they don't overcook.

Teriyaki Squid

Surprisingly, you don't see teriyaki-style squid all that often. Bland and chewy squid is the perfect canvas to soak up the salty-sweet teriyaki marinade, and it chars nicely on the grill. You can also pair the marinade with your choice of meat, fish, or shrimp and feel free to adjust the sugar and ginger according to taste. Try using pineapple juice or honey instead of brown sugar to sweeten the marinade with a different depth of flavor.

Time: 30 minutes plus marinating
Makes: 4 to 6 servings as part of a multicourse family-style meal

> 1½ pounds (12 small) fresh or previously frozen whole calamari squid (tubes and tentacles), cleaned
>
> ⅔ cup Japanese soy sauce
>
> ½ cup brown sugar
>
> ¼ cup mirin, sake, dry sherry, or vermouth
>
> 1 tablespoon vegetable oil
>
> 1 teaspoon grated fresh ginger (from a ½-inch piece)
>
> 2 cloves garlic, smashed with the flat part of a cleaver or large knife

❀ Rinse the squid under cold running water and pat dry with paper towels.

❀ In a small saucepan, mix together the soy sauce, sugar, mirin, oil, ginger, and garlic, and bring to a boil over high heat. Simmer over medium heat for 10 minutes to reduce slightly. Remove from the heat and let cool. Reserve ¼ cup of the teriyaki sauce to serve with the rice.

❀ Place the squid in a large container with a tight-fitting lid. Pour the marinade over and toss to coat. Cover and marinate in the refrigerator for at least 2 hours, turning halfway through the marinating time.

❀ Prepare a very hot charcoal fire (you can hold your hand over the rack for no more than 1 to 2 seconds) with the rack 4 to 6 inches from the coals, or preheat a gas grill to high.

❀ Drain the squid, reserving some marinade for basting.

❀ Brush the grilling rack with oil and grill the squid, pressing down with a spatula, and turning once, until opaque and firm to the bite, 2 to 3 minutes. Baste with the marinade once on each side at the beginning of cooking to form a glaze. Do not overcook or the squid will be rubbery. Discard the remaining marinade.

❀ Cut the squid tubes into rings and serve with rice drizzled with reserved sauce.

Variations: To make teriyaki kebabs, cut chicken, pork, or beef into 1-inch chunks, marinate, and thread onto skewers. For vegetarian kebabs, cut firm tofu, red bell peppers, onions, and/or pineapple into chunks.

Pat's Notes: Small squid with bodies 3 to 4 inches long are super tender and cook quickly. Any bigger and the meat can be tough and rubbery.

Profile of a Grandma: NELLIE WONG

If you're looking for a surrogate grandmother to teach you how to cook, Nellie Wong would be happy to oblige.

Nellie, who lives in California's Bay Area, has no lack of students within her family (she has three daughters and six grandchildren) but she believes that her cooking skills are a gift meant to be shared.

For over 15 years, Nellie taught Chinese cooking classes at the Indiana University Adult Extension Program in South Bend, Indiana, where her husband, Warren, was a mathematics professor at the University of Notre Dame. On occasion, Nellie also taught her friends' college-bound children how to cook.

In the 1980s, people in the Midwest were very interested in cooking Chinese food, says Nellie. In a town of 100,000 people, Nellie made a name for herself. "Even when Warren became head of the math department, people would ask him, 'Is your wife Nellie Wong?'"

For Nellie, this was very significant. She was finally being recognized. Born into a traditional Chinese family, she was the second youngest of nine children, and she was female. In a time and culture where girls were low on the totem pole and sons were revered, Nellie says, "I didn't make my mark until I was able to leave home."

Yet, Nellie was destined to leave her mark.

It was 1938—World War II was looming. Nellie's very pregnant mother (with Nellie in her belly), father, and extended family of about 20 relatives fled Canton, China, on foot.

On their way south to Hong Kong, Nellie's father planned to catch a train to scout out a hospital in the next village, but the train was disrupted. It turned out to be a blessing in disguise: a few days later the hospital was bombed. Instead, a lucky Nellie was delivered by her father in a house in Wun Foa.

The family eventually made it safely to New Zealand where Nellie lived (except for a brief return to China) until she migrated to the United States in 1964.

At thirteen, Nellie learned how to cook and was put in charge of preparing the evening meal. Between her parents, she picked up all the culinary knowledge she needed. Her dad was Cantonese (the Cantonese are famous for their cuisine) and really loved food, so he introduced her to fine ingredients and first-rate cuisine. "Dad was a gourmet eater and demanded good food." From her mom, she learned knife skills. "She told me that cutting was very important, that's a basic."

On the day I meet her, a neatly coiffed Nellie is wearing a fuchsia blouse, pearls strung around her neck. As she sniffs at the bowl of filling she's making for her STUFFED EGG-CREPE ROLLS (page 211), she describes how her mom taught her to season with smell. "If you're cooking fish and it's strong, you add more sherry and ginger. So you just go by smell."

Ginger is one of Nellie's oft-used seasonings. "Every day I'm going like this," she says as she smacks the rhizome with her cleaver. Wham! She tells me that once her neighbor in their duplex came over and asked, "Nellie, what do you do every day at five o'clock? I hear that loud smash." And Nellie told her with a smile, "I crush garlic and I smash ginger."

Nellie didn't just smack ginger in the kitchen. Until recently, the active grandmother also smacked balls around the tennis court and to this day is still refining her piano lessons. Above all, Nellie enjoys connecting her grandkids with their culture by teaching them to make traditional Chinese foods like wontons and CHINESE PICKLES (page 133), and reading books on the subject to them. "I hope to continue as they grow older," she says earnestly.

Nellie realizes that because her children grew up outside the Chinese community (aside from attending Chinese camp), they might not feel fully equipped to communicate this culture to the next generation. Thus, she wants to take on this role: "It's something that I can pass on that will be eternal."

7

FEEDING A CROWD: POTLUCKS, PARTIES, AND FESTIVALS

Asians like to eat, and they like to get together. And no Asian gathering is complete without a generous spread of food. Whether it's a simple birthday celebration, a community potluck, or a festival like Lunar New Year or Eid ul-Fitr, which celebrates the end of Ramadan, food is always at the center of the celebration and many favored and familiar dishes are served. Each community has a signature dish: Vietnamese Americans usually celebrate Tet (Vietnamese New Year) with a braised dish like CARAMELIZED PORK BELLY AND EGGS BRAISED IN COCONUT WATER (page 227); SOMEN SALAD (page 242) is a must-have for Japanese American potlucks; and FROM-SCRATCH POT STICKERS (page 236) are requisite at Chinese New Year. Over the generations, dishes like STICKY RICE STUFFING (page 244) have evolved and been incorporated into Western holiday traditions like Thanksgiving and Christmas. As the chapter title indicates, the following recipes are meant to serve large groups, but feel free to halve the portions.

Somen Salad

Amma's Rice (Biryani)

Caramelized Pork Belly and Eggs Braised in
Coconut Water (*Thit Kho*)

Chicken Delight

Chinese Chicken Salad

Easy Lechón

Filipino Fried Noodles (*Pancit*)

From-Scratch Pot Stickers (*Guotieh*)

Honeyed Chicken Wings

Long-Life Noodles

Somen Salad

Sticky Rice Stuffing (*Naw Mai Fun*)

Stir-Fried Glass Noodles (*Japchae*)

White Chicken with Ginger-Garlic Sauce (*Bai Chit Gai*)

Yellow Coconut Rice (*Nasi Kuning*)

Amma's Rice (Biryani)

Amma means "mother" and this recipe is named for Munni Khursheed Ashraf, the late matriarch of the Ashraf-Siddiqui family and Arman Siddiqui's grandmother. The recipe was never written down so the Lynnwood, Washington, teenager set out one afternoon to recreate the recipe in his Aunt Samia's kitchen with his Aunt Fazi, who was visiting from Holland. The final outcome is Fazi's interpretation of Munni's dish, with a little tweaking by Samia. Biryani is a sumptuous Pakistani/Indian dish often reserved for special occasions such as weddings, parties, or holidays like Eid. Samia remembers it as her mom's go-to dish when expecting company.

Time: 2½ hours (1½ hours active)
Makes: 6 to 8 servings

  3 cups basmati rice

  ½ teaspoon saffron threads

  ¼ cup boiling water

  ½ cup plus 1 tablespoon ghee or butter, divided

  2 large white onions, halved and cut into thin crescents

  1 head garlic (8 to 10 cloves), minced

  3-inch piece fresh ginger (3 ounces), peeled and minced

  Whole spices: 12 black peppercorns, 8 whole cloves, seeds from 10 cardamom pods, and three 3-inch sticks of cinnamon

  Ground spices: 2 teaspoons ground cumin, 1 teaspoon ground coriander, and ½ teaspoon garam masala (see page 8)

  Salt

  2 pounds boneless chicken breasts or thighs, cut into 1-inch chunks

  ½ cup yogurt, divided

  1 tablespoon olive oil

  4½ cups cold water

  Raita (recipe follows)

  Mango or your favorite chutney, for serving

❧ Wash the rice in 2 or 3 changes of water until the water almost runs clear (see page 37). Let soak in fresh cold water until required. Place the saffron threads in a small bowl and add the boiling water; set aside.

❈ In a large, wide-mouthed heavy-bottomed pot or Dutch oven, melt ½ cup ghee over medium heat. Add the onions and cook until soft and translucent, 5 to 6 minutes. Throw in the garlic and ginger and cook for 30 seconds. Toss in the whole spices and stir well. Add the ground spices and 2 teaspoons salt and stir for another 30 to 45 seconds. Tumble in the chicken and toss to coat with the seasonings and spices. Cook and stir until the chicken is no longer pink, about 8 minutes. Stir in ¼ cup of the yogurt and mix well. Reduce the heat to low. Cover and cook for about 30 minutes, or until the liquid evaporates and the oil starts to separate from the chicken. Turn off the heat and leave the pot on the stove covered.

❈ Meanwhile, drain the rice well in a colander. In a medium pot, heat the oil over medium-high heat until it becomes runny and starts to shimmer. Tip the rice into the pot and stir for 2 to 3 minutes. Add the water, the remaining ghee, and a pinch of salt. Bring everything to a gentle boil. Reduce the heat to low. Cover and simmer for 20 minutes, or until the rice kernels are tender and separate. Set aside covered.

❈ Uncover the chicken and spread the pieces evenly around the bottom of the pot. Smooth the remaining yogurt evenly over the chicken. Layer the cooked rice on top of the chicken and yogurt as evenly as possible, smoothing down any clumps. Drizzle the saffron liquid, including the threads, over the rice. Cover and cook over low heat for 20 minutes to allow the flavors to meld.

❈ Spoon the chicken and rice onto a rimmed platter and mix thoroughly. Pick out the large spices and discard. Serve with the raita and chutney.

Pat's Notes: For convenience, mince the garlic and ginger together in a food processor. Substitute lamb for the chicken, as Samia does.

Basmati rice, with its thin fine grains, is the ideal variety to use. If unavailable, long-grain rice is the next best thing; don't use short-grain rice, as it will result in mushy rice.

Grandma Says: Buy free-range, organic chicken. They have not been injected with water like many chickens sold at supermarkets. You *don't* want a watery biryani.

Raita

Raita (pronounced *wry-tah*) is an integral part of any Pakistani or Indian meal. The type of yogurt used is key. With great consistency, and a tangy and well-balanced flavor, Greek yogurt is your best bet. Use either whole-milk or low-fat yogurt, but never nonfat.

Time: 5 minutes plus chilling
Makes: 2 cups

> 2 cups yogurt
> ½ teaspoon ground cumin
> Pinch of salt

❧ In a small bowl, mix together the yogurt, cumin, and salt with a fork until smooth and lump-free. Refrigerate for 30 minutes and serve chilled.

Caramelized Pork Belly and Eggs Braised in Coconut Water (*Thit Kho*)

Thit kho is one of those dishes rarely found in restaurants but eaten in all Vietnamese homes. A meal during Tet (the Vietnamese Lunar New Year) would be incomplete without a *kho* (as savory-sweet braised dishes based in a caramel sauce are called), and this pork and egg version is a favorite among Southern Vietnamese. Serve hot with a side of store-bought pickled mustard greens and freshly steamed rice.

Time: 2 hours (30 minutes active)
Makes: 4 to 6 servings as part of a multicourse family-style meal

> 2 pounds skin-on pork belly or pork shoulder (see Pat's Notes)
> 2 tablespoons sugar
> 5 Asian shallots, sliced (⅓ cup)
> 3 large cloves garlic, sliced
> 3 tablespoons fish sauce
> ¼ teaspoon freshly ground black pepper
> 1½ cups coconut water, strained of any meat (see page 6)
> 6 hard-boiled eggs, peeled

❧ Using a sharp knife, scrape off any stray hairs from the pork skin and cut the meat along the grain into 2-inch-wide strips and then crosswise into 1-inch-thick chunks with layers of meat, fat, and skin.

❧ In a medium heavy-bottomed pot or Dutch oven, heat the sugar over medium-high heat without stirring. After 1 to 2 minutes, the sugar will start to clump together then melt into a syrup and form globules. Continue cooking until the syrup turns a light golden hue and eventually caramelizes into a thick amber liquid, 2 to 3 minutes. You will also smell a pleasant burnt sugar aroma. Tumble in the pork and raise the heat to high. Stir for 1 minute to render some fat. Throw in the shallots and garlic and stir and cook until the pork browns but is not cooked through, about 5 minutes. Reduce the heat to medium. Add the fish sauce and pepper and toss for 1 minute to evenly coat the meat.

❧ Pour in the coconut water. The liquid should barely cover the pork. Bring to a boil and add the eggs. Cover and simmer over low heat for at least 1 hour (1½ hours or longer if you want the meat melt-in-your-mouth tender), stirring occasionally to ensure that the eggs and meat are evenly coated with sauce. Pierce the meat with the tip of a knife to test for tenderness. If at anytime the level of the sauce becomes less than one-third the level of the pork, add water, ¼ cup at a time. Uncover and cook until the liquid is reduced to about 1 cup or one-third the level of the pork.

❧ Remove from the heat and let the dish stand for 10 minutes. Skim the fat off the surface. (If you can wait, refrigerate the dish overnight. The fat will congeal on the surface, making this task much easier.) Reheat over medium-low, taste the sauce, and adjust the seasonings if desired.

Pat's Notes: Pork belly is essentially the raw version of the part of the pig that is usually cured and smoked for bacon. It is the desired and traditional cut for this dish because it has the perfect balance of lean meat to fat. However, you may substitute the leaner pork shoulder or use a mix of cuts. But try not to use all lean meat—the unctuous skin and fat are essential for the rich, velvety texture of this dish. Pork belly comes with or without the skin and is commonly sold at Asian markets. With its increasing popularity, you should be able to special order pork belly from your local butcher, or try online sources like Flying Pigs Farm (www.flyingpigsfarm.com) and Niman Ranch (www.nimanranch.com).

Look for belly pieces that are 2 to 3 inches thick and choose pieces that come from the front belly, as opposed to the back belly, for a good balance of meat and fat. How can you tell? Look carefully at the layers and select a slab that is about 50/50 lean meat to fat.

Chicken Delight

This scrumptious crispy-on-the-outside, succulent-on-the-inside Filipino fried chicken comes from Consolacion Mejia Yaranon, also known as Aunty Neneng. Known as Yummy Yummy Chicken to her grandkids, it is a favorite at children's parties and fiestas and also perfect anytime you'd like a spot of comfort food. If you don't feel like dealing with kitchen-splattering, calorie-laden oil, you can bake the chicken in the oven at 375 degrees F for about 45 minutes. It doesn't turn out as crispy or juicy, but still tastes pretty good.

Time: 1 hour plus marinating
Makes: 6 to 8 servings as part of a multicourse family-style meal

> 3½ to 4 pounds chicken pieces (drumsticks, wings, breasts, thighs)
> 1 tablespoon soy or fish sauce
> Juice from 2 small lemons (¼ cup)
> 1 teaspoon freshly ground black pepper
> 2 eggs
> ½ cup all-purpose flour
> 1 teaspoon salt
> 3 cups (or as needed) vegetable oil for deep-frying

❧ Wash the chicken pieces and place in a large bowl. Add the soy sauce, lemon juice, and black pepper and mix well. Cover and marinate in the refrigerator for at least 30 minutes or up to 1 hour.

❧ Preheat the oven to 250 degrees F. Line a plate with paper towels.

❧ Just before frying the chicken, crack the eggs into a large bowl. Add the flour and salt and beat well. Add the chicken and toss until well coated.

🌿 In a large wok, heavy skillet, or Dutch oven, heat the oil over high heat until it reaches 375 degrees F on a deep-fry thermometer (see page xiii for deep-frying tips). Reduce the heat to medium-high. Using tongs, pick up the chicken pieces one at a time and allow the excess batter to drip off. Gently lower the chicken into the oil and fry in a batch of 4 to 5 pieces until all sides are evenly golden brown and the chicken is cooked through (cut into a piece to test), 10 to 15 minutes. Remove the chicken with a slotted spoon, shaking off excess oil, and drain on paper towels. Keep warm in the oven.

🌿 Use a slotted spoon or a wire mesh strainer to remove any debris from the oil and bring back to 375 degrees F before frying the next batch. Repeat with remaining chicken. Serve hot.

Chinese Chicken Salad

Despite its name, this dish has always been a popular fixture at Japanese American potlucks. Erica Sugita's mother, who was born in Hawaii and raised in Japan, used to make the Chinese-influenced salad for all occasions. The sweet and tangy salad was one of the few vegetable dishes Erica and her siblings willingly ate. Feel free to mix and match the ingredients; chopped water chestnuts and blanched Chinese cabbage also work well in the salad.

Time: 30 minutes
Makes: 8 servings as part of a multicourse family-style meal

2 cups (or as needed) vegetable oil for deep-frying

1 ounce dried rice vermicelli

8 ounces skinless, boneless chicken breasts, cooked as desired and shredded

1 medium head iceberg or romaine lettuce, cut into ¼-inch strips (8 cups)

1 cup canned Mandarin orange segments, drained

½ cup cooked green peas

¼ cup toasted almonds

4 green onions, white and green parts, chopped

Dressing:

¼ cup sugar

¼ cup vegetable oil

Juice of 1 large lemon (3 tablespoons)

2 tablespoons distilled white vinegar

2 tablespoons toasted sesame seeds

½ teaspoon grated fresh ginger (from ¼-inch piece)

1 teaspoon salt

¼ teaspoon ground white pepper

* To deep-fry the rice vermicelli, heat the oil in a large wok, heavy skillet, or Dutch oven over high heat until it reaches 350 degrees F on a deep-fry thermometer (see page xiii for deep-frying tips).

* Line a plate with paper towels.

* Throw in a few noodles to test—they should puff up immediately. Reduce the heat to medium-high. Break the noodles into small handfuls. Place a handful into a wire mesh strainer or slotted spoon and plunge into the hot oil until all the noodles puff up to more than double their original size and are crunchy, 5 to 10 seconds. Remove immediately and drain on paper towels. Do not let them brown. Repeat with remaining noodles.

* In a large bowl, combine the chicken, lettuce, oranges, peas, almonds, and green onions.

* To make the dressing, combine the sugar, oil, lemon juice, vinegar, sesame seeds, ginger, salt, and pepper in a bottle. Cover tightly and shake well. (Alternately, whisk everything together in a bowl.)

* Just before serving, pour the dressing over the salad and toss to mix well. Add the rice noodles and fold in gently.

Pat's Notes: Store-bought fried Chinese noodles (the Chung King brand) can be substituted for the homemade fried rice noodles.

Easy Lechón

In the Philippines, *lechón*, a spit-roasted suckling pig, is often the highlight of national festivities (known as fiestas), holidays, and other special occasions like weddings, birthdays, and baptisms. In this simplified version from siblings Mike and Leah Tolosa, fresh ham (uncured pork from the hind leg of a hog) is used instead of a whole pig. The ham is first slow cooked until tender, then roasted to a crisp in the oven. Note there is only one ingredient, so the recipe's success lies in the technique. Lechón is usually served with a sweet-tart sauce made with liver and breadcrumbs and the commercially prepared Mang Tomas Lechon Sauce is convenient and tasty. It is available in most Asian or Filipino stores.

Time: 8 hours (20 minutes active)
Makes: 16 to 20 servings as part of a multicourse family-style meal

> 8- to 10-pound bone-in, skin-on fresh ham, preferably the shank end

❀ Wash the ham thoroughly with cold water and pat dry with paper towels. With a sharp knife, make a clean cut on the underside of the ham (where it is narrowest) down the entire length parallel to the bone, penetrating until the point where the skin meets the fat. This prevents the skin from splitting while cooking.

❀ Place the ham, cut-skin-side down, in a large slow cooker. Cover and cook on medium until fork tender, 6 to 7 hours, or until a meat thermometer inserted in the thickest part of the meat registers 155 degrees F. (Or cook, covered, in a heavy-bottomed pot or Dutch oven on the stove over low heat for the same amount of time.) The skin should be tender, which will develop into crispy cracklings in the oven (it is not lechón if the skin is chewy).

❀ Adjust your oven rack to the lowest position and preheat the oven to 400 degrees F.

❀ Remove the cooked ham from the slow cooker, allowing excess fat to drip off, and place in a roasting pan, cut-skin-side down. Let the ham sit for about 15 minutes to air dry. The skin should be completely dry before it goes into the oven to ensure crispy cracklings. Score the ham by carefully slicing through skin and fat to make a 1-inch diamond pattern. Be careful not to cut into the flesh itself.

⅛ Roast the ham for 20 to 25 minutes, or until the skin is golden brown and crispy. Let rest for 10 to 15 minutes. Transfer the ham to a serving platter and carve at the table. Make sure each diner gets some cracklings with the meat.

Pat's Notes: Fresh ham, which can be special-ordered from most butchers, has the pale pink or beige color of a fresh pork roast before cooking. Its flavor is quite unlike smoked or cured hams. Rather, it has an intense pork flavor similar to pork loin.

Filipino Fried Noodles (*Pancit*)

Pancit is probably one of the most well-known Filipino dishes. In the Filipino vernacular, pancit simply refers to noodles. This version (*pancit bam-i*) uses both rice vermicelli (*bihon*) and Chinese wheat noodles (*pancit canton*), but you can make the dish with either type of noodle, or flat egg noodles (*pancit miki*) and cellophane noodles (*sotanghon*). Just like fried rice, you can add any combination of meat, seafood, and vegetables—everything from shrimp to Chinese sausage to mung bean sprouts.

Time: 35 minutes
Makes: 6 to 8 servings

8 ounces dried rice vermicelli

Warm water

8 ounces dried Chinese wheat noodles (pancit canton)

2 tablespoons vegetable oil, plus more as needed

1 small yellow onion, finely chopped (¾ cup)

3 cloves garlic, minced (1 tablespoon)

1 pound skinless boneless chicken breasts or thighs, cut into bite-sized pieces

¼ cup citrus soy sauce (see page 23)

¼ cup regular soy sauce

1 small head cabbage, shredded (4 cups)

2 large carrots, peeled and shredded (2 cups)

2 stalks celery, trimmed and chopped (1 cup)

Chopped green onions for garnish

Filipino Fried Noodles

- In a heatproof bowl, soak the rice vermicelli in warm water for 10 to 15 minutes until soft and pliable. Cut into 4-inch lengths, drain, and set aside. Cook the wheat noodles in a large pot of boiling water according to package directions until al dente. Tip into a colander over the sink and rinse under cold running water. Drain and set aside.

- Preheat a large wok or skillet over medium-high heat for 1 minute. Swirl in the oil and heat until it becomes runny and starts to shimmer. Throw in the onion and garlic and cook until the onion is soft and translucent, 2 to 3 minutes. Add the chicken and stir and cook until no longer pink, 2 to 3 minutes. Add the citrus soy sauce and regular soy sauce and toss to coat. Toss in the cabbage, carrots, and celery and stir and cook until the cabbage wilts, 2 to 3 minutes.

- Throw in the vermicelli and noodles and stir everything swiftly around the wok until well mixed and heated through (use a spatula in each hand to evenly toss the noodles if necessary), 4 to 5 minutes. Bite into a rice noodle to see if it's tender. Adjust seasonings if necessary. If the noodles are looking a little dry, add water or chicken stock a few tablespoons at a time. If the noodles start to stick to the wok, add more oil. Transfer the noodles to a serving platter, scatter with green onions, and serve.

Grandma Says: For an even tastier dish, soak the rice vermicelli in warm chicken stock instead of water so it absorbs all that flavor.

From-Scratch Pot Stickers (*Guotieh*)

Made with pork and cabbage, two cheap and common ingredients, pot stickers may be considered peasant food. But this humble snack is an important fixture in many Chinese households during the Lunar New Year. Grandma Ellen Shyu Chou (see page 72) makes her pot stickers, including the skins, from scratch. Let me tell you, the skins really make the dumpling. Nothing beats the texture of homemade skins. Store-bought skins, like fresh pasta sheets, are thin and flat, while homemade have some heft to them and are thicker in the middle to endure the heat of cooking and to protect the filling.

Time: 2½ hours
Makes: About 40 dumplings (8 to 10 servings as a snack or appetizer)

Dough:

    2 cups all-purpose flour, plus more for dusting

    ¾ to 1 cup lukewarm water

Filling:

    2 cups finely chopped Chinese cabbage (½ small cabbage)

    2¼ teaspoons salt, divided

    1 pound ground pork

    1 green onion, white and green parts, finely chopped

    1 tablespoon soy sauce

    1 teaspoon minced fresh ginger (from a ½-inch piece)

    1 teaspoon sesame oil

    ¼ teaspoon ground white pepper

    Vegetable oil for pan-frying

    Soy-Ginger Dipping Sauce (recipe follows)

❧ To make the dough, combine the flour and ¾ cup water in a large bowl. Mix well with a wooden spoon until it starts to come together, adding more water if necessary. With your hands, form the dough into a rough ball. You want the dough to be pliable but not stick to your fingers. Sprinkle with a little more flour if the dough is too wet. The dough won't feel smooth at this point. Set the dough back in the bowl, cover with a damp towel, and let rest while you make the filling.

❧ To make the filling, place the cabbage in a medium bowl and sprinkle with 2 teaspoons salt. Mix well. Taking a handful of cabbage at a time, squeeze out as much water as you can. Or wrap the cabbage in a cheesecloth or non-terry towel and gently wring as much water out.

❧ In a large bowl, combine the cabbage, pork, green onion, soy sauce, ginger, sesame oil, pepper, and remaining salt. Mix well with chopsticks or clean hands. Set aside.

❧ To form the dumpling skins, knead the dough on a lightly floured surface until it is smooth all over, about 5 minutes. Divide into 4 equal balls. Knead each ball individually for about 30 seconds. Roll each portion into a log about 8 inches long and ½ inch in diameter. Pinch off 10 even, walnut-sized pieces from each log. Dust with flour as needed to prevent them from sticking to the work surface.

❧ Roll a piece into a ball and flatten into a disk between your palms. Place the flattened disk on a well-floured surface. Using a Chinese rolling pin (see Pat's Notes), start at the bottom right edge of the disk and roll from the outside of the circle in. Use your right hand to roll the pin over the edge of the disk as your left hand turns it counterclockwise. (Do the opposite if you are left-handed). Keep rolling and turning until it becomes a circle about 3 inches in diameter. Don't worry about making a perfect circle. Ideally, the skin will be thicker in the middle than at the edge. Repeat to make the remaining skins. Dust the skins with flour so they won't stick to each other. Cover them with a damp cloth as you make the dumplings.

❧ Spoon about 2 teaspoons filling into the center of one skin. Fold up the sides of the dumpling to form a half-moon pocket. The simplest way to seal the dumpling is to pinch it shut along the curved edge with your thumb and forefinger to create a flat seam. It will look like a turnover. Or, if you are good at crimping, you can create a pleated edge: Pinch the center shut. Start from one corner of the half-moon and make your way to the center, making 3 to 4 accordion pleats. Then work from the other corner to the center creating another 3 to 4 pleats. Press the pleated side of the dough firmly against the flat side and seal the entire dumpling. If there is too much filling, the dumpling cannot be properly sealed. Remove the extra filling to prevent leakage during cooking.

✤ On a parchment-lined tray dusted lightly with flour, set the dumpling firmly down seam-side up so that it sits flat. Repeat until all the dough or filling is used.

✤ Preheat an 8- to 10-inch nonstick skillet over medium-high heat for 1 minute. Swirl in 2 to 3 tablespoons of oil. Place about a dozen dumplings in a single layer seam-side up in the skillet and brown them for about 1 minute. Pour in about ¾ cup water to reach about ¼ inch up the sides of the dumplings. Cover immediately and steam for 9 to 10 minutes, or until all the water evaporates and the filling is cooked through. Remove the pot stickers with a spatula and arrange on a serving platter bottom sides up. The bottoms of the pot stickers should be golden brown and crisp but not burned.

✤ Wipe the skillet dry with paper towels and repeat with the remaining dumplings or freeze them (see Pat's Notes). Serve with the dipping sauce.

Variations: Japanese gyoza is an adaptation of Chinese pot stickers. Instead of green onions, add chopped leeks or perilla (*shiso*) leaves and add about 2 teaspoons of mirin.

For a vegetarian version, substitute spinach (given the same treatment as the cabbage), scrambled eggs, and/or cellophane noodles for the pork.

Pat's Notes: Chinese rolling pins are skinnier and don't have handles. They're available in Asian markets, or get a ¾- to 1-inch wooden dowel from the hardware store.

If you are using store-bought dumpling skins, you will have to wet the edge of the dough to seal the dumplings.

To freeze uncooked pot stickers, arrange them in a single layer on a baking tray and freeze until firm so they don't stick to each other (30 to 45 minutes will do). Tip into zip-top bags, seal, and freeze for up to a month. Do not defrost before cooking. Brown as instructed but steam for 10 to 11 minutes.

To reheat cooked pot stickers, heat 1 tablespoon oil in a skillet. Arrange the pot stickers in one layer and pour in 2 tablespoons water. Cover and steam until heated through, about 2 minutes.

Soy-Ginger Dipping Sauce

Try this tasty sauce with LUMPIA (page 61) or grilled meats as well as the pot stickers. It will keep in a sealed container in the refrigerator for several days.

Time: 10 minutes
Makes: ¾ cup

¼ cup soy sauce

¼ cup rice vinegar

¼ cup loosely packed cilantro, chopped (1 tablespoon)

1 green onion, white and green parts, finely chopped (1 tablespoon)

1 teaspoon grated fresh ginger (from a ½-inch piece)

1 clove garlic, smashed

¼ teaspoon chili sauce

In a small bowl, combine the soy sauce, rice vinegar, cilantro, green onion, ginger, garlic, and chili sauce.

Honeyed Chicken Wings

These sweet and savory chicken wings are a real crowd-pleaser among both kids and adults. The portions can be easily upped to feed a crowd, making them great for parties. Try them on the grill as well.

Time: 45 minutes (5 minutes active) plus marinating
Makes: 4 appetizer servings

1 cup vegetable oil

¼ cup plus 2 tablespoons honey

¼ cup soy sauce

¼ cup Shaoxing rice wine or dry sherry

6 cloves garlic, smashed with the flat part of a cleaver or a large knife

1 tablespoon brown sugar

1½ teaspoons salt

3 pounds (10 to 12) chicken wings, whole or separated at the joint into wings and drumettes

❧ In a large bowl, mix together the oil, honey, soy sauce, rice wine, garlic, brown sugar, and salt. Tumble in the chicken wings and prick them all over with a fork. Toss to coat the chicken evenly with the marinade. Cover and marinate in the refrigerator for 12 hours.

❧ Preheat the oven to 400 degrees F. Line a baking pan with foil.

❧ Arrange the chicken wings in the prepared pan. Bake for 40 minutes, turning halfway, until the skin is a glossy, golden brown. Check for doneness by cutting into a piece—the meat should not be pink.

Long-Life Noodles

Noodle dishes are always served during birthdays and Chinese New Year because the Chinese believe they symbolize good fortune, prosperity, and longevity. The longer the noodles, the longer (and luckier) your life will be—so don't cut them! This dish is made with long, flat egg noodles (called *e-fu* noodles, see page 13). Studded with three different kinds of mushrooms and Chinese chives, the noodles in this dish are not as dry as fried chow mein, but lightly coated with sauce.

Time: 30 minutes
Makes: 4 to 6 servings as part of a multicourse family-style meal

> Two 9-ounce packages fresh egg noodles or one 8-ounce package dried egg noodles
>
> 3 tablespoons vegetable oil, divided
>
> 1 tablespoon soy sauce
>
> Salt
>
> 3 cloves garlic, minced (1 tablespoon)
>
> 3 Asian shallots, chopped (3 tablespoons)
>
> 8 medium dried black mushrooms, rehydrated (see page 11; reserve about 1 cup of the soaking liquid) and cut into ¼-inch slices (1 cup)
>
> 4 ounces button mushrooms, trimmed and sliced (1 cup)
>
> 2 ounces enoki mushrooms, trimmed and separated (1 cup) (see Pat's Notes)
>
> 3 tablespoons oyster sauce
>
> 5 Chinese chives or skinny green onions, cut into 2 inch lengths (1 cup)
>
> Freshly ground black pepper

❧ Prepare the noodles according to package directions. Tip into a colander over the sink and rinse under cold running water. Place the noodles in a large bowl. Sprinkle with 1 tablespoon oil, the soy sauce, and a pinch of salt. Toss and set aside.

❧ Preheat a large wok or skillet over medium-high heat for 1 minute. Swirl in the remaining oil and heat until it becomes runny and starts to shimmer. Stir in the garlic and shallots and cook until fragrant, 30 to 45 seconds. Toss in the black mushrooms and button mushrooms and cook and stir until the mushrooms are almost cooked, 2 minutes. Add the enoki mushrooms followed by the reserved mushroom liquid. Sprinkle with the oyster sauce and 1 teaspoon salt. Add the chives followed by the noodles. Stir everything swiftly around the wok until well mixed and heated through (use a spatula in each hand to evenly toss the noodles if necessary). Season with salt and pepper to taste and toss with a couple more flourishes. Serve hot.

Pat's Notes: Enoki mushrooms have a mild but delightful flavor and a pleasantly crunchy texture. Cut off and discard the bottom of the cluster of mushrooms (up to the point where individual mushroom stems separate). No washing is necessary. The stems are generally left long.

Somen Salad

You probably won't find somen salad on the menu in a Japanese restaurant. However, it's a popular potluck dish in Japanese American communities and, as expected, feeds many. This recipe from Daisy Kushino (see page 200) calls for *kamaboko* (Japanese fish cake) but you can use surimi (imitation crab meat) instead. Like any salad, feel free to substitute or change proportions to taste. The dressing goes fabulously with field greens too.

Time: 40 minutes
Makes: 8 to 10 servings as part of a multicourse family-style meal

> 1 pound dried somen noodles
>
> 2 eggs
>
> Pinch of salt
>
> Vegetable oil for brushing
>
> ½ medium head iceberg or romaine lettuce, shredded (3 to 4 cups)
>
> 8 ounces Chinese Barbecued Pork (page 165) or Virginia ham, cut into julienne pieces (2 cups)
>
> 6-ounce package kamaboko, cut into julienne pieces
>
> 2 green onions, white and green parts, chopped
>
> Soy-Sesame Dressing (recipe follows)

- Cook the noodles according to package directions until tender yet firm and still chewy. Do not overcook or the noodles will be soggy. Tip into a colander over the sink and rinse under cold running water. Drain and set aside.

- To make the omelets, beat the eggs in a small bowl with the salt. Lightly brush the bottom of an 8-inch nonstick skillet with oil and heat over medium for 1 minute. Swirl in half the eggs to coat the bottom of the skillet in a thin, even layer. Cook until the omelet surface is nearly dry and the underside is light golden, 1½ to 2 minutes. Lift the edge of the omelet to check. Flip and cook for another 1 minute or so. Slide onto a plate. Repeat with the remaining eggs. When cool, roll the omelets into fat cigars and cut crosswise into very fine strips.

- Transfer the noodles to a large platter and arrange the lettuce, meat, kamaboko, green onions, and egg strips on top. Just before serving, pour the dressing over the salad. Toss and serve.

Soy-Sesame Dressing

Time: 5 minutes
Makes: ¾ cup

¼ cup canola oil

3 tablespoons rice vinegar or distilled white vinegar

2 tablespoons sesame seeds, toasted

2 tablespoons soy sauce

2 tablespoons sugar

1 teaspoon salt

- Combine the oil, vinegar, sesame seeds, soy sauce, sugar, and salt in a jar with a screw-top lid. Cover and shake well. (Alternatively, whisk together all the ingredients in a medium bowl.)

Sticky Rice Stuffing (*Naw Mai Fun*)

Many Chinese American families have incorporated this Chinese-style stuffing into their Thanksgiving tradition, serving it alongside steamed turkey (instead of roasted), which is the traditional way to cook chicken or duck. This stuffing was probably adapted from a traditional Cantonese dish called *lo mai gai*—glutinous rice, black mushrooms, and Chinese sausage wrapped in a dried lotus leaf and steamed. Pearl Fong, a Chinese American of Cantonese descent who lives in New Jersey, blends both traditional Thanksgiving ingredients (chestnuts) with traditional Chinese ones (water chestnuts) to create stuffing that is delicious any time of the year.

Time: 1¼ hours (45 minutes active) plus soaking
Makes: 8 to 10 servings as part of a multicourse family-style meal

> 1½ cups white glutinous rice
>
> 1½ cups long-grain rice
>
> 3¾ cups water or chicken stock (recipe on page 42)
>
> 1½ teaspoons salt, divided
>
> 1 tablespoon vegetable oil
>
> 1 medium yellow onion, chopped (1 cup)
>
> 6 ounces (about 4) Chinese sausages, steamed (see page 20) and cut into ¼-inch diagonal slices
>
> 8 medium dried black mushrooms, rehydrated (see page 11; reserve the soaking liquid) and cut into ¼-inch-thick slices
>
> ½ cup (2 ounces) chopped peeled water chestnuts (canned is okay)
>
> 15 (4 ounces) peeled, cooked chestnuts (see Pat's Notes), chopped
>
> 2 tablespoons soy sauce
>
> 2 teaspoons sesame oil (optional)
>
> ½ teaspoon freshly ground black pepper

❧ Combine the glutinous rice and long-grain rice in a large pot and wash in 2 to 3 changes of water, until the water almost runs clear (see page 37). Drain and add the water and ½ teaspoon salt. Let soak for 1 hour.

❧ Set the pot of rice on the stove and bring to a boil over high heat. Reduce the heat to medium and cook until the water is partially absorbed, 8 to 10 minutes.

❧ In a small skillet, heat the oil over medium-high heat until it becomes runny and starts to shimmer. Add the onion and cook until soft and translucent, 2 to 3 minutes.

❧ Place the onion, sausages, mushrooms, water chestnuts, and regular chestnuts on top of the rice and cover with a tight-fitting lid. Reduce the heat to medium-low and steam for 15 to 20 minutes. Add the soy sauce, sesame oil, black pepper, and remaining salt. Stir from the bottom to distribute the ingredients. Cover and cook for another 10 minutes, or until the rice is tender but not mushy; the grains should be separated. If the rice is still hard, make a well in the center of the pot and add a little water, stock, or mushroom-soaking liquid. Raise the heat to high to generate more steam, then reduce to medium-low and cook a few more minutes.

❧ Moisten the rice stuffing with turkey drippings and/or chicken stock and serve as a side dish with turkey.

Pat's Notes: You can use fresh, canned, or vacuum-packed chestnuts. If using fresh chestnuts, soak them in cold water for at least 6 hours. Cut a cross into the flat side of their shells with a sharp paring knife. Place the chestnuts in a medium saucepan and pour in enough water to cover. Bring to a boil over high heat and continue boiling for 20 to 25 minutes, or until the chestnuts are tender when pierced with a knife. Take the saucepan off the stove and pour in enough cold water for the water to be warm yet cool enough to handle. Keep the chestnuts submerged in the warm water while shelling and peeling the inner skin (pellicle).

Stir-Fried Glass Noodles (*Japchae*)

Japchae is one Korean dish that's never absent from a feast table. Vegetables, meat, and glass-like sweet potato noodles are separately precooked, then tossed together in a wok to create a harmony of colors, textures, and flavors. Japchae is perfect for parties because it can be prepared ahead and served at room temperature. This recipe comes from Susan C. Kim, a corporate lawyer–turned–features writer based in San Francisco, via her grandmother, Sang Jung Choi (see page 252).

Time: 30 minutes plus soaking
Makes: 6 to 8 servings as part of a multicourse family-style meal

> 1 pound dried Korean sweet potato noodles
>
> Hot water
>
> 8 ounces spinach, trimmed (4 to 5 cups)
>
> 2 tablespoons vegetable oil, plus more as needed
>
> 6 medium dried black mushrooms, rehydrated (see page 11) and cut into thin slices (¾ cup)
>
> 1 small yellow onion, halved and cut into thin crescents
>
> 2 medium carrots, peeled and cut into julienne pieces (1¼ cups)
>
> 3 green onions, white and green parts, cut into 1-inch lengths
>
> 2 cloves garlic, minced
>
> ⅓ cup soy sauce
>
> 3 tablespoons brown sugar
>
> 1 tablespoon sesame oil
>
> 1 tablespoon toasted sesame seeds

❧ Place the noodles in a heatproof bowl and soak in hot water for 15 minutes. With kitchen shears, cut into 3- to 4-inch pieces. You just want the noodles to be manageable so don't worry about getting exact lengths. Drain and set aside.

❧ Place the spinach in a heatproof bowl and soak in very hot water for 1 to 2 minutes until wilted but not fully cooked. Rinse under cold running water and drain. Gently squeeze the water from the spinach and cut into 3 sections.

❧ Preheat a large wok or skillet over medium-high heat for 1 minute. Swirl in the oil and heat until it becomes runny and starts to shimmer. Add the mushrooms, onion, carrots, green onions, and garlic and stir and cook until the carrots are crisp tender, 2 to 3 minutes. Reduce the heat to medium and toss in the noodles. Add the soy sauce, brown sugar, and sesame oil. Stir everything swiftly around the wok for 3 to 4 minutes, coating the noodles evenly with the seasonings. Add more oil if the noodles stick to the bottom of the wok. Taste and adjust seasonings if desired. Mix in the spinach and sesame seeds at the very end and toss with a couple more flourishes. Serve hot or let cool to room temperature.

Pat's Notes: Korean sweet potato noodles, long and chewy, are made from sweet potato starch and used in stir-fries. Before cooking, the noodles should be soaked in hot water for about 10 minutes. Then, add the softened noodles as well as some broth to the dish. Substitute the fattest cellophane noodles you can find if sweet potato noodles aren't available. Follow the package directions to cook.

Japchae keeps well and can stay fresh for up to a week in the refrigerator. To reheat, cook in a skillet and add sesame oil until the noodles are supple and heated through.

White Chicken with Ginger-Garlic Sauce
(*Bai Chit Gai*)

Every Cantonese cook has their own way of poaching chicken for this dish. However, there is one commonality: a low, slow heat which is necessary for a moist, tender bird. Find the freshest chicken possible—preferably organic—as you want the flavor of the meat to stand on its own. The bold and fresh flavors of the sauce accentuate the chicken's simple preparation method.

Time: 2 hours (30 minutes active) plus salting
Makes: 4 to 6 servings as part of a multicourse family-style meal

> 3½-pound whole chicken, trimmed of fat (preferably fryer and not previously frozen)
>
> 3½ tablespoons sea or kosher salt (1 tablespoon for every pound of chicken)
>
> 4 cloves garlic, minced (1 tablespoon)
>
> 2 green onions, white and green parts, chopped
>
> 3-inch piece fresh ginger, peeled and shredded
>
> ½ cup vegetable oil
>
> 2 tablespoons soy sauce

❧ Rinse the chicken and pat dry with paper towels. Rub the salt evenly all over the chicken, including inside the cavity. Cover and refrigerate for 2 to 3 days, turning once every day.

❧ Rinse the salted chicken thoroughly with cold water and drain in a colander or on a rack over the sink.

❧ In a large pot, pour in enough water to completely submerge the chicken (about 12 cups). Bring the water to a rolling boil over high heat. Carefully lower the chicken, breast-side up, into the water, adding boiling water if necessary to submerge it. Cover and bring to a rolling boil again.

❧ Turn off the heat and let the chicken stand on the stove for about 1 hour and 20 minutes. Do not lift the lid once the chicken goes in! To test for doneness, poke the chicken in the meatiest part of the thigh with a chopstick. If the juices run clear, the chicken is done. (Or insert a meat thermometer into the thigh. It should register at least 165 degrees F.) If the chicken isn't done, simmer over low heat for a few more minutes.

❧ Using two large spoons, carefully remove the chicken from the pot and drain in a colander. Transfer the chicken to a chopping board and allow it to cool slightly. Reserve the stock for another use.

❧ While the chicken is cooling, make the sauce. Place the garlic, green onions, and ginger in a heatproof bowl. In a small saucepan, heat the oil over medium heat until it starts to bubble gently, 2 to 3 minutes. Don't let it smoke. Pour the oil carefully over the ingredients. It might sizzle and splatter so stand back. Stir in the soy sauce.

❧ When it is cool enough to handle, cut the chicken through the bone into small pieces with a cleaver or large knife. Or simply disjoint it into serving pieces, if you prefer. Arrange the chicken pieces on a platter. Pour the ginger-garlic sauce over the chicken and serve warm with freshly steamed rice or at room temperature as a Chinese "cold dish."

Yellow Coconut Rice (*Nasi Kuning*)

Nasi kuning, literally "yellow rice" in Indonesian, gets its festive golden color from turmeric. As the showpiece of a major celebration such as a wedding or anniversary, the rice is molded into an inverted cone and served on a bed of banana leaves together with a grand spread of meat and vegetable dishes. Yellow coconut rice is also a humble accompaniment for almost any dish served with white rice.

Time: 45 minutes plus frying shallots
Makes: 6 to 8 servings as a as part of a multicourse family-style meal

> 2½ teaspoons ground turmeric
>
> 1 teaspoon salt
>
> 1 cup warm water
>
> 1½ cups coconut milk
>
> 1 plump stalk lemongrass, bruised (see page 10) and tied into a knot
>
> 1 salam leaf

Yellow Coconut Rice

4 kaffir lime leaves, crumpled
2½ cups long-grain rice
2 cups water
Fried shallots (see page 22) for garnish

❦ Dissolve the turmeric and salt in the warm water.

❦ In a large pot, bring the coconut milk, lemongrass, salam leaf, and kaffir lime leaves to a gentle boil over medium-high heat. Reduce the heat to medium-low. Add the turmeric water. Tip the rice into the pot and add the water. Bring to a gentle boil, stirring occasionally. Simmer uncovered until the liquid has just been absorbed, about 10 minutes. Reduce the heat to low. Cover and cook for 15 to 20 minutes, or until the rice is tender but not mushy; the rice grains should still be separated. If the rice is still hard, make a well in the center of the pot, add a little water, and cook a few more minutes.

❦ Halfway through the estimated cooking time, gently fluff the rice with a fork or chopsticks.

❦ Let the rice cool. Fish out the lemongrass, salam leaf, and lime leaves and discard.

❦ On a large serving platter, mound the rice into the shape of an inverted cone. Garnish with fried shallots.

Profile of a Grandma: SANG JUNG CHOI

As told by Susan C. Kim

My 90-year-old grandmother, Sang Jung Choi, grew up in Korea during the Japanese occupation. As a result, her language skills, and her cooking, are Japanese-influenced.

At thirteen, my grandmother started working in a silk weaving factory to help support her family, and she continued to work even after she married. When her husband died early, she became the sole breadwinner and worked even harder to support her four young children. In fact, my grandmother won an award for her diligence, never having missed a day of work in her 20 years with the factory.

Since she worked from a young age, my grandmother didn't learn to cook until she was about twenty, considered late for Korean women back then. She didn't have formal training, but rather perfected her skills over the years by tasting other people's cooking, tweaking ingredients, and, of course, practicing. A lot.

In the 1970s, my grandmother moved to the United States and worked at my aunt's Korean market in Troy, Michigan. Most Korean markets in the United States, as well as in Korea, sell home-cooked foods along with groceries. My grandmother ran the back kitchen and whipped up popular dishes such as KOREAN BARBECUED BEEF SHORT RIBS (page 154), SEAWEED-WRAPPED RICE AND VEGETABLE ROLLS (page 276), and STIR-FRIED GLASS NOODLES (page 246) on a daily basis. Customers loved to stop in and pick up her daily specials, wrapped up fresh and hot and ready to go, along with their groceries.

My grandmother also catered for Korean parties and events. She made large quantities of everyday foods as well as special occasion dishes. One example was sweet rice dumplings, a popular item for a Korean baby's first birthday (actually celebrated when the child is 100 days old). People ordered them in huge quantities, and my grandmother formed each and every dumpling by hand.

In fact, everything she made was homemade and handmade—no food processors, no prepackaged anything. I remember watching in awe as my tiny, old grandmother hauled vats of boiling water across the kitchen, or stirred a thick gelatin with a wooden spoon for hours on end.

My grandmother was, and still is, an absolute perfectionist in the kitchen. She slices, dices, wraps, stirs, and fries with exact precision. And if something doesn't look perfect, she makes me eat it so that she doesn't have to serve it.

When I was young, my grandmother would have dishes like short ribs and glass noodles waiting for me when I arrived home from school each day. She even timed it so that the food would be hot off the stove right when I walked through the door. To her, serving cold food is unacceptable.

Today, even my non-Asian neighborhood friends remember my grandmother's cooking. They would sample her food as they ran through our kitchen, even if they had no idea what it was. They tried foods their parents weren't even aware of at the time, such as rice rolls wrapped in nori (seaweed). (Before sushi became en vogue, black sheets of nori were a little intimidating for many American palates.) My playmates were too young to know any better, but now, as adults, many brag that they've been eating Korean cuisine since they were kids. One Jewish boy used to come over and devour an entire jar of kimchi, plain, without rice. We would stand there horrified. Not even Koreans would do that! But the fiendish boy loved the hot, spicy sourness of the famous pickled cabbage.

My happiest memories are of sitting on the kitchen floor with my mother, grandmother, and siblings wrapping *mandu* (Korean dumplings), cleaning soybeans, slicing cabbage, and sharing the day's stories. Those moments were more than about making things to eat; cooking was a family gathering ritual, a methodical rhythm of comfort, and, most important, a way to share one's love with others.

8

COMFORT FOOD AND
ONE-WOK MEALS

Comfort food has always been a staple of home cooking and it varies from culture to culture, individual to individual. Yet there is a common thread. Imbued with familiarity, emotional security, and the pleasant memories of childhood, the nostalgic and sentimental appeal of comfort food never fails to envelop you in a sense of well-being and comfort.

Comfort food often takes the form of one-wok meals that feature carbohydrates, protein, and vegetables all in one dish. The Japanese have a name for their version: *nabemono*, one-pot dishes that are cooked in a *donabe* (clay pot, see page xix) or *suki-yaki* (round cast-iron pot), and are favored for family dining and entertaining guests.

Compared to the macaroni and cheese and chicken pot pie we know in the West, Asian versions take more unconventional forms such as STUFFED POTATO FLATBREAD (page 281) and GRANDMA MIYOSHI'S DUMPLING SOUP (page 268). Some are simple to make and others can be a wee-bit complicated. Regardless, recreating any of these dishes will provide a filling and satisfying meal reminiscent of Grandma's cooking and Grandma's love.

Chicken Coconut Noodle Soup

Bibimbap (Seasoned Vegetables over Rice)

Chicken and Egg over Rice (*Oyako Donburi*)

Chicken Coconut Noodle Soup (*Ohn No Khauk Swe*)

Clay Pot "Black Pork" (*Hong Bak*)

Fat Noodles in Miso Soup (*Miso Udon*)

Filipino Meatloaf (*Embutido*)

Grandma Miyoshi's Dumpling Soup (*Dango Jiru*)

Japanese Beef and Vegetable Hot Pot (*Sukiyaki*)

Japanese-Style Beef Stew (*Nikujaga*)

Leftover Thanksgiving Turkey–Rice Porridge (*Jook*)

Rice Cooker Casserole

Seaweed-Wrapped Rice and Vegetable Rolls (*Kimbap*)

Soft Noodles Tossed with Duck Eggs and Oyster Mushrooms

Special Indonesian Fried Rice (*Nasi Goreng Istimewa*)

Stuffed Potato Flatbread (*Aloo Paratha*)

Sweet and Savory Rice Noodles (*Pad See Ew*)

Vietnamese Crab Noodle Soup (*Bun Rieu Cua*)

Wide Rice Noodles Smothered in Rich Gravy (*Rad Nah*)

Wok-Tossed Rice Vermicelli with Eggs and Chives

Bibimbap (Seasoned Vegetables over Rice)

This homestyle Korean dish literally means to stir (*bibim*) rice (*bap*). There are two different ways to serve bibimbap. In restaurants, bibimbap is sometimes served in a stone bowl heated over a burner so that a layer of crispy, burnt rice forms on the bottom. Yangja Cho Im makes a simpler version topped with any vegetable side dish she may have on hand. You can use just about any meat or vegetable dish: everything from Korean barbecued beef (*bulgogi*) to DEEP-FRIED TOFU (page 122) to steamed vegetables, or even FROM-SCRATCH POT STICKERS (page 236) and STIR-FRIED GLASS NOODLES (page 246). It's a great way to use up leftovers and with the immense number of combinations, you'll never make it the same way twice.

Time: 10 minutes
Makes: 1 serving

1½ cups warm cooked Japanese short-grain rice

¼ cup Cabbage Kimchi (page 131)

¼ cup Spicy Korean Oyster Salad (page 139)

¼ cup Soybean Sprout Salad (page 138)

1 egg, cooked over easy

½ teaspoon sesame oil

1 teaspoon Korean red pepper paste (*koch'ujang*), or to taste

Scoop the rice into a big bowl with a wide mouth. Arrange the vegetables in neat piles on top of the rice. Top with the fried egg, drizzle the sesame oil over, and spoon a little red pepper paste on top. Mix well and serve warm or at room temperature.

Chicken and Egg over Rice (*Oyako Donburi*)

Literally, *oyako donburi* means "parent and child bowl," the parent and child being chicken and egg, sitting atop a mound of rice. Though not very traditional, you can add sliced onions, julienned carrots, snow peas, or green peas to the mix for a true one-pot meal. This recipe makes an individual serving but you can easily double or quadruple it to feed your family (see Pat's Notes). You can also substitute beef for the chicken for *gyutama donburi*, or "stranger and child bowl."

Time: 20 minutes
Makes: 1 serving

> ½ cup dashi (recipe on page 40) or chicken stock (recipe on page 42)
>
> 2 teaspoons Japanese soy sauce
>
> 2 teaspoons mirin or sake
>
> 2 teaspoons sugar
>
> 2 ounces boneless, skinless chicken breast, cut into thin diagonal bite-sized pieces
>
> 2 medium fresh shiitake mushrooms or rehydrated dried black mushrooms (see page 11), stemmed and halved
>
> 1 green onion, white and green parts, trimmed and cut into 1-inch lengths (reserve some for garnish)
>
> 1 egg
>
> 1 cup hot cooked Japanese short-grain rice

❀ In a small saucepan, combine the dashi, soy sauce, mirin, and sugar, and bring to a boil over medium-high heat. Add the chicken and mushrooms and simmer until the chicken is no longer pink, about 2 minutes. (If you use a larger saucepan, you may need more liquid to cover the ingredients, but add sparingly.) Skim off any scum or foam that rises to the surface. Add the green onion and cook for another 1 minute.

❀ Crack the egg into a small bowl and stir with chopsticks or a fork until well mixed but not foamy. Pour the egg into the sauce in light trickles, using chopsticks to slow down the flow, and cover the entire surface of the pan. Don't stir. Cover and cook until the egg is just set, 30 to 45 seconds. The egg will be like a soggy omelet. (You can cook it to desired doneness but I recommend no more than 1 minute.)

❧ Scoop the rice into a donburi (Japanese earthenware bowl) or any large bowl with a wide mouth. Ladle the chicken and egg mixture, including desired amount of sauce, over the rice. Sprinkle with the reserved green onion and serve immediately.

Pat's Notes: For more than one serving, simply repeat the recipe. Or, multiply the ingredients by the number of servings (but no more than 4) and cook all at once in a single saucepan; then divide the mixture among separate bowls of rice.

Chicken Coconut Noodle Soup (*Ohn No Khauk Swe*)

This popular Burmese dish features noodles doused in a mild curry sauce with a consistency that's somewhere between soup and gravy. Topped with different accompaniments of contrasting textures and flavors, it's a one-dish meal that's perfect for everyday eating and when entertaining guests. Grandma Alvina Mangrai (see page 292) likes to eat it with egg noodles, but you can use rice vermicelli too.

Time: 1½ hours (1 hour active)
Makes: 6 to 8 servings

> 3 tablespoons fish sauce
>
> 3 tablespoons soy sauce
>
> 3 cloves garlic, chopped (1 tablespoon)
>
> 2-inch piece fresh ginger, peeled and grated (2 tablespoons)
>
> 2 teaspoons ground turmeric
>
> 2 pounds boneless chicken thighs or breasts, cut into 1-inch cubes
>
> ¼ cup vegetable oil
>
> 2 medium yellow onions, chopped (2 cups)
>
> 2 teaspoons ground paprika
>
> Three 13½-ounce cans coconut milk (5 cups)
>
> 7 cups chicken stock (recipe on page 42)
>
> ½ cup garbanzo bean flour whisked into ½ cup warm water to make a smooth, runny paste
>
> 2 pounds fresh or 1 pound dried thin Chinese egg noodles (like chow mein noodles)

Garnishes:

> 6 hard-boiled eggs, peeled and cut crosswise into ¼-inch-thick slices
>
> 4 tablespoons ground dried red chilies, pan-roasted until dark and fragrant
>
> 1 large sweet onion, halved, cut into thin crescents, and soaked in water
>
> 2 green onions, white and green parts, chopped
>
> 1 cup cilantro sprigs
>
> 3 limes, quartered
>
> Fish sauce

※ In a medium bowl, combine the fish sauce, soy sauce, garlic, ginger, and turmeric. Add the chicken and mix well with your hands (use gloves to prevent your nails from being stained ochre by the turmeric). Set aside.

※ In a medium heavy-bottomed pot or Dutch oven, heat the oil over medium-high heat until it becomes runny and starts to shimmer. Stir in the onions and cook until soft and translucent, 3 to 4 minutes. Add the paprika and mix until the onions are well coated.

※ Tumble in the chicken and raise the heat to medium-high. Stir and cook until the chicken is no longer pink, 4 to 5 minutes. Add the coconut milk and stock and bring to a gentle boil, stirring constantly to prevent the mixture from curdling. Reduce the heat to medium-low, cover, and simmer gently for 20 minutes to allow the flavors to meld.

※ Stir in the garbanzo bean flour paste and return to a boil. Simmer over medium-low heat until the sauce is thick like heavy cream, 5 to 10 minutes. Adjust the consistency with more stock for a thinner gravy or more garbanzo bean flour for a thicker gravy. Taste and add more fish or soy sauce if necessary. Reduce the heat to very low and keep warm until ready to serve.

※ Just before serving, cook the noodles in a large pot of water according to package directions. Tip into a colander over the sink and rinse under cold running water. Drain and place in a bowl. Toss in a little oil to prevent sticking.

※ Divide the noodles among individual bowls and ladle about 1½ cups sauce over them. Garnish with eggs, chilies, onions, cilantro, limes, and fish sauce as desired.

Clay Pot "Black Pork" (*Hong Bak*)

This Singapore version of red-cooked pork comes with the addition of crispy fried shallots, courtesy of Dorothy Ho's mother, Yuh-Wan Chiang. When Dorothy was growing up, her mom often made this dish, and it's still a must-have on the menu when she comes to visit. It's quite time-consuming to make, but after the initial steps, you can just leave the dish to stew on the stove in a clay pot, imparting a deep, smoky flavor into every bite.

Time: 1½ to 2 hours (30 minutes active)
Makes: 4 to 6 servings as part of a multicourse family-style meal

> 1 cup (or as needed) vegetable oil for shallow-frying
>
> 15 (12 ounces) Asian shallots, peeled and cut into paper-thin slices
>
> 3 cloves garlic, chopped (1 tablespoon)
>
> 1 tablespoon sugar
>
> 3 tablespoons dark soy sauce
>
> 1 pound boneless pork shoulder, cut into 1½-inch cubes
>
> Regular soy sauce
>
> ¾ cup water, plus more as needed
>
> 4 hard-boiled eggs
>
> 14-ounce block fried tofu (or see recipe on page 122 to fry your own tofu), cut into 8 to 10 pieces

❧ In a large wok or skillet, heat the oil over medium-high heat until it becomes runny and starts to shimmer. Add the shallots and cook and stir continuously until evenly golden brown and crispy, 3 to 4 minutes (the timing will depend on how thin the slices are and how hot the oil is). With a slotted spoon, transfer the fried shallots to a plate lined with paper towels and set aside.

❧ Pour out the oil until about 1 tablespoon remains in the wok. Reduce the heat to medium, add the garlic to the leftover oil, and cook until fragrant, 15 to 30 seconds. Add the sugar and stir continuously until the sugar melts and caramelizes to form brown globules, 3 to 4 minutes. The caramel-coated garlic will clump together and the oil will separate. If the garlic starts to burn, reduce the heat.

🍴 Stir in the dark soy sauce, then add the pork. Stir and cook until the pork is well coated with the sauce, about 3 minutes. Add 3 tablespoons regular soy sauce, followed by the fried shallots and stir and cook for 2 to 3 minutes. Add the water and bring to a boil.

🍴 Transfer the pork mixture to a clay pot or Dutch oven (or leave it in the wok). Cover and simmer over medium-low heat for 30 minutes. Add the eggs and tofu. Stir gently to mix and spoon some sauce over the eggs and tofu to evenly color them. Simmer the dish for another 30 minutes to 1 hour, or until the pork has reached desired tenderness. Every 15 minutes, stir and check that the bottom of the pot is covered with sauce. Add water ¼ cup at a time if necessary. You don't want the meat to burn. Stir in more soy sauce to taste before turning off the heat. Serve with freshly steamed rice and a vegetable side dish.

Pat's Notes: Hong bak is the Fujian (a southeast coastal province of China) name for this dish, and means "red meat." Yuh-Wah calls it "black pork" probably because the dark soy sauce turns the meat a rich, almost black color.

Grandma Says: Never add salt. If you add salt, you will notice that it makes the dark soy sauce color "run," so your meat won't have the nice dark color.

Fat Noodles in Miso Soup (*Miso Udon*)

Udon is a thick Japanese wheat noodle usually served hot in soup. Packaged noodles can be bought dried, or fresh (cooked or uncooked) as *nama udon*. Udon broth comes in many varieties, including soy sauce and this miso broth.

Time: 1 hour
Makes: 4 servings

> 1 pound chicken thighs, or any other bone-in parts
>
> 5 cups water
>
> 4 dried black mushrooms, rehydrated (see page 11) and cut into quarters (reserve the soaking liquid)
>
> 8 ounces dried udon, or 2 pounds fresh nama udon
>
> 6 tablespoons miso
>
> 2 green onions, white and green parts, cut into ¼-inch lengths

In a large saucepan, combine the chicken, water, and mushroom soaking liquid and bring to a boil over high heat. Reduce the heat to medium and cover. Simmer 20 to 30 minutes, or until the chicken is tender and no longer pink. Skim off any scum or foam that rises to the surface.

Remove the chicken and scrape the meat from the bones. Cut the meat into 1-inch chunks. Discard the bones and return the meat to the soup.

To cook dried udon, bring a large pot of water to boil. Reduce the heat to medium and add the noodles. Return to a boil. Add 1 cup of cold water and bring back to a boil. Repeat two times, adding 3 cups of cold water total. Test the noodles and if necessary boil for 2 or 3 minutes more until tender. Do not overcook or they will become mushy. Tip into a colander over the sink and rinse under cold running water. Drain.

To cook nama udon, put the noodles in a heatproof bowl and pour boiling water over them. Let soak for a few minutes, just long enough to heat through. Separate the noodles gently with chopsticks while in the water. Tip into a colander over the sink and rinse under cold running water. Drain.

In a small bowl, mix the miso with a little soup from the saucepan until a smooth paste forms. Add the miso mixture to the soup and stir to mix. Add the noodles, mushrooms, and green onions and simmer gently over medium-low heat for 2 to 3 minutes. Serve in Japanese *donburi* (earthenware bowls).

Variations: Instead of using chicken and making chicken stock, use 5 cups DASHI (page 40) and add any of the following: fried tofu (*abura age*) cut into triangles and simmered in hot water for 5 minutes; fish cake slices (*kamaboko*); cubed silken tofu; julienned carrots; or chopped greens (watercress, arugula, or spinach).

Filipino Meatloaf (*Embutido*)

Raisins and sweet relish may seem odd in meatloaf, but the combination of sweet and savory are delightful in Leah Tolosa's Filipino take on a very American comfort food. Leah has fleeting memories of her late grandmother, whom she called Apu. Leah's Apu cooked many favorites for the family, including embutido. She also cooked for a living, running a *karinderia* (eatery) and peddling snacks such as *bibingka* (see page 301), fried green papaya empanadas (turnovers), *suman* (see page 330), and tamales (savory ground rice topped with dried shrimp and boiled egg wrapped in banana leaves) outside the local church after Christmas pre-dawn masses. Leah's recipe makes three loaves wrapped in aluminum foil to be baked. But you can also bake the entire recipe in a large loaf pan.

Time: 1 hour 40 minutes (40 minutes active) plus cooling
Makes: 6 to 8 servings as part of a multicourse family-style meal

> 2 slices white bread, cut into cubes (2 cups)
> ½ cup milk
> 1 egg, beaten
> 1 tablespoon vegetable oil
> 1 small onion, chopped (¾ cup)
> 1 clove garlic, minced
> 1 medium carrot, peeled and grated (½ cup)
> ½ small red bell pepper, chopped (½ cup)
> 1½ pounds ground meat of your choice (chicken, turkey, pork, veal, or beef)
> ½ cup raisins
> ⅓ cup prepared sweet relish
> 1½ teaspoons freshly ground black pepper
> 1 teaspoon salt
> 3 hard-boiled eggs, halved
> Banana ketchup (see Pat's Notes) or Thai sweet chili sauce for serving

❦ Preheat the oven to 375 degrees F.

❦ In a large bowl, soak the bread cubes in the milk until soft, about 5 minutes. Mix in the beaten egg and set aside.

꙳ In a medium skillet, heat the oil over medium heat until it becomes runny and starts to shimmer. Add the onion and garlic and cook until the onion is soft and translucent, 2 to 3 minutes. Add the carrot and bell pepper and cook until heated through, another 1 to 2 minutes. Let the vegetable mixture cool for about 5 minutes.

꙳ Add the vegetable mixture to the bread mixture followed by the ground meat, raisins, relish, pepper, and salt. Mix well.

꙳ To assemble the embutido, lay a 12-inch-square sheet of aluminum foil on the counter. Scoop one-third of the meat mixture (about 2 cups) onto the center of foil. Shape into a 9- by 5-inch rectangle. Lay 2 egg halves, cut-side down, on top of the meat mound. Fold up the sides of the foil and shape the meat mixture into a log, hiding the eggs in the middle. Wrap it completely with foil and roll into a tightly packed log 2 to 3 inches in diameter. Secure by twisting the ends shut. Repeat with the remaining meat mixture and eggs to form 2 more logs.

꙳ Place the wrapped logs on a baking sheet or pan and bake for 1 hour, or until the center is no longer pink.

꙳ Cool completely before serving. To serve, unwrap the foil and cut the embutido into 1-inch-thick slices. Arrange at an angle on a platter to display the hard-boiled egg centers. Serve with banana ketchup or Thai sweet chili sauce.

Pat's Notes: Banana ketchup is a condiment made from bananas, sugar, vinegar, and spices. A cheaper substitute for tomato ketchup, it is popular in the Philippines.

Grandma Miyoshi's Dumpling Soup (*Dango Jiru*)

Every time Lisa Nakamura, a classically trained chef of Japanese descent, makes *dango jiru*, she is transported back to her late grandmother's kitchen in Kapoho, Hawaii. Dango refers to dumplings that plump up in a delicious broth; most traditional recipes call for dumplings made with sweet rice flour (mochiko flour). Grandma Miyoshi's version differs from the original Japanese version in that it has wheat noodles instead of mochiko dumplings, and is studded with chunks of pork luncheon meat (aka Spam)! Luncheon meat was introduced to Hawaii during World War II and became popular because it is nonperishable and very versatile. Today it is synonymous with Hawaiian cuisine.

Time: 1½ hours
Makes: 4 to 6 servings as part of a multicourse family-style meal

> 7 cups water, divided
>
> 2 to 2¼ cups all-purpose flour, plus more for dusting
>
> 12-ounce can luncheon meat (such as Spam), cut into ½-inch cubes
>
> 1 medium yellow onion, halved and cut into thin crescents
>
> 1 large carrot, peeled and cut into thin coins (1 cup)
>
> 1 (8-ounce) bunch Asian mustard greens, trimmed and cut into thirds (5 to 6 cups)
>
> 1 (8-ounce) bunch mizuna or arugula, trimmed (2 to 3 cups)
>
> 1 (8-ounce) bunch watercress, trimmed and cut in half (2 to 3 cups)
>
> 1 teaspoon soy sauce
>
> 1 teaspoon sugar
>
> 1 teaspoon salt
>
> Chopped green onions for garnish
>
> Chinese hot mustard paste and soy sauce for dipping

❧ Put 1 cup cold water in a large mixing bowl and add 1½ cups flour. Mix well with your hands to form a sticky dough. Sprinkle in the remaining flour a little at a time and knead the dough in the bowl until it is as soft as your earlobe (Grandma Miyoshi's poetic description!) and no longer sticks to your hands.

❦ Sprinkle flour liberally on a dry work surface and glove your hands in flour. Take the dough out of the bowl and knead until it is smooth and springy, about 5 minutes. Cover the dough with a kitchen towel and let it rest for 30 minutes.

❦ While the dough is resting, make the soup: In a large pot, bring 6 cups of water to a boil over high heat. Add the luncheon meat, onion, and carrot and return to a boil. Reduce the heat to medium-low, cover, and simmer for 30 minutes. Add the mustard greens, mizuna, and watercress and cook until they are just tender, 1 to 2 minutes. Add the soy sauce, sugar, and salt.

❦ Using a rolling pin dusted with flour, roll the dough out into a 12-inch square about ⅛ inch thick. Cut the dough into 1-inch-wide strips, dusting with dough as necessary. Pull gently on each noodle to stretch and thin it out. The noodles will be pretty long, but you can cut them in half if desired.

❦ Raise the heat to medium-high and return the soup to a boil. Lower the noodles one at a time into the bubbling soup; don't let them bunch up. Cook until they're tender yet firm and still chewy (bear in mind that pasta made with all-purpose flour will have a softer texture than semolina-based pasta), 6 to 8 minutes.

❦ Ladle the soup and noodles into big bowls and sprinkle with green onions. Serve steaming hot with Chinese mustard paste and extra soy sauce in dipping dishes. To eat, dip the noodles, luncheon meat, or vegetables into the mustard paste and soy sauce.

Pat's Notes: You can precook the noodles in another pot of boiling water before adding to the soup just before serving to avoid overcrowding the pot. The delicious soup is meant to be jam-packed with meat and vegetables; add more water if you prefer.

Japanese Beef and Vegetable Hot Pot

Japanese Beef and Vegetable Hot Pot (*Sukiyaki*)

Sukiyaki was one of the few Japanese dishes Grandma Kimiye Hayashi (see page 44) cooked for her children when they were growing up. She would throw in whatever vegetables were available—mostly carrots and celery—despite the fact her kids didn't care too much for them. Sukiyaki is a versatile dish and traditional ingredients include tofu, Japanese scallions (*negi*), and chrysanthemum leaves (*shungiku*), but you can add bamboo shoots and any leafy vegetable such as Chinese cabbage or spinach. Traditionally, sukiyaki is cooked at the table in a sukiyaki pan that has been greased with suet (beef fat). In this "modern" method, the sukiyaki is cooked in the kitchen and served from a Dutch oven or crock pot to retain the heat.

Time: 45 minutes
Makes: 6 to 8 servings as part of a multicourse family-style meal

Sukiyaki Sauce:

> 1 cup dashi (recipe on page 40) or chicken stock (recipe on page 42)
>
> ½ cup Japanese soy sauce
>
> ½ cup mirin or sake
>
> ¼ cup sugar

Hot Pot:

> 4 ounces *shirataki* (see Pat's Notes) or cellophane noodles
>
> Boiling water
>
> 2 tablespoons vegetable oil, divided, plus more as needed
>
> 1 pound well-marbled tender beef (sirloin tip, top sirloin, or tenderloin), sliced paper-thin across the grain, then cut into bite-sized pieces
>
> 1 large yellow onion, halved and cut into thin crescents
>
> 4 ounces (1 cup) fresh shiitake, enoki, or button mushrooms
>
> 2 medium carrots, peeled and cut into ¼-inch diagonal slices (1 cup)
>
> 2 stalks celery, cut into ¼-inch diagonal slices (1 cup)
>
> 5 green onions, white and green parts, cut into 2-inch diagonal lengths
>
> 9-ounce package broiled tofu (*yakitofu*), cut into 16 pieces

✀ To make the sukiyaki sauce, mix together the dashi, soy sauce, mirin, and sugar in a bowl. Taste and adjust seasonings if desired. Set aside.

❧ In a heatproof bowl, soak the noodles in boiling water for 1 minute. Tip into a colander over the sink and rinse under cold running water. Cut them in half.

❧ In a medium Dutch oven or heavy-bottomed pot, heat 1 tablespoon of the oil over high heat until it becomes runny and starts to shimmer. Add half of the beef and stir until the meat is no longer pink, 2 to 3 minutes. Transfer to a plate. Repeat with the remaining beef, adding more oil if necessary.

❧ In the same Dutch oven, heat the remaining 1 tablespoon oil over medium-high heat. Add the onion, mushrooms, carrots, and celery and stir and cook until just wilted, about 4 minutes. Add the green onions and stir until they turn bright green, about 30 seconds. Add the sukiyaki sauce, noodles, cooked beef, and tofu. Mix well and bring to a gentle boil over medium heat. Cook until all the ingredients are heated through, 1 to 2 minutes. Serve hot with Japanese rice.

Optional: For a very traditional serving method (and only if the sukiyaki is kept bubbling over a brazier or hot plate at the table), crack one egg for each diner into individual bowls and beat with chopsticks. At the table, lift out pieces of beef, vegetables or noodle and dip in the egg before eating. This transfers the heat to the egg so you don't scald your mouth.

Pat's Notes: The quality of beef in sukiyaki is very important. I use a cut called "Korean barbecue beef," available in Asian markets, which are thin slices of sirloin or another prime cut of beef. Or ask your butcher to slice any tender, well-marbled beef into very thin slices.

The noodle known as shirataki, literally "shining waterfall," is made from the root of an aroid called devil's tongue or snake palm. It can be found in Japanese markets and online at www.asianfoodgrocer.com.

Japanese-Style Beef Stew (*Nikujaga*)

Nikujaga—which refers to its ingredients, meat (*niku*) and potatoes (*jagaimo*)—is one of the mainstays of Japanese comfort food known as *ofukuro no aji* ("mother's taste"). Like the comfort foods of any cuisine, it's simple, filling, and homey. Yuki Morishima makes this dish whenever she wants a taste of home. Yuki's recipe uses very little meat, as with all traditional Japanese dishes. You can add more at will. The stew reheats very well.

Time: 40 minutes
Makes: 4 servings as part of a multicourse family-style meal

> 8 ounces beef sirloin tip or tenderloin, trimmed of fat
>
> 2¼ cups dashi (recipe on page 40)
>
> ¼ cup Japanese soy sauce
>
> 1 tablespoon mirin
>
> 1 tablespoon sugar
>
> 2 medium (about 1¼ pounds) russet potatoes, peeled and each cut into 6 to 8 equal pieces
>
> 1 medium yellow onion, cut into 8 wedges and separated
>
> 2 large carrots, peeled and cut into ½-inch-thick coins

❧ Handle the beef partially frozen so that it is easier to cut (if it's fresh, place in the freezer for about 30 minutes). Cut the beef along the grain into 1½-inch-thick strips. Then, with your knife at an angle almost parallel to the cutting surface, slice the meat diagonally across the grain into ⅛-inch-thick slices.

❧ In a 10- to 12-inch skillet or wide saucepan at least 3 inches deep, combine the dashi, soy sauce, mirin, and sugar and stir to mix. Add the beef, potatoes, onion, and carrots and stir to coat evenly with sauce. Place an *otoshibuta* (see Pat's Notes) on top of the ingredients and cover the pan with a lid. Simmer over medium-low heat for 15 to 20 minutes, or until the potatoes are tender and infused with a golden hue.

❧ Serve with Japanese short-grain rice and steamed green leafy vegetables.

Variation: Add ½ cup green peas to the stew for color and vegetable variety.

Pat's Notes: An otoshibuta, or literally "dropped lid," is uniquely Japanese. It is placed on top of ingredients in a pan while they are cooking to allow heat to circulate evenly, effectively cooking ingredients with little liquid. Some Japanese pans actually come with a second lid—usually made of wood—for this purpose. You can improvise one by cutting a piece of parchment paper or aluminum foil into a circle with a diameter just a wee bit smaller than your pot. Fold the circle into quarters and cut the corner off to form a hole in the middle of the circle to let out steam.

Leftover Thanksgiving Turkey–Rice Porridge (*Jook*)

Turkey is not a bird typically eaten by Asians, but Asian Americans make turkey for Thanksgiving too. The day after Thanksgiving, the carcass, scraped clean of meat for leftovers, is cooked with rice and water to make rice porridge. You can make this delicious comfort food, which is also a soothing meal for sick ones, any time. Simply use a chicken carcass (or chicken pieces), or the meaty bone from last night's ham dinner instead of Thanksgiving leftovers.

Time: 4 hours (15 minutes active)
Makes: 4 servings

> 1½ cups long-grain rice
> 1 turkey carcass (from a 12- to 14-pound turkey)
> Salt

Garnishes:
> Leftover turkey meat
> Chinese Barbecued Pork (page 165)
> Soy sauce
> Sesame oil
> Cilantro leaves
> Green onions
> Tianjin preserved vegetables (see Pat's Notes on page 291)
> Ground white pepper

❧ Wash the rice in 2 to 3 changes of water until the water almost runs clear (see page 37). Drain.

🍴 Put the turkey carcass in a large stockpot and add enough water to submerge by 1 inch (12 to 14 cups water). Bring to a boil over high heat and skim off any scum or foam that rises to the surface. Add the rice and return to a rolling boil.

🍴 Reduce the heat to low and cover. Simmer for 3 to 4 hours, stirring occasionally so that the rice doesn't stick to the bottom of pot and scorch, until the rice grains are swollen and the porridge is as thick as cooked oatmeal. If it gets too thick for your liking, add more water. If it's too thin, cook the porridge a little longer until it reaches the desired smoothness and thickness.

🍴 Remove the carcass and fish out any stray bones. Add salt to taste. Ladle into individual bowls and garnish with turkey, pork, soy sauce, sesame oil, cilantro, green onions, vegetables, and pepper as desired.

Pat's Notes: The more frequently you stir the rice porridge, the faster the rice grains will break down and the smoother the porridge will be.

Rice Cooker Casserole

Wondering what to do with leftovers from CHICKEN ADOBO (page 182) or CARAMELIZED PORK BELLY AND EGGS BRAISED IN COCONUT WATER (page 227)? Make this easy casserole in your rice cooker. Feel free to improvise on the ingredients, all you need is 3½ to 4 cups of meat and vegetables.

Time: 40 minutes (20 minutes active)
Makes: 4 servings

> 2 cups long-grain rice
>
> 2 cups water
>
> 3 Chinese sausages, steamed (see page 20) and cut into ½-inch diagonal slices (1 cup)
>
> 1 cup cooked leftover meat cut into bite-sized pieces, plus ½ cup leftover sauce or gravy (or chicken stock)
>
> 6 medium dried black mushrooms, rehydrated (see page 11) and cut into ¼-inch slices (¾ cup)
>
> 1 tablespoon sesame oil (optional)
>
> 2 cloves garlic, minced

1 teaspoon salt

6 ounces medium (36/40 count) shrimp, peeled, deveined and halved (1 cup)

Chopped green onions for garnish

❧ Wash the rice in 2 to 3 changes of water until the water almost runs clear (see page 37). Drain and put in a rice cooker bowl. Add the water, sausages, meat and sauce, mushrooms, sesame oil, garlic, and salt. Stir to mix.

❧ Place the bowl in the rice cooker and start to cook. Five minutes before the rice is done (usually about 15 minutes into the cooking process but all rice cookers are different), add the shrimp and give a good stir. Continue cooking until the shrimp is cooked through and the rice is tender. Sprinkle with green onions and serve.

Pat's Notes: To make this dish on the stovetop, bring the rice and water to a boil in a 4-quart pot. Add all the ingredients except the shrimp and green onions and stir to mix. Return to a boil then reduce the heat to low. Cover and simmer for 20 minutes, or until almost all the water has been absorbed. Add the shrimp and give a good stir. Cover, turn off the heat, and steam until the shrimp is cooked through and the rice is tender, 8 to 10 more minutes.

Seaweed-Wrapped Rice and Vegetable Rolls (*Kimbap*)

Similar to Japanese sushi, *kimbap* (literally, "seaweed rice") is a common lunchbox meal, eaten largely for ease, and also a great picnic food. Unlike sushi, the rice is not highly seasoned and according to Susan C. Kim who got this recipe from her grandma, Sang Jung Choi (see page 252), dipping the rolls into any sauce—soy or otherwise—is a definite no-no.

Time: 45 minutes
Makes: 4 to 6 servings

4 cups freshly cooked Japanese short-grain rice

1 teaspoon rice vinegar or distilled white vinegar

1½ teaspoons soy sauce, divided, plus more for brushing

1½ teaspoons toasted sesame oil, divided

4 ounces spinach

Boiling water

1 medium carrot, peeled and cut into ¼-inch julienned strips

Vegetable oil for brushing

2 eggs, beaten with a pinch of salt

Four ¼-inch-thick slices pickled yellow radish (labeled *dakkwang* in Korean or *takuwan* in Japanese)

Four 7- by 8-inch roasted seaweed sheets (*nori*)

1 tablespoon toasted sesame seeds

Special tools: Bamboo mat for rolling

❧ While the rice is still hot, gently fold in the vinegar, 1 teaspoon soy sauce, and 1 teaspoon sesame oil. Let cool.

❧ In a heatproof bowl, soak the spinach in boiling water for 1 to 2 minutes until just wilted. Rinse under cold running water and drain. Repeat with the carrots, soaking them until they are soft but still crunchy, 3 to 4 minutes.

❧ In a small bowl, mix the spinach with the remaining sesame oil and soy sauce.

❧ To make the egg strips, lightly brush the bottom of an 8-inch nonstick skillet with oil. Set over medium heat for 1 minute. Swirl in the eggs to coat the bottom of the skillet in a thin, even layer. Cook until the omelet surface is nearly dry and the underside is light golden, 1½ to 2 minutes. Lift the edge of the omelet to check. Flip and cook for another 1 minute or so. Slide onto a plate. When cool, roll the omelet into a fat cigar and cut into ¼-inch-wide strips.

❧ To assemble the kimbap, arrange the rice, spinach, carrot, egg strips, and pickled radish within easy reach on a work surface and divide each into 4 portions. Prepare a bowl of water to wet your fingers when they get sticky while handling the rice.

❧ Lay a sheet of seaweed on a bamboo mat with the shorter end parallel to your body. Spread 1 cup of seasoned rice evenly over the lower two-thirds of the seaweed. Lay one portion each of spinach, carrots, egg, and pickled radish in the center of the rice parallel to your body. Sprinkle with sesame seeds. Start from the end closest to you and roll the mat with the ingredients inside into a log, using your fingers to keep the filling ingredients where they are and squeezing to tighten as you go. When done, give the bamboo mat a squeeze around the roll to tighten. Gently release the mat, remove the roll, and place on a plate seam side down. Repeat with remaining ingredients.

Brush each roll lightly with sesame oil. Cut crosswise into ½-inch pieces. After every cut, moisten the knife with water to help keep each cut clean.

Pat's Notes: Don't fret if your first attempt at kimbap is lopsided—you can still eat it. Keep practicing and you'll soon get the hang of it.

If you don't have a rolling mat, you can use parchment or wax paper.

Soft Noodles Tossed with Duck Eggs and Oyster Mushrooms

In Vietnam, duck eggs are often preserved and salted, and fertilized duck eggs are especially prized. But here, rich, fresh duck eggs are wok-tossed with delicate oyster mushrooms and egg noodles. The recipe comes courtesy of Eric Banh, co-owner of Monsoon restaurant and Baguette Box in Seattle. From the time you fire up your wok, the cooking process takes only about 3 minutes, so have everything ready because things move very quickly.

Time: 20 minutes
Makes: 2 servings

> 8 ounces fresh Chinese egg noodles (like chow mein noodles)
>
> 3 tablespoons vegetable oil
>
> 2 duck eggs, lightly beaten
>
> 4 ounces fresh oyster mushrooms, each shredded into 2 to 3 pieces with your fingers
>
> 1 tablespoon soy sauce
>
> 1 tablespoon oyster sauce
>
> 2 tablespoons unsalted butter
>
> Pinch of kosher salt
>
> Freshly ground black pepper
>
> 2 green onions, green parts only, halved lengthwise and cut crosswise into 3-inch lengths

🍂 Cook the noodles in a large pot of boiling water according to package directions until tender yet firm and still chewy. Tip into a colander over the sink and rinse under cold running water, separating the individual strands as much as possible.

🍂 Preheat a large wok or skillet over high heat for about 1 minute. Swirl in the oil and heat until it starts to smoke. Immediately add the eggs and oyster mushrooms. Stir and cook for 10 seconds. Add the noodles, soy sauce, oyster sauce, butter, salt, and pepper to taste. Stir everything swiftly around the wok until well mixed. Add the green onions and stir with a couple more flourishes. When the eggs are cooked but still creamy, 2 to 3 minutes, remove from the heat and serve immediately.

Pat's Notes: If you can't find duck eggs, use 3 chicken eggs instead. Feel free to use any mushroom in season; using chanterelles turns this into a special occasion dish.

Special Indonesian Fried Rice (*Nasi Goreng Istimewa*)

In Indonesia, fried rice, a common breakfast, is usually a simple dish without the fixings. This recipe, using meat and shrimp, is the "special" (*istimewa*) version. It's a favorite one-meal deal for lunch or dinner. Javanese fried rice, *nasi goreng jawa*, uses shrimp paste but Chinese immigrants to Indonesia concocted their own *nasi goreng cina* (Chinese fried rice) that omits it. Unlike Chinese fried rice where the egg is scrambled into the dish, the Indonesian rendition is either topped with a fried egg or strewn with shredded omelet—and sprinkled with fried shallots, of course.

Time: 50 minutes plus frying shallots
Makes: 4 servings

> 5 cups cooked long-grain white rice, leftover from the day before or refrigerated for at least 2 hours
>
> 2 tablespoons vegetable oil, plus more as needed
>
> 5 Asian shallots or ½ small yellow onion, coarsely chopped (⅓ cup)
>
> 2 cloves garlic, minced
>
> 1 long fresh red chili (such as Holland or Fresno) cut into thin rings on the diagonal; or about 2 teaspoons prepared chili paste

1 teaspoon dried shrimp paste (optional)

8 ounces boneless, skinless chicken thighs, cut into 1-inch chunks

4 ounces medium (36/40 count) shrimp, peeled and deveined

2 tablespoons Indonesian sweet soy sauce (see page 24)

1½ tablespoons regular soy sauce

1 teaspoon salt

½ teaspoon ground white pepper

Garnishes:

4 fried eggs

Sliced cucumbers

Sliced tomatoes

Shrimp chips (optional, see Pat's Notes)

Fried shallots (see page 22)

❧ Break up large clumps of the rice and separate the grains with wet fingers. Set aside.

❧ Preheat a large wok or skillet over high heat for about 1 minute. Swirl in the oil and heat until it becomes runny and starts to shimmer. Reduce the heat to medium and add the shallots, garlic, chili, and shrimp paste. Cook and stir until the shallots are fragrant and softened and the pungent smell of the shrimp paste has mellowed, 2 to 3 minutes. (When frying chilies, the volatile oils will permeate the air so it's a good idea to have your air vent on high and your windows open). Use your spatula to squish the shrimp paste as you go and scrape it off the bottom of the wok to prevent it from sticking.

❧ Raise the heat to high, add the chicken, and cook and stir until no longer pink, 1 to 2 minutes. Add the shrimp and continue stirring until they just begin to turn pink, 20 to 30 seconds. Add the cooked rice, using your spatula to break up any clumps. Add the sweet and regular soy sauces, salt, and white pepper. Stir everything swiftly around the wok until the rice is well-coated and well-colored (little bits of white here and there are okay), and the chicken and shrimp are cooked through, 4 to 5 minutes. Add more oil if the rice begins to stick to the wok; or reduce the heat if it starts to scorch. Taste and adjust the seasonings if desired.

❧ Divide the fried rice among 4 serving plates. Top each serving with a fried egg and garnish with cucumber, tomato, and shrimp chips. Sprinkle with fried shallots and serve immediately.

Pat's Notes: Shrimp chips (*krupuk udang*), made from dried shrimp, tapioca flour, and eggs, are sold raw as flat and hard pale pink disks, or ready-fried as curvy, crunchy chips. If you decide to deep-fry them yourself, do so before starting on the main recipe so that they're ready to garnish the fried rice hot from the wok.

Stuffed Potato Flatbread (*Aloo Paratha*)

Whenever Champa Ramakrishna doesn't feel like preparing the requisite three dishes per meal, she makes *aloo paratha*. Easy to make and nutritious, the one-dish Indian meal can be eaten for breakfast, lunch, or dinner. While Champa can churn out perfect parathas in a matter of minutes, making them symmetrical takes some practice—so don't be discouraged if your first few don't turn out quite right. Instead of the yogurt dip, you can serve the flatbread with your favorite pickle or chutney.

Time: 2 hours
Makes: 10 parathas, 4 to 5 servings

> 2 cups Indian whole wheat flour (*atta*), or a combination of 1 cup whole wheat pastry flour and 1 cup all-purpose white flour, plus more as needed
>
> 1 tablespoon vegetable oil, plus more for drizzling
>
> Salt
>
> ¾ to 1 cup lukewarm water
>
> 1 pound Yukon gold potatoes
>
> 1 small yellow onion, finely chopped (¾ cup)
>
> 1 tablespoon finely chopped cilantro leaves
>
> ½ teaspoon ground dried red chilies or crushed red chili flakes
>
> ½ teaspoon cumin seeds
>
> ½ teaspoon ground cumin
>
> Yogurt Dip (recipe follows)

❧ In a large mixing bowl, mix the flour, oil, and a pinch of salt. Add the water a little at a time and knead into a soft, pliable dough. Once the dough starts to pull easily away from the side of the bowl, knead it on a lightly floured surface until smooth, 1 to 2 minutes. Cover with a damp cloth and set aside for 30 minutes.

❧ Meanwhile, put the potatoes in a medium saucepan with enough water to cover. Bring to a boil then reduce the heat. Cover and simmer for 15 to 20 minutes, or until a fork can prick them easily. The potatoes should still be somewhat firm and not too soft. Drain in a colander and let cool.

❧ When the potatoes have reached room temperature, peel and grate them. You should have about 2 cups. In a large bowl, combine the potatoes, onion, cilantro, ground chilies, cumin seeds, ground cumin, and 1 teaspoon salt. Mix thoroughly with your hands. Taste and adjust the seasonings.

❧ Divide the dough into 10 equal 1½-inch balls (an easy way to do this is to divide the dough in half, then each half into 5 balls). Divide the potato filling into 10 equal portions. Prepare a plate with about 1 cup flour for dusting.

❧ Sprinkle flour liberally onto a work surface and roll a ball into a disk about 4 inches in diameter with a rolling pin. Place 1 portion of filling in the center and gather the edges up and around it, stretching the dough if necessary. Pinch to seal securely at the top so that the filling is entirely enclosed. It will look like a fat dumpling.

❧ Gently flatten the dumpling into a thick patty, being careful not to let the filling escape. Dip both sides in the flour. Lay the patty seam side down and carefully roll it out into a circle 5 to 6 inches in diameter and about ⅛ inch thick. Don't worry if a little filling pops out. Just pat it back inside the paratha as best as you can.

❧ Repeat with the remaining dough and filling, dusting with flour as needed. Place the parathas on a plate, layering them between parchment paper to prevent them from sticking together before cooking.

❧ Preheat a heavy griddle or 8-inch nonstick skillet. Place 1 paratha on the ungreased griddle and cook over medium-high heat until the underside is speckled with golden brown spots, about 3 minutes. Flip and drizzle the top with oil (about ½ teaspoon). Smear the oil all over the surface with a spatula and press down to ensure even browning. Flip again, drizzle more oil on top, and repeat the smearing process. Cook for another 2 to 3 minutes, flipping every minute or so, until the paratha is evenly browned on both sides.

❧ Slide onto a plate and keep warm in a low oven while you cook the remaining parathas. To eat, tear off bite-sized pieces of paratha and dip into the yogurt mixture.

Variations: Add any of the following cooked ingredients to, or in lieu of, the potato filling: grated cauliflower, mashed lentils or mung beans, and Indian cheese (paneer).

Pat's Notes: Atta (sometimes called chapati flour) is a very finely ground whole wheat flour made from hard wheat. With a high protein content and just enough bran to give it body without making it too coarse for soft pliable Indian breads, atta flour is also strong and dough made from it can be rolled out very thin. It is available at South Asian markets.

Parathas freeze well. Just cook them without oil and freeze, placing wax or parchment paper in between each paratha. When ready to use, defrost and reheat the paratha on the griddle with some oil.

Grandma Says: Grate the cooked potatoes instead of mashing so there will be no lumps.

Yogurt Dip

Have everyone make individual servings and tailor the dip to their personal taste.

Makes: 1 serving

> ½ cup homemade or Greek yogurt
> Ground cumin
> Ground dried red chilies
> Salt

❧ Spoon the yogurt into an individual dish. Sprinkle ground cumin, ground chilies, and salt to taste (I recommended pinches to start with). Mix well.

Sweet and Savory Rice Noodles (*Pad See Ew*)

When Churairat Huyakorn owned a Thai restaurant in Bremerton, Washington, *pad see ew* was one of her most popular dishes. She developed a system for standardizing every order: Per order, she would add 2 dashes fish sauce, 2 drops vinegar, etc. With easy-to-follow measurements, this dish is easy to make and tastes delicious—anyone can give it a whirl. Ideally, purchase fresh rice sheets (available in Asian markets) so you can cut them to the desired width. If not, the precut ones will do (they are usually about ¾-inch wide). As a last resort, dried rice sticks work as well. Have all the ingredients ready before you start cooking as things move very quickly once you get going.

Time: 30 minutes
Makes: 2 servings

1 pound fresh rice sheets, or 7 ounces large dried rice sticks

8 ounces pork shoulder (chicken, beef, and shrimp work as well)

8 ounces Chinese broccoli

Boiling water

¼ cup vegetable oil, plus more as needed

3 cloves garlic, minced (1 tablespoon)

1½ tablespoons fish sauce, divided, plus more for serving

2 eggs

2 tablespoons sweet soy sauce (see page 24)

1 tablespoon oyster sauce

1 tablespoon sugar

1½ tablespoons distilled white vinegar, plus more for serving

Ground white pepper

Crushed dried red chilies for serving

❧ Cut the fresh rice sheets into 2-inch-wide strands and separate them. (If using dried rice sticks, soak them in hot water for 6 to 8 minutes. You want them soft and pliable but not falling apart. Tip into a colander over the sink, rinse under cold running water, and drain.) Set aside.

❧ Handle the pork partially frozen so that it is easier to cut (if it's fresh, place in the freezer for about 30 minutes). Cut the pork along the grain into

1½-inch-thick strips. Then, with your knife at an angle almost parallel to the cutting surface, slice the meat diagonally across the grain into ⅛-inch-thick slices.

🍴 Separate the Chinese broccoli into leaf and stem pieces. Cut the stems into 2-inch pieces and halve the thicker ones lengthwise as they take longer to cook. In a heatproof bowl, soak the broccoli in boiling water until wilted but not fully cooked, about 30 seconds. Rinse under cold running water and drain.

🍴 Preheat a large wok or skillet over very high heat for about 30 seconds. Swirl in the oil and heat until smoking. Add the meat followed by the garlic and ½ tablespoon of the fish sauce to flavor the meat. Stir and cook until the meat is no longer pink, about 1 minute. Push the meat to one side and crack in the eggs. Let the eggs cook undisturbed until the whites start to turn opaque, about 15 seconds, then stir to mix with the meat. Push the meat and egg mixture up one side of the wok.

🍴 Toss in the noodles and spread them across the bottom of the wok to make as much contact with the hot surface as possible. That's how you get the nice charred noodle bits and the unmistakable burnt flavor peculiar to foods fried in a searing hot wok. Add more oil if the noodles stick to the wok. Mix the noodles with the meat and eggs and stir everything swiftly around the wok.

🍴 Add the remaining fish sauce, the sweet soy sauce, oyster sauce, and sugar. Sliding your spatula to the bottom of the wok, turn and toss all the ingredients to coat evenly with the seasonings. Add the Chinese broccoli and vinegar and toss with a couple more flourishes until well mixed and the broccoli is cooked through but the stems are still crunchy, 1 to 2 minutes. Taste and adjust seasonings if desired.

🍴 Divide the noodles between 2 plates and sprinkle with white pepper. Serve with fish sauce, vinegar, and crushed chilies on the side.

🍴 To make more servings, rinse the wok with hot water (no soap required) and give it a quick scrub just to remove the brown bits stuck to the bottom. Wipe with a paper towel and set the wok back over the heat to dry completely before carrying on.

Variation: For a vegetarian version, skip the meat and add firm tofu, or just make it with the eggs. One difference: Add the eggs first, then the garlic to prevent it from burning in the ultra-hot wok.

Pat's Notes: Dark sweet soy sauce gives the noodles color, while fish sauce and oyster sauce season the dish.

Grandma Says: Use the widest noodles possible; they will break easily if they're not big enough. If you have a strong fire, the noodles won't break.

Vietnamese Crab Noodle Soup (*Bun Rieu Cua*)

In Vietnam, mud crabs (a type of soft-shell crab) are often caught in rice paddy fields for this dish. To extract the crab "juice" that is essential to the soup, their top shells are removed and pounded with salt. Water is then added, and the resulting liquid strained through a sieve. Thanh Nguyen, who migrated to the United States in the 1970s, proposes a more modern method: whirling the crabs in a blender and then straining. You can find frozen soft-shell crabs at Asian markets, or use Dungeness or blue crabmeat instead.

Time: 3 hours (1 hour active)
Makes: 6 to 8 servings

> 1½ pounds pork spareribs, cut into individual 1-inch pieces (available at Asian butchers)
>
> 1 cup dried shrimp, rinsed and ground to a coarse powder in a food processor
>
> 2 tablespoons vegetable oil, divided
>
> 2 cloves garlic, cut into thin slices
>
> 1 teaspoon ground paprika
>
> 4 medium tomatoes, each cut into 4 wedges then halved crosswise (3 red and 1 green for crispness)
>
> 1 whole (8 ounces) soft-shell crab
>
> 2 tablespoons tamarind paste (see page 25)
>
> ½ cup warm water
>
> 4 eggs
>
> 8 ounces ground pork

½ cup (half a 7-ounce bottle) shrimp paste in soybean oil
(see Pat's Notes)

¼ cup fish sauce

Salt

1 pound small or medium round rice noodles (bun) or rice
vermicelli, cooked according to package directions

Garnishes:

2 cups (6 ounces) fresh mung bean sprouts, tails snapped off

1 cup shredded cabbage or lettuce

1 cup cilantro sprigs

1 cup Vietnamese balm leaves (see Pat's Notes)

1 cup spearmint leaves

1 jalapeño, cut into rings

Chopped green onions

3 limes, cut into wedges

❊ In a large stockpot, bring 10 cups water to a rolling boil over high heat with
the pork ribs and dried shrimp. Reduce the heat to medium and simmer for
2 hours, or until the meat is tender.

❊ In a small skillet, heat 1 tablespoon of the oil until it becomes runny and
starts to shimmer. Add the garlic and cook until fragrant, 15 to 30 seconds.
Add the paprika and stir for another 10 seconds. Add the garlic mixture to
the stockpot.

❊ In the same skillet, heat the remaining oil over medium heat until it
becomes runny and starts to shimmer. Add the tomatoes and stir and cook
for 1 minute; add to the stockpot.

❊ In a blender, whirl the soft-shell crab, shells and all, with 1½ cups water for
15 to 20 seconds, or until the shells are crushed and the meat is puréed.
Strain the juice and add to the stockpot. Add 1 more cup water to the
blender and pulse 2 to 3 times to absorb any remaining flavor. Strain and
add to the stockpot. Discard the shells and meat.

❊ Mix the tamarind paste with the warm water and add to the stockpot.

❊ In a medium bowl, mix the eggs and pork with chopsticks or a fork until
well combined. Stir in the shrimp paste and mix well. Slowly add the egg

and pork mixture to the soup. Do not stir, allowing the meat to cook in clusters for 8 to 10 minutes. Sprinkle with the fish sauce and salt and stir gently so that the meat clusters remain intact.

Divide the cooked rice noodles among individual bowls and garnish with mung bean sprouts, cabbage, cilantro, balm leaves, spearmint leaves, jalapeño, green onions, and limes as desired. Pour 2 cups of hot soup over each bowl of noodles, including one or two pork ribs and some pork clusters.

Pat's Notes: Shrimp paste in soybean oil is a prepared sauce of shrimp, garlic, white pepper, soybean oil, paprika, and fish sauce. Don't confuse this with shrimp paste (see page 23). They are different in both texture and color. A staple of southern Thailand, it is added to fried rice, noodles, stir-fried vegetables, and seafood dishes. Store up to 6 months in the refrigerator once opened. Thanh Nguyen uses Pantainorasingh brand, available at www.templeofthai.com.

Vietnamese balm (*kinh gioi*) has a concentrated fragrance and flavor akin to that of lemon balm. The small serrated leaves have a lavender center. Sold in small plastic bags, they will keep for 3 or 4 days in the refrigerator.

Wide Rice Noodles Smothered in Rich Gravy (*Rad Nah*)

Pad Thai may be Thailand's most famous dish in the United States, but when it comes to noodles, *rad nah* reigns in Panee Lertpanyavit's kitchen. A key ingredient in this recipe is broad bean sauce. Panee prefers to buy the paste with broken beans rather than whole beans which she believes tastes better.

Time: 30 minutes
Makes: 4 servings

8 ounces flank steak or sirloin (or any meat of your choice)

2 tablespoons tapioca starch, divided, plus more as needed

1 pound Chinese broccoli

3 tablespoons vegetable oil, divided

2 pounds fresh wide rice noodles, rinsed and separated into individual strands

1 tablespoon dark soy sauce

2 tablespoons broad bean sauce

2 cloves garlic, minced

2 cups water

2 tablespoons oyster sauce

1 tablespoon soy sauce

2 teaspoons sugar

Ground white or black pepper

Pickled Green Chilies (recipe follows)

❧ Handle the beef partially frozen so that it is easier to cut (if it's fresh, place in the freezer for about 30 minutes). Cut the beef along the grain into 1½-inch-thick strips. Then, with your knife at an angle almost parallel to the cutting surface, slice the meat diagonally across the grain into ⅛-inch-thick slices.

❧ Coat the beef with 1 tablespoon of the tapioca starch and set aside. In a small bowl, combine the remaining tapioca starch with 2 tablespoons water and mix into a slurry.

❧ Separate the Chinese broccoli into leaf and stem pieces. Cut the stems into 2-inch pieces and halve the thicker ones lengthwise as they take longer to cook.

❧ Preheat a large wok or skillet over high heat for about 1 minute. Swirl in 2 tablespoons of the oil and heat until smoking. Toss in the noodles and stir until golden brown, 2 to 3 minutes. Drizzle the dark soy sauce over the noodles, slide your spatula to the bottom of the wok, and turn and toss to coat the noodles. You want to coat the noodles evenly with soy sauce for color, but don't fret if there are still patches of white. Transfer the noodles to a rimmed platter.

❧ In the same wok, swirl in the remaining oil and heat over high heat until it becomes runny and starts to shimmer. Add the broad bean sauce and garlic, followed by the beef. Stir and cook for 1 minute. Throw in the Chinese broccoli and stir and cook until the beef is no longer pink and the broccoli is bright green and just wilted, about 2 minutes.

❧ Add 2 cups water. Stir in the oyster sauce, soy sauce, and sugar and mix well. Bring to a boil. Give the tapioca starch slurry a quick stir and pour it into the wok, stirring constantly. Allow the sauce to bubble until it thickens to the consistency of beef gravy, about 2 minutes. If the sauce is not thick enough, add more tapioca starch slurry. If you prefer a thinner sauce, add water and adjust the seasonings. Remove from the heat. Pour the sauce over the noodles and sprinkle with pepper. Serve immediately with pickled chilies.

Pickled Green Chilies

Green chilies soaked in vinegar add both heat and tang to every bite of rad nah. You can use any mild chili, just not the very spicy Thai chilies!

Makes: 4 servings

>   2 jalapeños, cut into rings
>   ⅓ cup vinegar

* In a nonreactive container with a tight-fitting lid, soak the chilies in vinegar for at least 12 hours. Serve in individual small dishes.

* Pickles will keep for 2 to 3 days at room temperature.

Wok-Tossed Rice Vermicelli with Eggs and Chives

My grandfather taught my mom how to make this simple dish and it has become a staple in my kitchen. When you crave a satisfying breakfast or a light lunch, this fits the bill perfectly. All you need are a few simple ingredients to toss in the wok. Garnish with CHINESE BARBECUED PORK (page 165) or steamed vegetables if you'd like a little more variety. Note that the Tianjin preserved vegetables are super salty so use sparingly.

Time: 20 minutes
Makes: 2 servings

>   8 ounces rice vermicelli
>   Hot water
>   1 tablespoon vegetable oil
>   2 cloves garlic, chopped
>   3 eggs

2 cups chicken or vegetable stock, plus more as needed

1 tablespoon Tianjin preserved vegetables (see Pat's Notes)

1 tablespoon fish sauce

½ teaspoon salt

¼ teaspoon white pepper

4 Chinese chives or skinny green onions, cut into 1-inch lengths

In a medium bowl, soak the rice vermicelli in hot water for 5 to 10 minutes until soft and pliable. Tip into a colander over the sink and separate the strands.

Preheat a large wok or skillet over medium heat for about 1 minute. Swirl in the oil and heat until it becomes runny and starts to shimmer. Stir in the garlic and cook until fragrant, 15 to 30 seconds.

Raise the heat to high and crack the eggs into the wok and scramble until they just begin to set, 45 seconds to 1 minute. Add the vermicelli followed by the stock. Stir the noodles swiftly around the wok to mix. Add the preserved vegetables, fish sauce, salt, and pepper and continue to stir and toss. Bring to a boil and cook until the noodles are tender but still chewy to the bite and the liquid has reduced to about 1 cup, a total of 3 to 4 minutes. The final dish should be a little soupy, add more stock if necessary. Throw in the chives, toss with a couple more flourishes to heat through, and serve immediately.

Pat's Notes: The Chinese characters on the label read "Tianjin winter vegetables." This pickled condiment originated in Tianjin, China, and is made of Chinese cabbage, salt, and often garlic. Sold in earthen crocks and plastic bags in Asian markets, it adds flavor to soups and noodle dishes.

Profile of a Grandma: ALVINA MANGRAI

Little girls often dream of marrying a prince. Alvina Mangrai actually did. Alvina's real-life Prince Charming was Sao Kawn Kiao Mangrai, a descendent of King Mangrai (1239–1311), the founder of the Lan Na Kingdom of Chiang Mai.

Born to a middle-class family in Burma (now Myanmar) in 1936 during British rule (Burma gained independence in 1948), Alvina studied commerce, accounting, and economics at Rangoon University in Rangoon (now Yangon). Upon graduation in 1961, she quickly found a job teaching English at the university. There she met Sao, a fellow tutor. A humble man, Sao did not reveal his royal links until just before they said "I do" in 1962.

While this story may seem like a fairy tale come true, things didn't quite go according to plan.

The same year Alvina and Sao married, the military junta took over the government. Industries were nationalized, foreign companies were expelled, and the Burmese language was reinstated as the official language. "Writing and speaking (Burmese) was difficult for me since I spoke English at home and at school," Alvina explains.

Things got even more complicated under the junta's rule. Several members of Sao's family were thrown in jail because they were considered the ruling class. Alvina and Sao made up their minds to leave the country before his turn came. In March 1972, the couple and their four children moved to the San Francisco Bay Area.

Life in the United States was very different. Alvina hadn't learned how to cook because in Burma they had servants, cooks, and butlers to see to their every need. But where there's a will, there's a way. "I learned because I was missing my food," says Alvina.

Surrounded by the sizeable Burmese community in the Bay Area, Alvina picked up recipes from friends and acquaintances. She also recalled the tricks and tips the cooks had used at home in Burma.

Despite her daily hour-long commute to work as a city and county retirement analyst, Alvina always made it home in time to cook for her husband and children. She cooked mostly Burmese cuisine, with steak or spaghetti thrown into the mix once in awhile.

Alvina takes pride in her curry dishes, especially her shrimp curry and BURMESE PORK CURRY (page 163). When her children were growing up, their friends would often pop by after school for a bite of curry. Alvina did have to make a few minor changes. In Burma, curries were drowned in oil to prevent the meat from going bad (most people didn't have refrigeration, and oil preserves food for several days). Alvina's children didn't like the oil-laden curries, so she made it a point to drain as much oil as possible before serving.

Burmese curries are not too spicy; instead, they are eaten with condiments that more than make up for it. Fresh hot green chilies are pounded into a paste and red chilies are fried with dried prawns and shrimp paste (*ngapi* in Burmese) "to give that hot flavor." The somewhat odorous shrimp paste and fermented anchovies were quite displeasing to Alvina's children. "Manda [her youngest daughter] used to say, 'It stinks!'" So Alvina did what any loving Burmese mom would do—she minimized the offensive smell by adding a hint of lemongrass.

Yes, Alvina's children were quite the critics. But it was her late husband (Sao passed away unexpectedly three days after Christmas in 1997) who helped her improve her cooking with his refined native palate. With his encouragement and by subscribing to her credo, "the more you cook the better you become," Alvina developed her own personal cooking style.

And when relatives visiting from Burma tasted her cooking and proclaimed it was delicious, Alvina knew she had arrived.

9

SWEETS, SIPS, AND SLURPS

In Asia, instead of rich—and often too-sweet—desserts, fresh fruit is eaten as a palate refresher to end a meal. Don't be mistaken, there's a never-ending array of Asian sweets out there, but they aren't usually eaten after dinner. Rather, an Asian sweet tends to be a tide-me-over between meals, or an after-nap snack.

Asian sweets run the gamut from cakes and cookies to more indigenous sweet soups and shaved ice beverages. Techniques used range from baking and deep-frying, to steaming and boiling. Colonization has ensured a Western influence, but these East-meets-West creations have all evolved with a twist. A flan is flecked with cardamom; a sponge cake is steamed on the stove. Diverse ingredients like coconut milk, salted eggs, feta cheese, and butter appear side by side. Above all, Asian sweets are lighter and less cloying than your typical American cheesecake.

Gathered from grandmothers, aunts, and mothers across all Asian communities, this chapter gives a cross section of the many sweets and beverages enjoyed as snacks or a hot tisane to soothe a sore throat. Some have been hybridized to suit the palate of foreign-born children and grandchildren, while others are still traditional. But they are all delicious and reflect Lola's or Popo's loving touch.

Crispy Fried Bananas with Coconut Flakes and Sesame Seeds

Cakes and Cookies

Cantonese-Style Steamed Cake (*Ma Lai Go*)

Coconut Bread Pudding (*Klappertaart*)

Filipino Sweet and Savory Flat Cake (*Bibingka*)

Japanese Sweet Bean Cookies (*Yaki Manju*)

Kimiye's Unfruitcake

Semolina Coconut Cake (*Sarnwin Makin*)

Stuffed Pancakes (*Dorayaki*)

Custards and Jellies

Cardamom-Studded Flan

Lychee Agar Agar

Pumpkin Custard (*Num Sang Khya L'peou*)

Drinks and Sweet Soups

Black Glutinous Rice Porridge (*Bubur Pulot Hitam*)

Ginger Tea (*Wedang Jahe*)

Spiced Milk Tea (*Chai*)

Sweet Melon and Tapioca Pearls in Coconut Milk

Three-Bean Coconut Milk Parfait (*Che Ba Mau*)

In a Class of Their Own

Brown Sugar Banana Spring Rolls (*Turon*)

Crispy Fried Bananas with Coconut Flakes and Sesame Seeds
(*Kleuy Tod*)

Festive Dumplings (*Tang Yuan*)

Lola's Sweet Rice Rolls (*Suman Sa Gata*)

✒ Cakes and Cookies ✒

Cantonese-Style Steamed Cake (*Ma Lai Go*)

This sponge cake is almost as light and springy as an angel food cake but uses whole eggs instead of just the whites. You'll sometimes find it at dim sum restaurants. Hong Kong–born Pearlie Wong ascribes to the principles of feng shui when making this cake. She always cooks it in a round pan because "round means smooth for everyone," while sharp edges emit negative energy. Try the cake with whipped cream—the way Pearlie's grandkids like it!

Time: 40 minutes (15 minutes active)
Makes: One 8-inch round cake (8 servings)

> 4 eggs
> 1 cup sugar
> 1 cup all-purpose flour

✒ Set up your steamer (see page xv for other steaming options). Fill the steamer pan half full of water and bring to a rolling boil over high heat. Reduce the heat to medium until you are ready to steam.

✒ In a medium bowl, beat the eggs and sugar with a hand mixer until the sugar completely dissolves, about 2 minutes. Test with your fingers to see if any granules are left. Add the flour and beat until pale and fluffy, 4 to 5 minutes. Pour the batter into an 8-inch round glass casserole or soufflé dish.

✒ Return the water in the steamer to a rolling boil. Set the batter in the steamer basket or rack and place on top of the steamer pan. Cover and steam over medium heat for 20 to 25 minutes, or until a knife inserted into the center comes out clean. The cake will also puff up and its surface will be covered with craters (like the moon).

✒ When done, turn off the heat and wait for the steam to subside before lifting the lid. Lift it away from you to prevent scalding yourself and to keep condensation from dripping onto the cake. Carefully remove the cake and cool completely before cutting into slices.

Grandma Says: Don't leave the batter to stand; the steamer must be ready when the batter is ready.

Coconut Bread Pudding (*Klappertaart*)

Indonesia was a Dutch colony for 300 years and much of the cuisine has Dutch influences including *klappertaart*, which means "coconut tart." Most versions are more tart-like and don't include bread. So this variation is a bit of a misnomer as it's more of a bread pudding. The recipe is from Brigitta Suwandana, a Woodinville, Washington engineer and mother of two young boys who learned to make it from her late mother who grew up during the colonial Dutch period. It was originally written in the 1940s when it was customary to list the amount of ingredients according to how much they cost. The original recipe called for about 7 cents worth of bread!

Time: 1 hour 20 minutes (20 minutes active)
Makes: 6 to 8 servings

> 6 cups white bread torn roughly into bite-sized pieces (about 10 slices)
>
> Two 17 ½-ounce cans (about 4⅓ cups) young coconut water with meat
>
> 4 eggs
>
> ½ cup sugar (reduce if the coconut water contains a lot of sugar)
>
> 1 teaspoon vanilla extract
>
> 1 cup shredded young coconut meat
>
> 1 teaspoon whole milk powder
>
> 2 tablespoons unsalted butter, melted
>
> ½ cup raisins (optional)

❀ Preheat the oven to 350 degrees F. Grease a 2-quart baking dish.

❀ In a large bowl, soak the bread in the coconut water for about 5 minutes. Strain the bread through a sieve just until it's not swimming in liquid. The coconut meat will be caught in the sieve with the bread. Discard the coconut water.

❀ In a large mixing bowl, beat the eggs with the sugar and vanilla. Fold in the soaked bread and coconut meat, shredded young coconut, milk, and melted butter.

❀ Pour the mixture into the prepared baking dish and sprinkle the raisins on top. Bake until the top is golden brown, 50 to 60 minutes.

Pat's Notes: If you can find some and don't mind the trouble, crack open about 4 young coconuts, pour out the fresh liquid and use it to soak the bread as above. (The amount of water in a coconut varies greatly, anywhere from 1 to 4 cups.). Then scrape out the meat with a spoon for about 1½ cups of coconut meat.

Instead of milk powder, use ¼ cup whole or 2 percent milk. The texture will be a little softer but that's okay.

Try to find canned coconut water without added sugar, or with as little as possible. Adjust the amount of sugar in the recipe accordingly.

Filipino Sweet and Savory Flat Cake (*Bibingka*)

Mention *bibingka* to any Filipino and their eyes will probably light up. This traditional treat, integral to Filipino food heritage, is often made with ground rice, water, sugar, and sometimes coconut milk, with some variations. Grandma Gloria Santos (see page 332) remembers vendors lining the streets selling bibingka and other tasty, freshly steamed treats after midnight mass on Christmas Eve in the Philippines. When Gloria moved to the United States, she couldn't find the fresh stone-ground rice flour she was used to, so she devised this version instead. For special occasions, she adds salted egg slivers, and together with a topping of savory feta cheese, there's a surprise in every bite of bibingka!

Time: 1 hour (15 minutes active)
Makes: One 8-inch round cake (8 servings)

> 1 banana leaf cut into an 8-inch circle
>
> ½ precooked salted duck egg, cut lengthwise into 6 slices (optional)
>
> 1 cup premade baking mix (such as Bisquick or Krusteaz)
>
> 1 cup milk
>
> 1 egg
>
> ¾ cup sugar, plus more for sprinkling
>
> 2 ounces feta or other soft white cheese, cut into thin 1- by 2-inch slices
>
> 1 tablespoon unsalted butter, melted

✿ Preheat the oven to 325 degrees F.

- Line the bottom of an 8-inch round pan with a round piece of parchment paper followed by the banana leaf. Arrange the salted egg slices like the petals of a flower in the center of the pan with their tips touching in the middle.

- In a medium mixing bowl, beat the baking mix, milk, egg, and sugar together until most of the lumps are smoothed out. Immediately pour the batter into the pan and bake for 20 minutes. Remove the cake and lay the cheese evenly on top of the half-baked cake. You want cheese in every bite. Continue baking for another 20 minutes, or until the top is a nice golden brown. Brush the top with melted butter and sprinkle with sugar.

Pat's Notes: Gloria usually doubles the recipe and makes two 8-inch cakes.

Salt-cured duck eggs have a briny taste and aroma to them; a little goes a long way. They are available in Asian markets.

Grandma Says: Don't start mixing the batter until the oven is preheated. Once the batter is ready, put it in the oven immediately.

Japanese Sweet Bean Cookies (*Yaki Manju*)

Katie Kiyonaga's Aunty Shiz makes these sweet bean paste–filled cookies every holiday, preparing a number of varieties with different fillings and in different shapes—each an individual work of art. The recipe is deceptively simple because it doesn't reflect the years and years of experience it takes to develop the know-how of when the dough is exactly the right texture, how to get the knack for rolling the *manju* so that there are no gaps between filling and dough, and how to get that sweet potato shape just so. But keep practicing and you'll eventually get it right.

Time: 1½ hours
Makes: 3 to 3½ dozen cookies

> ½ cup (1 stick) unsalted butter, softened
>
> 1 cup sugar
>
> 1 egg
>
> 2 egg whites
>
> 2 tablespoons light corn syrup
>
> 3 cups all-purpose flour, or as needed

1 teaspoon baking soda

      ⅛ teaspoon salt

      6 drops soy sauce for color (optional)

      2½ to 3 cups Lima Bean Paste (recipe follows)

Glaze:

      1 egg yolk

      3 tablespoons soy sauce

      ¼ teaspoon evaporated milk (Carnation is the preferred brand)

❀ Preheat the oven to 375 degrees F. Lightly grease 2 baking sheets.

❀ In a large bowl, beat the butter and sugar together until light and fluffy. Beat in the egg and then the egg whites. Beat until smooth and well combined. Add the corn syrup and mix well. Stir in 2 cups of flour, the baking soda, and salt. Knead a smooth dough with your hands. Sprinkle in the remaining cup of flour, a little at a time, and knead until the dough pulls easily away from the side of the bowl and no longer sticks to your fingers. Add the soy sauce and knead into the dough to color it evenly.

❀ Pinch off a small portion of dough and roll it into a ball the size of a gumball (about 1 inch in diameter). Roll a portion of the bean paste into a ball of the same size. Flatten the dough ball between your palms and cup it in one hand. Place the bean paste ball in the middle. Stretch the dough over the bean paste ball and pinch the ends together to cover the filling completely. Shape as desired into a ball, egg shape, or sweet potato shape with two pointy ends. Repeat with the remaining dough and bean paste.

❀ To make the glaze, in a small bowl, mix together the egg yolk, soy sauce, and evaporated milk.

❀ Arrange the cookies on the prepared baking sheets about 1½ inches apart. Brush thickly with the glaze. Bake for 10 to 15 minutes, or until light golden.

❀ Remove the cookies gently with a spatula and let them cool completely on a wire rack. Repeat with the next batch until all the cookies are baked.

Grandma Says: Glaze the cookies again when they come out of the oven to give them a glossy shine. Bake again for 45 seconds to 1 minute.

    Don't use a mixer for any part of this recipe—the dough will get too soft.

Japanese Sweet Bean Cookies

Lima Bean Paste (*Shiro An*)

If you're short on time, or patience, lima bean paste is available in Asian markets that are well-stocked with Japanese items. The beauty of making it at home is you can control the amount of sugar. Lima bean paste keeps in the refrigerator for up to 1 week and in the freezer indefinitely.

Time: 2½ hours plus soaking
Makes: 4 cups

> 1 pound (3 cups) dried lima beans
> Boiling water
> 2 cups sugar
> Pinch of salt

❀ Place the lima beans in a large heatproof bowl and cover with boiling water. Soak for at least 3 hours, or up to 12 hours. Drain.

❀ Using your fingers, gently slip the skins off—they will pop off easily—and discard. Remove any sprouts. The beans might split but that's okay.

❀ Transfer the beans to a medium saucepan and pour in enough water to cover them by an inch. Bring to a boil, skimming off any foam or scum that rises to the surface. Reduce the heat to medium and simmer for 1 to 1½ hours, or until the beans are fall-apart tender and crumble easily between your fingers. Replenish the water as it evaporates so that the beans are submerged at all times (you will probably add 1 to 2 cups), and stir often. If the beans scorch, they will turn an ugly brown and taste as bad as they look.

❀ When the beans are tender, mash them with a potato masher or large fork until the texture resembles chunky mashed potatoes. Working in batches, use a wooden spatula to press the bean mixture through a sieve. Add a little water if the mashed beans are having trouble going through. The sieved bean mixture should now resemble smooth mashed potatoes.

❀ Return the bean mixture to the same saucepan and add the sugar and salt. Cook over medium heat, stirring constantly, until the mixture starts to bubble. Reduce the heat to low. Simmer for 15 to 20 minutes, stirring constantly to prevent scorching. Run your wooden spatula through the paste and if the paste holds it shape and remains parted for a few seconds, it is ready. The paste will thicken as it cools anyway, so don't worry about cooking it down until it's really thick.

🌸 Remove from the heat and cool before using as a filling for confections.

Kimiye's Unfruitcake

This confection from Grandma Kimiye Hayashi (see page 44) isn't so much a cake as a plethora of candied fruit and nuts bound together by the thinnest of cake batters. When her children were growing up, they didn't like dates, so Kimiye added more nuts instead. And when the mood struck, she would use green and red candied cherries for a Christmas theme. Unlike the fruitcake often vilified as an evil holiday concoction, this is a wonderful treat anytime.

Time: 1 ¾ hours (30 minutes active)
Makes: Two 9-inch cakes

> 2 cups all-purpose flour
> 2 teaspoons baking powder
> ½ teaspoon salt
> 1 pound dried pineapple chunks
> 1 pound dried cherries
> 1¼ pounds pitted dried dates, coarsely chopped
> 4 eggs
> 1 cup sugar
> 2 pounds (about 8 cups) unsalted mixed raw nuts, coarsely
> chopped

🌸 Preheat the oven to 275 degrees F. Grease two 9-inch springform pans and line the bottoms and sides with parchment paper.

🌸 Sift the flour, baking powder, and salt into a large mixing bowl. Add the pineapple, cherries, and dates and mix with your hands, coating each piece of fruit with flour.

🌸 In a small bowl, whisk the eggs until the yolks and whites are well combined. Add the sugar and continue whisking until the mixture turns pale yellow, about 2 minutes. Pour the egg and sugar mixture over the fruit and mix well with your hands. Mix in the nuts.

🌸 Press the mixture firmly into the prepared pans. Bake for 1 to 1¼ hours, or until the tops are golden brown.

🌸 Let the cakes cool in the pans for 15 to 30 minutes before turning them out onto a wire rack. Remove the parchment paper and let cool completely. The cake can be eaten immediately.

Pat's Notes: I think this fruitcake is just like a PowerBar, chock full of energy-giving fruit and nuts and good for you, but much tastier!

Use whatever combination of fruit your family likes and add some rum or brandy if desired.

Grandma Says: I only used fruits my kids love—that's what makes the fruit cake taste good.

Semolina Coconut Cake (*Sarnwin Makin*)

We know semolina, or *shwegi* in Burmese, as coarsely ground durum wheat that is made into pasta. It looks like cornmeal but bakes up into a cake with a grainy texture quite unlike cakes baked with regular wheat flour. Grandma Alvina Mangrai (see page 292) likes her semolina cakes sweet sweet, so feel free to decrease the amount of sugar here. Add golden raisins to the batter or sprinkle with white poppy seeds instead of coconut.

Time: 1 hour (30 minutes active)
Makes: One 13- by 9-inch cake (10 to 12 servings)

> Two 13½-ounce cans coconut milk
> 1 can whole or 2 percent milk (use the coconut milk can to measure)
> 1½ cups sugar
> 5 eggs at room temperature, lightly beaten
> 2 cups semolina flour
> 1 teaspoon vanilla extract
> ¼ cup (½ stick) unsalted butter, melted

¼ cup sweetened shredded coconut

¼ cup slivered blanched almonds

❀ Preheat the oven to 400 degrees F. Grease a 13- x 9- x 2-inch baking pan.

❀ In a large saucepan, heat the coconut milk, milk, and sugar over medium-high heat. Just before it comes to a boil (bubbles will start gathering at the edge of the pan), reduce the heat to medium-low. Temper the eggs by drizzling 3 to 4 tablespoons of hot—not boiling—milk from the saucepan into the eggs and whisk together. Gradually add the tempered egg mixture to the milk mixture in the saucepan, whisking continuously to avoid lumps. By doing this, the eggs won't scramble and the milk won't curdle.

❀ Continue to cook until the custard starts to thicken and bubble, 3 to 4 minutes. Gradually add the semolina. Stir continuously with a wooden spoon, squishing lumps against the side of the pan. The batter will start to clump together and pull easily away from the side of the pan, resembling a thick oatmeal, after 8 to 10 minutes. Add the vanilla right at the end and mix well.

❀ Pour the batter into the prepared baking pan. Bake for 25 to 30 minutes, or until a toothpick inserted into the center comes out clean. Remove the cake from the oven and raise the heat to 450 degrees F, or switch to broiler mode. Pour melted butter over each cake and shower with the coconut and almonds. Bake for another 3 to 4 minutes, or until the tops are golden brown.

❀ Let the cake cool completely in the pan on a wire rack. Cut the cake vertically into 1½-inch-wide strips and then diagonally into diamonds. The cake will be sticky and chewy.

Pat's Notes: Use a light colored—preferably stainless steel—saucepan with thick, straight sides to prevent burning.

Stuffed Pancakes (*Dorayaki*)

A popular snack, *dorayaki* probably gets its name from the Japanese word *dora*, which means "gong." Indeed, it is a confection of two pancakes sandwiched together in the shape of a gong; inside you'll discover a delightfully sweet azuki bean filling.

Time: 35 minutes, plus making bean paste
Makes: 8 stuffed pancakes

> 1 cup all-purpose flour, sifted
>
> ½ cup sugar
>
> ½ teaspoon baking soda
>
> ½ teaspoon baking powder
>
> 2 eggs
>
> ⅓ cup water
>
> 2 teaspoons honey
>
> 1½ teaspoons sake
>
> ⅛ teaspoon Japanese soy sauce (optional)
>
> Vegetable oil for brushing
>
> 1 cup Azuki Bean Paste (recipe follows)

✤ Preheat the oven to 200 degrees F. Line a baking sheet with paper towels.

✤ In a large bowl, whisk together the flour, sugar, baking soda, and baking powder. In a separate bowl, beat the eggs well. Stir in the water, honey, sake, and soy sauce and mix well to combine. Pour the wet ingredients over the dry ingredients and stir just until the dry mixture is moistened.

✤ Preheat a griddle over medium heat. Sprinkle with a few drops of water; if they dance across the surface, the griddle is ready. Lightly brush with oil. Pour 2 tablespoons of batter onto the griddle to form a circle about 4 inches in diameter. Make as many pancakes as will fit comfortably on the griddle. Cook until the cakes start to bubble on the surface, 1½ minutes. Flip to brown the second sides for another minute or so.

✤ Place the cooked pancakes in a single layer on the lined baking sheet and keep warm in the oven. Don't stack warm pancakes or they'll become limp and soggy. Repeat with the remaining batter to make 16 pancakes total.

Place 2 tablespoons of bean paste in the center of a warm pancake. Place another warm pancake on top and pinch with your fingertips all around the edge to seal. Repeat to make 8 stuffed pancakes. Serve immediately.

Pat's Notes: Instead of azuki bean paste, try using cream cheese or crème de marron (chestnut cream) instead.

Azuki Bean Paste (*Tsubushi An*)

There are two types of azuki bean paste: *tsubushi an* (or *anko*) is more rustic with a coarser texture and some beans left whole; *koshi an* is pressed through a sieve to remove the hulls, resulting in a smooth, refined paste. Both are used as a filling for confections. Store-bought versions tend to be supersweet.

Time: 1½ hours plus soaking
Makes: 2 cups

> 1 cup azuki beans
> ½ to ¾ cup sugar
> ¼ teaspoon salt

Soak the azuki beans in a large bowl of water for 12 hours. Drain.

Place the beans in a large saucepan and pour in enough water to cover. Bring to a boil over high heat. Reduce the heat to medium and simmer for 10 minutes. Drain the water to remove foam and scum. Repeat three times, using a fresh batch of water each time. After the fourth round, cook the beans over medium heat until they are tender and squish easily between your fingers, 10 to 15 minutes. Replenish the water as it evaporates to keep the beans covered and stir occasionally to prevent scorching.

When the beans are tender, add the sugar and salt and cook over medium-low heat, stirring constantly to dissolve the sugar and prevent the beans from scorching. When the mixture starts to bubble, reduce the heat to low. Cook until the paste is shiny, 15 to 20 minutes. Mash the beans roughly as you cook, leaving some beans whole.

Remove from the heat and transfer the paste to a heatproof container to cool before using as a filling for confections. Keep leftover azuki bean paste refrigerated for 3 to 4 days and freeze for up to 3 months.

Pat's Notes: The traditional Japanese method of making azuki bean paste is to reboil the beans in fresh water several times to remove scum and foam as well as to get rid of the "beany" taste and smell for better flavor. You can also reboil the beans just once. Or, if you are a minimalist, I've found that boiling the beans in water continuously for 45 minutes to 1 hour works fine, just as long as you diligently skim off any scum or foam that rises to the surface and keep adding water to the saucepan as it evaporates so that the beans don't scorch.

You can also cover the soaked beans with water and pressure cook for 8 to 10 minutes at high pressure. If you don't have time to soak the beans, pressure cook them for 15 to 20 minutes.

The azuki bean paste can also be used in THREE-BEAN COCONUT MILK PARFAIT (page 323).

Cardamom-Studded Flan

One wouldn't necessarily think of flan as an Indian dessert, but this fusion recipe has a fascinating provenance. It comes from Mumtaz Rahemtulla, a woman who is of Indian origin (from the western-most state of Gujarat) and a fourth-generation Kenyan. Both she and her husband were British nationals born in Kenya. But when Kenya gained independence, they opted for Kenyan citizenship. In the 1970s, they migrated to Canada, where their children were born, before moving again to the United States. Mumtaz usually steams her flan on the stove (over medium heat for about 30 minutes), but I choose to bake it in a water bath in the oven. Either way, you'll be rewarded with a rich, creamy treat harboring a surprise in every bite—a heady shot of cardamom.

Time: 1¼ hours (30 minutes active) plus chilling
Makes: 8 to 10 servings

½ cup sugar

2 cups 2 percent milk

12-ounce can evaporated milk

1 cup sweetened condensed milk

5 eggs at room temperature

1 teaspoon vanilla extract

1 teaspoon freshly grated nutmeg (⅓ of a nutmeg nut)

Seeds from 6 green cardamom pods, ground with a mortar and pestle (¼ teaspoon), plus more for garnish

Pinch of saffron

✌ In a small, heavy saucepan, heat the sugar without stirring over medium heat until it starts to melt around the edge of the pan, 5 to 7 minutes. Continue to cook, swirling the pan occasionally or stirring with a wooden spoon to encourage the rest of the sugar to melt. The light golden syrup will shift in color from lighter to darker shades of amber. After about 15 minutes total, the sugar will have completely melted into a thick, deep amber syrup. Don't step away from the stove during this process, even for a minute. If at any time you need to stop the caramelizing process abruptly, pull the pan off the stove and carefully immerse the bottom in a sink filled with cool water.

❀ Quickly pour the caramel into a 10-inch pie plate and swirl to coat the bottom. (If the caramel hardens before you're done, microwave the plate for 30 to 45 seconds until the caramel is runny again.) Set aside to cool.

❀ Preheat the oven to 325 degrees F.

❀ In a large bowl, whisk the 2 percent milk, evaporated milk, condensed milk, eggs, vanilla, nutmeg, cardamom, and saffron into a smooth custard. Pour the custard into the caramel-coated plate through a sieve to smooth out any lumps.

❀ Place the pie plate in a baking pan. Fill the pan with boiling water until it reaches halfway up the side of the pie plate to create a water bath.

❀ Bake for 45 minutes to 1 hour, or until the flan crinkles at the edges and is speckled with light brown spots. Insert a toothpick into the center and it should come out clean.

❀ Cool the flan to room temperature before chilling in the refrigerator overnight to set completely.

❀ When ready to serve, carefully loosen the flan by running a thin-bladed knife along the edge of the pie plate. Invert a serving platter on top of the flan and hold both firmly as you flip them over right side up. Shake gently until the flan pops out from the pie plate onto the platter.

Lychee Agar Agar

In Southeast Asia, *agar agar* (see page 2) is used to make multiple layers of a colorful gelatin-like confection or used as a topping for cakes. You can add just about any fruit or flavoring for a tasty, practically fat-free dessert. Or use milk instead of water for a richer taste and mouthfeel. There are endless ways to make agar agar, but using lychees is one of the most popular.

Time: 15 minutes plus chilling
Makes: 8 servings

> 20-ounce can lychees, drained and syrup reserved (you should have 1¼ cups lychee fruit and 1½ cups syrup)
>
> 2½ cups water
>
> ¼-ounce packet (1 tablespoon) agar agar powder
>
> ½ cup sugar

✣ In a medium pot, bring the lychee syrup and water to a boil over medium heat. Just as it comes to a gentle boil, gradually add the agar agar powder, stirring continuously to avoid lumps. Once the powder completely dissolves, stir in the sugar and cook until the sugar dissolves. Turn off the heat and let cool for 5 minutes.

✣ Rinse a gelatin mold with hot water. Arrange the lychee fruit on the bottom.

✣ Pour the agar agar mixture into the mold and leave to cool completely.

✣ Refrigerate until set, at least 3 hours. Carefully loosen the agar agar from the side of the container by running a thin-bladed knife along the edge. Dip the container briefly into warm water (to about the depth of the agar agar) and shake gently to loosen. Invert a serving platter on top of the agar agar and hold both firmly as you flip them over right-side up. Shake gently until the agar agar pops out from the container onto the platter. Cut into slices before serving.

Variation: For chocolate agar agar, whisk 3 tablespoons cocoa powder into ½ cup hot water (so there are no lumps), and combine with 2 cups whole or 2 percent milk, 1½ cups water, and 1 cup sugar. Omit the lychees.

Pat's Note: You can also use gelatin in this recipe but use two ¼ ounce packets instead.

Pumpkin Custard (*Num Sang Khya L'peou*)

Hollowed-out pumpkins are filled with coconut custard in this delightful dessert that Phiroum Svy learned to make from her grandma in Cambodia. Traditionally, larger pumpkins are used, but Phiroum likes to make this recipe with miniature ornamental pumpkins like We-Be-Little, Jack Be Little, and Sweetie Pie available in the fall. When they're not in season, use kabocha squash; it's sturdy and doesn't fall apart easily when steamed. When the pumpkin is cut, each wedge shows off the creamy yellow custard contrasting beautifully with the orange pumpkin flesh.

Time: 1 hour (20 minutes active) plus chilling
Makes: 4 to 6 servings

> Four ¾-pound miniature pumpkins (3 to 4 inches across) or one
> 2½- to 3-pound kabocha squash (6 to 7 inches across)
>
> 1 cup coconut milk
>
> 1 cup sugar
>
> 4 eggs

❧ Wipe the pumpkins with a damp cloth to remove any dust or dirt.

❧ Insert the tip of a sharp paring knife diagonally into the top of a pumpkin until it pierces through the skin and flesh and into the cavity. Make short cuts in a zigzag or hexagonal pattern around the stem in a circle to make a hole large enough to insert a teaspoon (1½ to 2 inches in diameter). With a smaller pumpkin, it might be easier just to slice off the top straight across. Lift off the lid and scrape out the seeds and stringy bits with a teaspoon. Repeat with the remaining pumpkins.

❧ Set up your steamer (see page xv for other steaming options). Fill the steamer pan half full of water and bring to a rolling boil over high heat. Reduce the heat to medium until you are ready to steam.

❧ In a medium bowl, whisk the coconut milk and sugar together. Crack the eggs into the bowl and whisk until just incorporated. Place the pumpkins in the top tier of the steamer with the pumpkin lids on the side. Using a ladle, carefully pour equal amounts of custard into each pumpkin cavity to only about three-quarters full (since the custard will rise and pouf up). Try not to spill any custard over the sides of the pumpkins. If you do, wipe clean with a damp cloth.

❧ Return the water in the steamer to a rolling boil. Set the steamer basket or rack on top of the steamer pan. Cover and steam over medium heat for 30 to 45 minutes (1¼ to 1½ hours for kabocha squash). The custard is set when it doesn't jiggle when shaken and a knife inserted into the center comes out clean. Don't steam for much longer than 45 minutes or the miniature pumpkins will fall apart.

❧ When done, turn off the heat and wait for the steam to subside before lifting the lid. Lift it away from you to prevent scalding yourself and to keep condensation from dripping onto the pumpkins. Carefully remove the steamer from the heat and let the pumpkins cool to room temperature. They will be quite fragile, so don't remove them from the basket until cooled. Refrigerate for 10 to 12 hours to let the custard set. Don't worry if the custard falls a little.

❧ Cut each pumpkin into 4 to 6 wedges and serve cold or warm (heat it up in the microwave). Use a spoon to scoop up some pumpkin flesh together with the custard, making sure you get a little of each with every bite.

Pat's Notes: This recipe makes about 2½ cups of custard. Pour any excess into ramekins and steam for 10 to 15 minutes.

The miniature pumpkins can also be cooked in the microwave on medium heat for 4 to 5 minutes.

Black Glutinous Rice Porridge (*Bubur Pulot Hitam*)

Not really black in color, but rather a deep, dark shade of burgundy, black glutinous rice has a nutty flavor that shines in this luscious sweet porridge. It's a favorite in Southeast Asia and can be enjoyed at any time: at breakfast, as a snack between meals, or as a dessert. Coconut cream is the thick, pasty layer that separates and rises to the top of coconut milk. It adds a rich creamy texture to the porridge, but if you can't find it, the thinner milk will do just fine.

Time: 1½ hours (30 minutes active) plus soaking
Makes: 4 to 6 servings

> 1 cup black glutinous (sticky) rice
> 5 cups water, plus more as needed
> 2 pandan leaves, trimmed and tied into separate knots
>   (see page 17)
> 1 cup unsweetened coconut cream
> ¼ teaspoon salt
> 4 ounces Indonesian palm sugar, chopped (¼ cup) (see page 17),
>   or dark brown sugar
> 2 tablespoons granulated sugar

❧ Put the rice in a large bowl. Pour in enough water to cover by 2 inches. Soak for at least 2 hours, or up to 12 hours. Drain before cooking.

❧ In a large saucepan, bring the rice, 5 cups water, and pandan leaves to a rolling boil over high heat. Reduce the heat to medium and simmer for 1 to 1½ hours. Stir frequently to keep the rice from scorching. Add more water if the mixture looks like it's drying out. The rice is done when it is soft and swollen and most of the water is absorbed. I like the texture as thick as oatmeal, but you can add more water for a thinner porridge, or raise the heat to boil it down at the end for a thicker porridge.

❧ When the rice is almost done, heat the coconut cream with the salt in a small saucepan over medium heat. Just as coconut mixture comes to a boil, reduce the heat to very low and keep warm.

- Once the rice has attained the desired texture, stir in the palm sugar and granulated sugar and cook until they completely dissolve, 4 to 5 minutes. Fish out the pandan leaves and discard.

- Spoon the rice porridge into individual bowls and drizzle coconut cream over each serving. Serve warm.

Ginger Tea (*Wedang Jahe*)

Juliana Suparman says this spicy ginger drink is a panacea for all ailments. More accurately described as a tisane than a tea, it's wonderfully soothing on a chilly wintry day or when you have a cold—the thick liquid coats a sore throat and warms the chest. It's pure liquid sunshine; you'll want to keep a pot stovetop throughout the winter!

Time: 45 minutes (10 minutes active)
Makes: 10 to 12 servings

> 8 ounces fresh ginger (about 2 knobby hands, each the size of your palm)
> 3 quarts water
> About 1½ cups Pandan Syrup (recipe follows)

- Place the ginger on a cutting board and smash with the flat blade of a cleaver, the bottom of a large glass, or a meat tenderizer until the skin splits open to expose the inner flesh and the juices start flowing.

- In a medium pot, combine the ginger, water, and syrup to taste. Bring to boil over high heat. Reduce the heat to medium-low and simmer for at least 45 minutes. The liquid will develop a golden yellow hue. The longer it simmers, the stronger the brew.

- Fish out the ginger, ladle the tea into individual mugs, and serve hot.

Pat's Notes: Ginger tea keeps for 2 days on the stovetop. Refrigerate for up to 1 week. I like to re-steep the ginger to make a second batch of tea. Steep it for longer or enjoy this second batch as a weaker concoction.

Pandan Syrup

Merely a simple syrup steeped with pandan leaves, this is used to sweeten many Southeast Asian drinks and desserts. The ratio of sugar to water is two to one, so you can adjust amounts according to your needs, using one pandan leaf for every cup of sugar. In my opinion, pandan leaves have no substitute. You can find pandan essence or flavoring in tiny bottles, but I'd rather go without than to use this usually artificial-tasting flavor.

Time: 15 minutes
Makes: 2 cups

2 cups sugar

1 cup water

2 pandan leaves, trimmed and tied into separate knots
(see page 17)

🌿 In a medium saucepan, combine the sugar, water, and pandan leaves. Bring to a boil over medium-high heat. Reduce the heat to medium-low and stir continuously until the sugar dissolves, leaving behind a crystal-clear syrup, 8 to 10 minutes.

🌿 Let the syrup cool completely. Fish out the leaves and use the syrup in desserts or drinks like THREE-BEAN COCONUT MILK PARFAIT (page 323), or transfer to a bottle, cover, and refrigerate indefinitely.

Spiced Milk Tea (*Chai*)

The spices in a *chai* vary from region to region and household to household in South Asia. However, the most common ones are cardamom, cinnamon, ginger, cloves, and peppercorns. This rendition comes from the Siddiqui family who hail from Pakistan. Regardless of the spice combination, the milky beverage has a warming, soothing effect and instills a sense of well-being, much like the embrace of a grandmother.

Time: 20 minutes
Makes: 4 to 6 servings

> 4 cups water
>
> 6 cardamom pods, crushed
>
> 4 whole cloves
>
> 1 teaspoon fennel seeds
>
> ¼ cup looseleaf strong black tea (Assam or Darjeeling are ideal) placed in a tea ball; or 4 teabags (with strings removed)
>
> 2 teaspoons sugar
>
> 1-inch stick cinnamon
>
> 1 paper-thin slice fresh ginger
>
> Pinch of ground cumin
>
> 4 cups whole or 2 percent milk

✽ In a large saucepan, bring the water to boil over high heat.

✽ Place the cardamom pods, cloves, and fennel seeds in a large tea ball or wrap in a 6-inch-square piece of muslin and tie the bundle into a pouch with kitchen twine. Lower the spice-filled tea ball into the water and add the tea, sugar, cinnamon, ginger, and cumin. Simmer over medium heat for 10 minutes.

✽ Pour in the milk and return to a boil. Watch carefully so that the chai doesn't boil over. Remove the tea and spices and discard.

✽ Ladle the chai into individual mugs and serve. Cover the saucepan and keep any remaining chai warm on the stove over low heat until it's all gone, up to 1 hour.

Sweet Melon and Tapioca Pearls in Coconut Milk

Sweet Melon and Tapioca Pearls in Coconut Milk

This is an easy-to-make, refreshing dessert perfect for a hot summer day. In Southeast Asia, pearl sago made from the sago palm (a tree found in Southeast Asia, New Guinea, and some islands in Polynesia) is more commonly used instead of tapioca pearls. Sago and tapioca pearls look alike and have similar properties, but tapioca pearls are easier to find in the United States. Tapioca pearls are available both at Asian markets and at corner supermarkets where they cost about three times as much. Be sure to buy the teeny-tiny white ones, not the larger brown ones used for making bubble tea. If you don't have a melon baller, simply cut the melon flesh into ½-inch cubes.

Time: 30 minutes
Makes: 8 servings

> 6 cups water
>
> 1 cup (4 ounces) dried small tapioca pearls, rinsed
>
> 3 cups (half a 5-pound melon) honeydew melon or cantaloupe scooped into balls
>
> 13½-ounce can (1½ cups) coconut milk
>
> ½ cup Pandan Syrup (page 319)
>
> Pinch of salt
>
> 2 cups ice cubes

❀ In a large saucepan, bring the water to boil over high heat. Stir in the tapioca pearls and reduce the heat to medium. Cook until the pearls turn clear with the barest speck of white in the middle, 15 to 20 minutes. Pour the tapioca into a sieve and rinse with cold running water to wash away the extra starch produced during boiling and to separate the individual pearls. Drain.

❀ In a large punch bowl, combine the tapioca, melon, coconut milk, syrup, salt, and ice cubes. Stir to mix well. Ladle into individual bowls and serve immediately.

Three-Bean Coconut Milk Parfait (*Che Ba Mau*)

This Vietnamese drink and dessert in one is also called "rainbow on ice" for obvious reasons: different colored beans are layered in a tall glass with crushed ice, tapioca pearls, coconut milk, and sugar. It's almost too pretty to eat!

Time: 2 hours plus soaking
Makes: 4 servings

> ¾ cup yellow hulled mung beans, soaked for at least 3 hours
> ¼ cup sugar
> ½ cup dried small tapioca pearls, rinsed
> 1 cup Azuki Bean Paste (page 310)
> Crushed or shaved ice
> 1 cup coconut milk
> ¼ cup Pandan Syrup (page 319)

❧ In a large saucepan, bring 2 cups of water to a boil over medium heat. Add the hulled mung beans and sugar. Cook, stirring constantly, until the water is completely absorbed, about 20 minutes. Let cool. Mash the mung beans with a spatula or a large fork into a coarse paste.

❧ Meanwhile, in a medium saucepan, bring 3 cups water to boil over high heat. Stir in the tapioca pearls and reduce the heat to medium. Cook until the pearls turn clear with the barest speck of white in the middle, 15 to 20 minutes. Pour the tapioca into a sieve and rinse with cold running water to wash away the extra starch produced during boiling and to separate the individual pearls. Drain.

❧ To assemble the dessert, layer ¼ cup each of the cooked mung beans, azuki bean paste, and tapioca pearls in a tall glass. Top with ice. Pour in ¼ cup coconut milk followed by 1 tablespoon of syrup (or to taste) and let it seep down. Repeat to make 3 more servings. Serve with long-handled spoons and straws. Just stir and eat!

⚘ In a Class of Their Own ⚘

Brown Sugar Banana Spring Rolls (*Turon*)

This delicious dessert is a study in contrasting textures. When the spring roll is fried, the brown sugar melts and melds with the *lumpia* wrapper, forming a crispy crust that's coated in sticky syrup. Once you sink your teeth into it, you are rewarded with the creamy softness of banana. Heavenly! Use cooking bananas—saba or burro bananas—or plantains if you can find them, but regular Cavendish (the popular Chiquita brand) bananas taste great too. Try to find bananas that are 4 to 5 inches in length. If not, just cut them to size.

Time: 30 minutes plus standing
Makes: 12 rolls

½ cup dark brown sugar

6 ripe saba bananas (they should be soft to the touch and have a yellow peel mottled with black spots), sliced in half lengthwise

12 lumpia or large spring roll wrappers

3 cups (or as needed) vegetable oil for deep-frying

⚘ Spread the brown sugar evenly on a large flat plate wide enough to fit the bananas. Press each banana half in the brown sugar and roll liberally to coat every square inch.

⚘ To assemble the rolls, prepare a small bowl of water for sealing. Cover the stack of lumpia wrappers with a damp towel to keep them moist. Carefully separate one wrapper from the stack and lay it on a dry work surface. (If you are using a square spring roll wrapper, lay it like a diamond with one corner pointing toward you.)

⚘ Place a banana half just below the center line of the wrapper parallel to your body. Fold the bottom edge of the circle (or corner) over the banana and tuck it in snugly. Roll once then fold the left and right sides in and continue to roll tightly into a cylinder. Before you reach the end of the wrapper, dab a little water along the top edge to seal. Repeat with the remaining banana halves and wrappers.

- Let the banana spring rolls "sweat" for at least 1 hour. The brown sugar will melt and beads of syrup will seep out onto the outer skin forming a sticky layer when fried.

- Line a plate with paper towels. In a large wok, heavy skillet, or Dutch oven, heat the oil over high heat until it reaches 350 degrees F on a deep-fry thermometer (see page xiii for deep-frying tips). Reduce the heat to medium-high. Using tongs, gently lower spring rolls into the oil one by one. Fry in a batch of 5 or 6 rolls until both sides are evenly golden brown, 45 seconds to 1 minute. When done, remove the spring rolls with a slotted spoon, shaking off excess oil, and drain on paper towels.

- Bring the temperature back to 350 degrees F before frying the next batch. Repeat with the remaining spring rolls. Serve immediately.

Pat's Notes: Popular in Southeast Asia, saba bananas are squat and angular, and they are often available in Asian markets. Red bananas from Central America sold at larger supermarkets have a similar taste and texture.

Crispy Fried Bananas with Coconut Flakes and Sesame Seeds (*Kleuy Tod*)

For this treat, creamy bananas are coated in a crispy batter studded with coconut flakes and sesame seeds for more crunch and flavor. It is especially good with coconut or vanilla ice cream. Aim for a batter that's not too thick but not runny. Although this is a Thai recipe, other Southeast Asian cultures have similar snacks. You can also try this with sweet potato chunks for some variety.

Time: 30 minutes plus standing
Makes: 4 to 6 servings

> 1 cup rice flour
> ½ cup less 1 tablespoon (7 tablespoons total) water
> 3 tablespoons sweetened coconut flakes
> 2 tablespoons sugar
> 1 tablespoon toasted sesame seeds
> ¼ teaspoon salt

3 large, ripe bananas (preferably cooking bananas like saba;
see Pat's Notes on page 325)

3 cups (or as needed) vegetable oil for deep-frying

❧ In a medium mixing bowl, mix together the rice flour, water, coconut flakes, sugar, sesame seeds, and salt into a smooth, lump-free batter. Add more water if you prefer a thinner batter. Cover and let stand at room temperature for 30 minutes.

❧ Halve each banana lengthwise and then into 2- to 3-inch pieces.

❧ Line a plate with paper towels. In a large wok, heavy skillet, or Dutch oven, heat the oil over high heat until it reaches 350 degrees F on a deep-fry thermometer (see page xiii for deep-frying tips). Reduce the heat to medium. Dip the banana pieces in the batter a few at a time and coat well. Using a tablespoon, gently lower the banana pieces into the oil one by one, drizzling some batter over each piece. Fry the banana pieces in a batch of 3 to 4 until both sides are evenly golden brown and crispy, 2 to 3 minutes. Remove the banana pieces with a slotted spoon, shaking off any excess oil, and drain on paper towels.

❧ Use a slotted spoon or a wire mesh strainer to remove any debris from the oil and bring back to 350 degrees F before frying the next batch. Repeat with the remaining banana pieces. Serve warm.

Pat's Notes: In Thailand, limestone water (*nahm bpoon daeng*) instead of tap water is widely used in batters for fried foods and pastries to promote crispiness. Pink limestone, available from Southeast Asian markets, is mixed with water to produce this natural mineral water. I have found that tap water works just fine though.

Festive Dumplings (*Tang Yuan*)

You'll love the warm burst of brown sugar in your mouth when you bite into one of these sticky, chewy balls. There are two delicious ways to finish the dumplings: coat them in a coconut-peanut mixture or float them in ginger syrup. The dessert is eaten during festivals and celebrations, including weddings and Chinese New Year, and is symbolic of family unity and harmony.

Time: 45 minutes
Makes: 35 to 40 dumplings (6 to 8 servings)

> 2 cups glutinous rice flour, plus more for dusting
> ⅓ to ½ cup cold water
> ¼ cup brown sugar
> Coconut-Peanut Crumble or Ginger Syrup (recipes follow)

❀ Put the rice flour in a mixing bowl. Gradually add water and mix until the dough is stiff and no longer sticks to your fingers. Keep in mind that the dough won't be as pliable as dough made with all-purpose flour. Cover the dough with a damp cloth as you work as it dries out very quickly.

❀ Dust a large plate with rice flour and glove your hands with flour. Pinch off a walnut-size piece of dough (about ¾ inch across) and flatten into a circle about 2 inches in diameter. Cup the dough in your palm and place ⅛ teaspoon brown sugar in the center. Pinch the edges together to fully enclose the sugar and then roll into a 1-inch ball. Place the dumpling on the plate. Repeat with the remaining dough and sugar.

❀ Fill a large bowl with cold water.

❀ Bring a large pot two-thirds full of water to a rolling boil over high heat. Reduce the heat to medium-high. Drop dumplings one by one into the pot, stirring to separate them. Cook the dumplings in several batches, depending on how large your pot is. When the dumplings bob to the surface, about 3 minutes, cook them for another 2 minutes.

❀ Scoop the dumplings out with a slotted spoon and dunk in the cold water so they don't stick together. Scoop them out again, draining as much water as possible, and place on a lightly greased plate to dry. Cover with a damp cloth as you finish cooking the remaining dumplings.

❧ To serve with the coconut-peanut crumble, spread 1 cup nut mixture on a large plate. Roll the dumplings in the mixture and arrange on a serving platter. Repeat with the remaining dumplings, replenishing the nut mixture as needed. Serve immediately and eat within the hour.

❧ To serve with the ginger syrup, put 6 dumplings in each of 6 bowls and add ½ cup hot syrup. Serve immediately.

Coconut-Peanut Crumble

What a wonderful contrast of flavors and textures! A coarse coating of crushed peanuts dancing with coconut and sugar gives way to the smooth stickiness of the rice ball. The mixture can be kept in an airtight container for 2 to 3 days.

Time: 15 minutes
Makes: 2 cups

> 1½ cups unsweetened grated coconut
>
> ¼ cup sugar
>
> ½ cup ground roasted peanuts
>
> 3 tablespoons toasted sesame seeds

❧ In an 8-inch heavy skillet, toast the coconut over medium heat until golden brown, 1 to 1½ minutes. Reduce the heat to low. Tip in the sugar and stir continuously until the sugar melts, 1½ to 2 minutes. Transfer to a medium bowl, add the peanuts and sesame seeds, and mix well.

Pat's Notes: The coated dumplings are best eaten warm and don't keep well as they'll turn hard after a few hours.

To roast your own peanuts, buy raw shelled peanuts. Remove their skins by soaking them in boiling water for about 3 minutes, then drain and dry on a paper towel before slipping the skins off. Roast the peanuts in a 350 degree F oven for 15 to 20 minutes, or until golden and crunchy. Grind in a food processor until fine, 30 seconds to 1 minute.

If you can't find unsweetened grated coconut, omit the sugar in the recipe and use sweetened shredded coconut. Toast the coconut in a skillet for 1 to 2 minutes and let cool. Then grind in a food processor for 30 to 45 seconds. It won't be as fine as grated coconut but that's okay.

Ginger Syrup

The dumpling plus ginger syrup combination is a staple at *Dong Zhi*, a Chinese festival celebrating the winter solstice.

Time: 35 minutes (5 minutes active)
Makes: 3½ cups syrup (6 servings)

> 4 cups water
>
> 5 ounces (1½ slabs) Chinese brown sugar (see Pat's Notes), or ½ cup light brown sugar
>
> 1-inch piece fresh ginger, cut into coins
>
> 1-inch-square piece dried tangerine peel (optional)

In a large saucepan, bring the water, brown sugar, ginger, and tangerine peel to a boil over high heat and cook until the brown sugar has completely dissolved. Reduce the heat to medium and simmer until the syrup is aromatic, about 30 minutes. Keep the syrup warm on the stove until ready to serve. Fish out the ginger and tangerine peel and discard.

Variation: Replace the ginger with 2 pandan leaves tied into knots for a Southeast Asian flavor.

Pat's Notes: Chinese brown sugar comes in slabs that are sold in 1-pound packages of 5 slabs.

Lola's Sweet Rice Rolls (*Suman Sa Gata*)

Suman refers to any cake that's wrapped in banana or coconut leaves, whether made from rice, grain, or root. The ingredients are few, the method simple, and it is one of the oldest and most popular Filipino snacks. In this version from Grandma Gloria Santos (see page 332), banana leaves imbue a sweet, tropical fragrance and flavor to coconut-soaked glutinous rice. Wrapping suman is a skill in itself and takes years of practice, as Gloria can attest to—she's been making them for decades. Today, her family and friends always look forward to unwrapping these neatly bound bundles and biting into the moist mound of sweet goodness hiding within. Don't be discouraged if your technique takes a while to perfect.

Time: 2½ hours (1½ hours active)
Makes: 30 rolls (12 to 15 servings)

> 2 cups white glutinous rice
>
> 2½ cups coconut milk (one-and-a-half 13½-ounce cans)
>
> ¾ cup sugar
>
> 1 teaspoon salt
>
> 2 to 3 banana leaves, fresh or thawed

❀ Wash the rice 3 to 4 times until the water almost runs clear. Drain.

❀ In a large wok or heavy-bottomed pot, bring the rice, coconut milk, sugar, and salt to a boil over high heat. Reduce the heat to medium and simmer for about 30 minutes, stirring constantly especially during the last 15 minutes of cooking. You don't want the rice to stick to the bottom of the pan and burn. Reduce the heat if the rice mixture starts to scorch at any point. After about 20 minutes, the oil from the coconut milk will separate from the rice and coat the side of the wok in a thin film and the rice mixture will start to pull easily away from the side of the pan. The rice mixture is done when it is shiny, almost dry, and very sticky, like risotto. Let the rice cool in the wok.

❀ Wipe away any white residue on the banana leaves with a damp cloth. Remove the spine and cut the leaves into 4- by 7-inch rectangles with each longer edge going along the grain.

❀ Place a banana leaf rectangle on a dry work surface with the smooth, matte side up (the shiny side has faint ridges) and the long edge parallel to your body. Drop 1½ tablespoons of the rice mixture in the center of the leaf. Mold the rice into a mound about 1½ by 4 inches. Take the leaf edge closest to you and fold it over the rice. Using both sets of fingers, tuck the leaf edge under the rice and roll to enclose the filling completely. Roll the bundle as tightly as possible into a compact cylinder. With the seam-side down, smooth your fingers across the bundle to gently flatten it and fold both ends of the leaf snugly under. Place the packet seam-side down directly in a steamer basket or rack. Repeat until the rice mixture is finished, layering the packets neatly in a single layer and then one on top of the other if necessary.

❧ Set up a steamer (see page xv for other steaming options). Fill the steamer pan half full of water and bring to a rolling boil over high heat. Reduce the heat to medium until you are ready to steam.

❧ Return the water in the steamer to a rolling boil. Place the basket with the rice rolls on top of the pan. Cover and steam over medium-high heat for 45 minutes to 1 hour or until the rice is tender. Turn off the heat and wait for the steam to subside before lifting the lid. Lift it away from you to prevent scalding yourself and to keep condensation from dripping onto the rolls. Carefully remove the basket and set the rolls aside to cool. Eat warm or at room temperature.

Pat's Notes: Instead of folding the ends under, you can also tie the ends with kitchen twine or banana leaf threads torn along the grain to make a sweet wrapper.

The rice rolls keep at room temperature for 2 to 3 days. Do not refrigerate or they will harden.

Grandma Says: If the banana leaf tears while you're rolling the packet, place another layer on the inside to patch the hole.

Profile of a Grandma: GLORIA SANTOS

 "I'll be making *suman* for my grandchildren tomorrow and I'll save some ingredients to show you next week when you come," Gloria Santos's cheerful voice came through with a gentle lilt over the phone. *Suman sa gata* (see page 330) are Gloria's specialty, beloved by her grandchildren and her friends at her weekly prayer meetings.

Gloria was born in 1923 in the Manila suburb of Mandaluyong, but her youthful countenance and feisty spirit belie her several decades on this earth.

Growing up in the Philippines in the 1930s, Gloria never cooked—or did any housework for that matter. Like many middle class families of the time, maids did most of the work while the matriarch supervised. "I just looked at what my grandma was doing. I didn't know anything."

During World War II, things changed drastically. Gone was the hired help, and Gloria, age sixteen, was the one doing the cooking. With war-time rationing, food was scarce. She remembers congee (rice porridge) being on the menu for breakfast, lunch, *and* dinner. And it wasn't always made with rice. "Rice was very expensive and we used any substitute we could find. We even used corn and ground it."

This was also when, out of necessity, Gloria learned how to make her signature sweet. "I made suman and sold it to people because of the hardship," she explains.

Soon after the war, Gloria graduated from college with a degree in education and met and married her husband, Benjamin. She started teaching at twenty-two, and between her growing family and her budding career, she had no time to cook. "I would give the maid money to go marketing and when I came home from work, the food was ready."

In 1968, Gloria and her husband fled to the United States with their three teenaged children to escape the civil unrest in the Philippines.

Here, she had to juggle a job outside the home—first devising patient menus at the University of Washington Medical Center, and then teaching English as Second Language to newly arrived Asian students in public schools—and feeding her husband and three children. Fortunately, it wasn't too difficult to recall the cuisine she grew up with. "I asked my friends how to cook this and that, and I remembered from watching my grandma. I put the two together and I knew what to do." Gloria is now a pro at cooking traditional Filipino delights like *adobo* (see page 182 for a recipe), *kare kare* (a peanut-based stew), chicken *tinola*, and FILIPINO SWEET AND SAVORY FLAT CAKE (page 301).

To this day, Gloria still whips up family feasts at Thanksgiving and Christmas. She spends a week cooking and preparing enough food to feed close to 40 people. Although she acknowledges it's a lot of work, she's unwilling to leave this important task to anyone else. "If other people bring the food, they'll be late and we'll all be hungry!"

Gloria also loves to bake and has amassed an entire storage room of cake pans and decorating tools in her Kirkland, Washington, home. In fact, she's been busy baking since the day her first grandson, BJ, was born. "For 34 years, I made cakes for BJ. I made him Mickey Mouse and many others." She has baked a cake for every one of her five grandchildren's birthdays, and now she intends to continue that tradition with her great-granddaughter, Ligaya. She never strays from her favorite recipe: mocha chiffon cake with butter cream icing. And for good reason, she says: "If I change the recipe, people are not happy."

Sadly, not one of her children or grandchildren is interested in baking or learning to cook Filipino dishes. "They only want to eat!" Gloria declares with a sigh. The moment her grandchildren step into her house they chorus, "Lola, Lola [Grandma, Grandma], I want to eat!" and usually demand pork chops or hamburgers. In turn, she likes to tease them, often asking with a playful glint in her eye, "You want some tongue?" (Beef tongue is considered a Filipino delicacy.) They, of course, respond with a resounding "Eew!" and the looks on their faces are priceless.

BEYOND THIS COOKBOOK: RESOURCES

ONLINE REFERENCES

www.asiafood.org
A comprehensive Asian food glossary from the Asia Society.

www.foodsubs.com
The Cook's Thesaurus is a cooking encyclopedia that covers thousands of ingredients and kitchen tools. Entries include pictures, descriptions, synonyms, pronunciations, and suggested substitutions.

www.thaifoodandtravel.com
Cookbook author and cooking instructor Kasma Loha-unchit has a fabulous Web site pertaining to Thai food.

www.vietworldkitchen.com
Food writer and cooking instructor Andrea Nguyen has a fantastic site on Vietnamese cuisine, including a very detailed ingredient primer.

MARKETS

Asian markets may be operated by Chinese, Vietnamese, Thais, and Filipinos, but they often carry ingredients and products from the Asian smorgasbord. While they are often found in Chinatowns and communities with large Asian populations, I've also found decently stocked Asian markets in smaller towns.

Cities with substantial Asian communities will have large Asian markets like 99 Ranch Market (www.99ranch .com) and Uwajimaya (www.uwajimaya .com) on the West Coast, and Super 88 (www.super88market.com) in the East. I find that the best way to find a local Asian market is to ask at a Chinese or Thai restaurant. On the Web, www .thaifoodandtravel.com has a listing of Southeast Asian markets in the United States.

In addition, Latin, Middle Eastern, and Caribbean markets, along with health food stores, specialty markets, and the international sections of mainstream grocery store chains are likely to carry the basic ingredients you need.

Visit just about any farmers market in the United States and you're bound to find a Hmong, Lao, or Viet farmer selling just-picked Asian produce. In addition, non-Asian farmers are branching out and growing Asian vegetables and herbs like bok choy and Thai basil. Find local markets and farms at www.localharvest.org.

ONLINE AND MAIL-ORDER RESOURCES

If you don't have access to ingredients nearby, here are some mail-order and online resources worth trying out:

Gourmetsleuth.com

A great resource for items like tamarind paste, hard-to-find spices, and woks.
P.O. Box 508
Los Gatos, CA 95031
Ph: 408-354-8281
www.gourmetsleuth.com

Importfood.com

Online supermarket specializing in Thai (and Southeast Asian) ingredients and products.
P.O. Box 2054
Issaquah, WA 98027
Ph: 888-618-8424
www.importfood.com

Kalustyan's

A comprehensive source for international—especially South Asian—ingredients and gourmet foods.
123 Lexington Avenue
New York, NY 10016
Ph: 800-352-3451
www.kalustyans.com

Melissa's/World Variety Produce, Inc.

A great online source for Asian produce like fresh banana leaves, kaffir lime fruit and leaves, chiles, and Asian greens.
P.O. Box 21127
Los Angeles, CA 90021
Ph: 800-588-0151
www.melissas.com

Pacific Rim Gourmet

This online store carries ingredients and kitchenware from the Pacific Rim.
16417 Sherman Street
Volente, TX 78641
www.pacificrimgourmet.com

Temple of Thai

A great find for Thai and Vietnamese items like sauces, black glutinous rice, and dried shrimp.
14525 SW Millikan Way
RCM #10102
Beaverton, OR 97005
Ph: 877-811-8773
www.templeofthai.com

The Wok Shop

Find all your equipment from woks to cleavers to clay pots at this online store based in San Francisco's Chinatown.
718 Grant Avenue
San Francisco, CA 94108
Ph: 415-989-3797
www.wokshop.com

SELECTED BIBLIOGRAPHY

Besa, Amy, and Romy Dorotan
Memories of Philippine Kitchens
New York: Stewart, Tabori and Chang, 2006

Chiang, Cecilia, with Lisa Weiss
The Seventh Daughter: My Culinary Journey from Beijing to San Francisco
Berkeley: Ten Speed Press, 2007

The Chong Family
Just One More
Honolulu: The Chong Family, 1989

The Chong Family
Once Again at Popo's: Another Collection of Favorite Recipes from the Chong Family
Honolulu: The Chong Family, 2002

The Chong Family
Potluck at Popo's: A Collection of Favorite Recipes from All the Members of the Chong Family
Honolulu: The Chong Family, 1989

Cost, Bruce
Asian Ingredients: A Guide to the Foodstuffs of China, Japan, Korea, Thailand and Vietnam
New York: William Morrow Cookbooks, 2000

Deseran, Sara
Asian Vegetables: From Long Beans to Lemongrass, A Simple Guide to Asian Produce plus 50 Delicious Easy Recipes
San Francisco: Chronicle Books, 2001

Hepinstall, Hisoo Shin
Growing Up in a Korean Kitchen: A Cookbook
Berkeley: Ten Speed Press, 2001

Honpa Hongwanji Buddhist Temple, Honolulu, Hawaii
Favorite Island Cookery Book I, II, III
Honolulu: 1973, 1975, 1979

Jade Circle Chinese Women's Club, Seattle, Washington
Precious Chinese Recipes
Seattle: The Little Flower Letter Shop, 1963

Jaffrey, Madhur
Madhur Jaffrey Indian Cooking
New York: Barron's Educational Series, 1982

Japanese Baptist Church, Seattle, Washington
Potluck Favorites II
Seattle: Fundcraft Publishing Inc., 1978

Loha-unchit, Kasma
It Rains Fishes: Legends, Traditions, and the Joys of Thai Cooking
San Francisco: Pomegranate Communications, 1995

Nguyen, Andrea
Into the Vietnamese Kitchen: Treasured Foodways, Modern Flavors
Berkeley: Ten Speed Press, 2006

Nishikawa, Gayle (editor)
The Rice Cooker's Companion: Japanese American Food and Stories
San Francisco: Mango Press, 2000

Norman, Jill
Herbs & Spices: The Cook's Reference
New York: DK Publishing, 2002

Ortiz, Elisabeth Lambert, and Mitsuko Endo
The Complete Book of Japanese Cooking
New York: M. Evans and Company, 1976

Oseland, James
Cradle of Flavor: Home Cooking from the Spice Islands of Indonesia, Singapore and Malaysia
New York: W. W. Norton, 2006

Pham, Mai
Pleasures of the Vietnamese Table
New York: William Morrow Cookbooks, 2001

Routhier, Nicole
The Foods of Vietnam
New York: Stewart, Tabori and Chang, 1989

Saint Peter's Episcopal Churchwomen
Oriental Flavors Book I and II
Seattle: 1969, 1983

Solomon, Charmaine
Encyclopedia of Asian Food
Boston: Periplus Editions, 1996

Taik, Aung Aung
Under the Golden Pagoda: The Best of Burmese Cooking
San Francisco: Chronicle Books, 1993

Thaitawat, Nusara
The Cuisine of Cambodia
Bangkok: Nusara and Friends, 2000

Young, Grace
The Wisdom of the Chinese Kitchen: Classic Family Recipes for Celebration or Healing
New York: Simon and Schuster, 1999

CONVERSION TABLES

Standard Measurements

1 gallon = 4 quarts = 3.785 liters

1 quart = 4 cups = .946 liter

1 cup = 16 tablespoons =
    24 centiliters = 240 milliliters

1 tablespoon = 3 teaspoons =
    15 milliliters

1 teaspoon = 5 milliliters

1 fluid ounce = 30 milliliters

1 pound = 454 grams

Weight

1 ounce = 28.35 grams

1 pound = 454 grams

1 gram = 0.035 ounce

100 grams = 3.5 ounces

1 kilogram = 35 ounces =
    2.2 pounds

Volume

1 milliliter = ⅕ teaspoon =
    0.03 fluid ounce

1 teaspoon = 5 milliliters

1 tablespoon = 15 milliliters

1 fluid ounce = 30 milliliters

1 cup = 237 milliliters

1 quart = 946 milliliters

1 liter = 34 fluid ounces =
    4.2 cups = 2.1 pints =
    1.06 quarts = 0.26 gallon

1 gallon = 3.8 liters

Temperature

Conversion formulas:

$°C = (°F - 32) × 5 ÷ 9$

$°F = (°C × 9 ÷ 5) + 32$

200°F = 93°C

225°F = 107°C

250°F = 121°C

275°F = 135°C

300°F = 149°C

325°F = 163°C

350°F = 177°C

375°F = 191°C

400°F = 204°C

425°F = 218°C

450°F = 232°C

475°F = 246°C

500°F = 260°C

Length

1 inch = 2.5 centimeters

1 centimeter = 0.4 inch

INDEX

Photographs are indicated by italics.

A

aduki (adzuki) beans, 2

agar agar (*kanten*), 2

Agar Agar, Lychee, 314

ajowan seeds, *xx*, 1, 98

asafetida, *xx*, 1, 98

atta, 283

Azuki Bean Paste (*Tsubushi An*), 310–11

azuki beans, 2

B

banana ketchup, 267

banana leaves, 2

Banana Spring Rolls, Brown Sugar (*Turon*), 324–25

Bananas, Crispy Fried, with Coconut Flakes and Sesame Seeds (*Kluay Tod*), *294*, 325–26

bananas, saba (red bananas), 325

basil, Thai (*bai horopa*), 2, *14*

bean sprouts

    Bibimbap (Seasoned Vegetables over Rice), 259

    Shrimp and Mung Bean Sprout Omelets, 207–8

    Soybean Sprout Salad (*Kong Namul Sangchae*), 138

    Stir-Fried Mung Bean Sprouts with Tofu and Chives (*Pad Tao Kua Tao Ngae*), 125–26

beans

    aduki (adzuki) beans, 2

    Azuki Bean Paste (*Tsubushi An*), 310–11

    Black Bean–Steamed Fish, 202–3

    broad bean sauce or paste (brown or yellow bean sauce), *xx*, 1, 3

    Chinese salted black beans (*dow see*), *xx*, 1, 4–5

    Japanese Sweet Bean Cookies (*Yaki Manju*), 302–6, *304*

    Layered Vegetable Stew (*Pinakbet*), 111–12

    Lima Bean Paste (*Shiro An*), 305–6

    mung beans, whole and hulled, 11

    Nepalese Nine-Bean Soup (*Kawatee*), 96, 97–98

    Shrimp with Homemade Black Bean Sauce, 210–11

    See also tofu (*dofu, dauhu*)

beef

    Beef, Tomato, and Pepper Stir-Fry, 147–49, *148*

    Filipino Meatloaf (*Embutido*), 266–67

    Fragrant Grilled Beef Bundles (*Bo Nuong La Lot*), 58–60

    Gingered Oxtail Stew, 150–51

    Grilled Beef Kebabs, Filipino Style (*Inasal*), 151–52

    Hearty Beef and Vegetable Soup, 87–88

    Japanese Beef and Vegetable Hot Pot (*Sukiyaki*), 270, *271*–72

    Japanese-Style Beef Stew (*Nikujaga*), 273–74

    Japanese-Style Hamburgers (*Wafu Hamburgers*), 153–54

    Korean barbecue beef, 272

    Korean Barbecued Beef Short Ribs (*Kalbi*), 154–56, *155*

    Korean Beef Stock (*Komt'ang*), 43

    Steamed Meatballs with Tangerine Peel (*Niu Rou Yuan*), 158–59

    Stir-Fried Beef with Mustard Greens, 160

    Wide Rice Noodles Smothered in Rich Gravy (*Rad Nah*), 288–90

besan, 8

betel leaves, wild, 60

Bibimbap (Seasoned Vegetables over Rice), 259

bok choy, 2, 114

bonito flakes (*katsuo bushi*), 3

breads and crackers

    Coconut Bread Pudding (*Klappertaart*), 300–1

    Roti (Indian Flatbread), 191–92

    Seaweed and Sesame Rice Crackers (*Furikake Mix Arare*), 52–53

    Shrimp Toast (*Banh Mi Tom Chien*), 46, 55–56

    Stuffed Potato Flatbread (*Aloo Paratha*), 281–83

broccoli, Chinese

    Chinese Broccoli in Oyster Sauce, 107–8

    cutting techniques, 114

    identifying and preparing, 3

    Mixed Medley Stir-Fry, 112–14

    Sweet and Savory Rice Noodles (*Pad See Ew*), 284–86

    Wide Rice Noodles Smothered in Rich Gravy (*Rad Nah*), 288–90

brown sugar, Chinese, 329

C

cabbage

    Bibimbap (Seasoned Vegetables over Rice), 259

    Cabbage Kimchi, *102*, 131–32

    Chinese cabbage (napa or Peking cabbage), 3, 291

    Chinese white cabbage (bok choy), 2, 114

    Eggy Stir-Fried Cabbage, 110

    Filipino Fried Noodles (*Pancit*), 233–35, *234*

    From-Scratch Pot Stickers (*Guotieh*), 236–39

    Hearty Beef and Vegetable Soup, 87–88

cakes

    Cantonese-Style Steamed Cake (*Ma Lai Go*), 299

    Coconut Bread Pudding (*Klappertaart*), 300–1

    Filipino Sweet and Savory Cake (*Bibingka*), 301–2

    Kimiye's Unfruitcake, 306–7

    Semolina Coconut Cake (*Samwin Makin*), 307–8

    Stuffed Pancakes (*Dorayaki*), 309–11

calamansi (calamondin), 9

cane vinegar, 183

cardamom (elaichi), 3

Cardamom-Studded Flan, 312–13

Casserole, Rice Cooker, 275–76

Casserole, Spicy Lamb (Gosht Ka Saalan), 157–58

chana dal (Bengal gram dal), 129

chapati flour (atta), 283

chicharron (bagnet), 112

chicken. See poultry

chickpea flour, 8

chilies, 3–4, 14

China grass (kanten), 2

Chinese keys (krachai, kachai), 79

chives, Chinese (koo chye), 5

Choi, Sang Jung

    Korean Barbecued Beef Short Ribs (Kalbi), 154–56, 155

    profile, 252–53

    Seaweed-Wrapped Rice and Vegetable Rolls (Kimbap), 276–78

    Stir-Fried Glass Noodles (Japchae), 246–47

Chou, Ellen Shyu

    From-Scratch Pot Stickers (Guotieh), 236–39

    Hot and Sour Soup (Suan La Tang), 80–81

    profile, 72–73

Choulaphan, Keo

    Lao Sausage (Sai Oua), 168–69

    profile, 176–77

cilantro, 5

clarified butter, 8–9

Clay Pot "Black Pork" (Hong Bak), 263–64

clay pot cooking techniques, xix

Clay Pot, Japanese Rice Cooked in a (Gohan), 34

Clay Pot Lemongrass-Steamed Fish (Pla Nueng Morh Din), 204, 205–6

coconut

    Caramelized Pork Belly and Eggs Braised in Coconut Water (Thit Kho), 227–29

Chicken Coconut Noodle Soup (Ohn No Khauk Swe), 254, 261–62

Chicken Coconut Soup (Tom Ka Kai), 84

Coconut Bread Pudding (Klappertaart), 300–1

coconut milk, 5

coconut water (coconut juice), 6

Festive Dumplings (Tang Yuan), 327–29

Semolina Coconut Cake (Sarnwin Makin), 307–8

Sweet Melon and Tapioca Pearls in Coconut Milk, 321, 322

Three-Bean Coconut Milk Parfait (Che Ba Mau), 323

Yellow Coconut Rice (Nasi Kuning), 249–51, 250

conversion tables, 339

Cookies, Japanese Sweet Bean (Yaki Manju), 302–6, 304

cooking intuitively, xi–xii

cooking techniques and equipment, xiii–xix, 238, 274

coriander, Mexican (culantro), 6, 14

coriander, Vietnamese (rau ram), 6

coriander leaves (cilantro), 5

coriander seeds (dhania), 6

Crab Noodle Soup, Vietnamese (Bun Rieu Cua), 286–88

Crackers, Seaweed and Sesame Rice (Furikake Mix Arare), 52–53

culantro, 6, 14

curry

    Burmese Pork Curry (Whethar Sebyan), 163–64

    Chicken and Eggs in a Golden Curry (Kuku Paka), 184–85

    Chicken Coconut Noodle Soup (Ohn No Khauk Swe), 254, 261–62

    Colonial Curried Chicken Soup (Mulligatawny Soup), 85–86

    curry paste, 6–7

    curry powder, 7, 199

    Eggplant Curry (Bagaara Baingan), 108–9

    Rick's Chicken Curry, 188–90

    Shrimp and Pineapple Red Curry (Kaeng Kue Sapparod), 209

    Vietnamese Chicken Curry (Ca Ri Ga), 198–99

    Yellow Split Pea Curry (Matar Dal), 130

Custard, Pumpkin (Num Sang Khya L'peou), 315–16

D

Dashi (Japanese Kelp and Fish Stock), 40–41

dates, red dried (Chinese dates), 7

deep-frying techniques, xiii–xv

Dressing, Soy-Sesame, 243

drinks

    Ginger Tea (Wedang Jahe), 318–19

    Spiced Milk Tea (Chai), 320

    Sweet Melon and Tapioca Pearls in Coconut Milk, 321, 322

    Three-Bean Coconut Milk Parfait (Che Ba Mau), 323

Duck, Teochew Braised (Lo Ack), 195–96, 197

dumpling skins, 7, 15

dumplings

    Festive Dumplings (Tang Yuan), 327–29

    From-Scratch Pot Stickers (Guotieh), 236–39

    Grandma Miyoshi's Dumpling Soup (Dango Jiru), 268–69

    Shanghai Soup Dumplings (Xiao Long Bao), 64–67

    Shiu Mai (Pork and Shrimp Cups), 68–69

    See also spring rolls

E

Eggplant Curry (Bagaara Baingan), 108–9

Eggplant with Sweet Miso Sauce (Nasu no Misoni), 125

eggs

    Caramelized Pork Belly and Eggs Braised in Coconut Water (Thit Kho), 227–29

    Chicken and Egg over Rice (Oyako Donburi), 260–61

Chicken and Eggs in a Golden Curry (*Kuku Paka*), 184–85

Eggy Stir-Fried Cabbage, 110

Marbled Tea Eggs, 51–52

salt-cured duck eggs, 302

Shrimp and Mung Bean Sprout Omelets, 207–8

Soft Noodles Tossed with Duck Eggs and Oyster Mushrooms, 278–79

Stuffed Egg-Crepe Rolls (*Yu Gun*), 211–13

Thai Stuffed Omelet (*Kai Yad Sai*), 70–71

Tofu Omelet with Sweet Peanut Sauce (*Tahu Telur*), 126–27

Wok-Tossed Rice Vermicelli with Eggs and Chives, 290–91

equipment and techniques, xiii–xix, 238, 274

F

fish

Black Bean–Steamed Fish, 202–3

Clay Pot Lemongrass-Steamed Fish (*Pla Nueng Morh Din*), 204, 205–6

Dashi (Japanese Kelp and Fish Stock), 40–41

Miso-Smothered Salmon, 206–7

Somen Salad, 220, 242–43

Stuffed Egg-Crepe Rolls (*Yu Gun*), 211–13

Sweet and Sour Fish Soup (*Canh Chua Ca*), 82–83

fish sauce (*nam pla, nuoc mam, patis*), 7–8, 28, 29

five-spice powder, 8

Flan, Cardamom-Studded, 312–13

flatbreads. *See* breads

flour, chapati (*atta*), 283

flour, garbanzo bean, 8

flour, rice (rice powder), 19

flour, tapioca, 25

G

galangal (galanga, *laos*), 8, 14

garam masala, 8

garbanzo bean flour, 8

ghee, 8–9

ginger, fresh, 9, 14

Ginger Syrup, 329

Ginger Tea (*Wedang Jahe*), 318–19

Gingered Oxtail Stew, 150–51

Ginger-Soy Dipping Sauce, 239

gram flour, 8

Green Onion Oil, 60

Gupta, Niloufer

profile, 140–41

Spiced Chayote and Peas (*Safed Kaddu aur Matar ki Sabzi*), 115–17, 116

Spiced Red Lentil Stew (*Palida*), 128–29

Spicy Lamb Casserole (*Gosht Ka Saalan*), 157–58

H

Hamburgers, Japanese-Style (*Wafu Hamburgers*), 153–54

Hayashi, Kimiye

Japanese Beef and Vegetable Hot Pot (*Sukiyaki*), 270, 271–72

Kimiye's Unfruitcake, 306–7

profile, 44–45

Hot and Sour Soup (*Suan La Tang*), 80–81

I, J, K

Indian bay leaves (salam leaves, *daun salam*), 14, 20

jujubes, 7

kaffir lime (*makrut*), 9, 14

kalamansi, 9

kale, Chinese. *See* broccoli, Chinese

kieffer lime (kaffir lime, *makrut*), 9, 14

kimchi. *See* pickles

Kushino, D aisy

Mochiko Fried Chicken, 187–88

profile, 200–1

Somen Salad, 220, 242–43

L

laksa leaves (*rau ram*), 6

Lamb Casserole, Spicy (*Gosht Ka Saalan*), 157–58

legumes

Spiced Red Lentil Stew (*Palida*), 128–29

Yellow Split Pea Curry (*Matar Dal*), 130

See also entries under bean

lemongrass (*serai, sereh*)

Caramelized Chicken with Lemongrass and Chilies (*Ga Xao Sa Ot Cay*), 179–81, 180

Clay Pot Lemongrass-Steamed Fish (*Pla Nueng Morh Din*), 204, 205–6

identifying and preparing, 9–10, 14

Lentil Stew, Spiced Red (*Palida*), 128–29

lily buds, dried, 81

Lima Bean Paste (*Shiro An*), 305–6

limestone water (pink limestone, *nahm bpoon daeng*), 326

Lumpia (Filipino Eggrolls), 61–63

Lychee Agar Agar, 314

M

Mangrai, Alvina

Burmese Pork Curry (*Whethar Sebyan*), 163–64

Chicken Coconut Noodle Soup (*Ohn No Khauk Swe*), 254, 261–62

profile, 292–93

Semolina Coconut Cake (*Sarnwin Makin*), 307–8

Marinade, Aged Chinese (*Lao Shui*) with Pork, 161–62

markets, Asian, 335

Meatballs, Crispy Fried (*Bakso Goreng*), 166–67

Meatballs, Steamed, with Tangerine Peel (*Niu Rou Yuan*), 158–59

Meatloaf, Filipino (*Embutido*), 266–67

menu planning, xi

mirin, 10

miso, 10

Miso Sauce, Sweet, Pan-Fried Tofu Simmered in, (*Tofu No Misoni*), 124–25

Miso Soup, Fat Noodles in (*Miso Udon*), 264–65

Miso Soup, Red and White (*Awase Miso Shiru*), 90

Miso-Smothered Salmon, 206–7

mizuna, 11, *14*

mortars and pestles, xix

mung beans, whole and hulled, 11

mushrooms

Brandied Chicken and Mushrooms in Oyster Sauce, 178–79

Chicken and Egg over Rice (*Oyako Donburi*), 260–61

cutting techniques, 114

dried black mushrooms (Chinese black mushrooms), *xx*, 1, 11

Fat Noodles in Miso Soup (*Miso Udon*), 264–65

Herb-Scented Chicken Soup (*S'ngao Chruok Moan*), 94–95

Hot and Sour Soup (*Suan La Tang*), 80–81

Japanese Beef and Vegetable Hot Pot (*Sukiyaki*), *270*, 271–72

Long-Life Noodles, 241–42

Rice Cooker Casserole, 275–76

Shiu Mai (Pork and Shrimp Cups), 68–69

Soft Noodles Tossed with Duck Eggs and Oyster Mushrooms, 278–79

Sticky Rice Stuffing (*Naw Mai Fun*), 244–45

Stir-Fried Glass Noodles (*Japchae*), 246–47

Stuffed Egg-Crepe Rolls (*Yu Gun*), 211–13

wood ear mushrooms, *xx*, 1, 12

mustard greens, Asian (mustard cabbage, *gai choy*)

Grandma Miyoshi's Dumpling Soup (*Dango Jiru*), 268–69

Stir-Fried Beef with Mustard Greens, 160

types of, 12, *14*

N

noodles

Chicken Coconut Noodle Soup (*Ohn No Khauk Swe*), *254*, 261–62

Fat Noodles in Miso Soup (*Miso Udon*), 264–65

Filipino Fried Noodles (*Pancit*), 233–35, *234*

Grandma Miyoshi's Dumpling Soup (*Dango Jiru*), 268–69

Japanese Beef and Vegetable Hot Pot (*Sukiyaki*), *270*, 271–72

Long-Life Noodles, 241–42

Soft Noodles Tossed with Duck Eggs and Oyster Mushrooms, 278–79

Somen Salad, 220, 242–43

Stir-Fried Glass Noodles (*Japchae*), 246–47

Sweet and Savory Rice Noodles (*Pad See Ew*), 284–86

types of, 12–13, *15*, 16

Vietnamese Crab Noodle Soup (*Bun Rieu Cua*), 286–88

Wide Rice Noodles Smothered in Rich Gravy (*Rad Nah*), 288–90

Wok-Tossed Rice Vermicelli with Eggs and Chives, 290–91

nori furikake, 53

O

Oil, Green Onion, 60

oils, tempering (*channa* or *tarka*), 98

oils, vegetable, xiii, 16

otoshibuta (drop-lids), 274

Oxtail Stew, Gingered, 150–51

Oyster Salad, Spicy Korean (*Kul Kimchi*), 139

oyster sauce, 16, *28*, 29

Oyster Sauce, Brandied Chicken and Mushrooms in, 178–79

P

pak choy (bok choy), 2, 114

palm sugar, *xx*, 1, 17

pandan leaves (pandanus leaves), *14*, 17

Pandan Syrup, 319

panko, 154

parsley, Chinese, 5

pea shoots, *14*, 121

Pea Shoots, Wok-Fried, *120*, 121

peppercorns, Sichuan, 17

pickles

Bibimbap (Seasoned Vegetables over Rice), 259

Cabbage Kimchi, *102*, 131–32

Chinese Pickles (*Liang Ban Huang Gua*), 133, 135

Eggplant Curry (*Bagaara Baingan*), 108–9

Indian Cucumber and Tomato Relish (*Kachumber*), 137

Pickled Green Chilies, 290

Spicy Korean Oyster Salad (*Kul Kimchi*), 139

Tianjin preserved vegetables, 291

pork

1-2-3-4-5 Sticky Spareribs (*Tang Chu Pai Gu*), 170

Aged Chinese Marinade (*Lao Shui*) with Pork, 161–62

Burmese Pork Curry (*Whethar Sebyan*), 163–64

Caramelized Pork Belly and Eggs Braised in Coconut Water (*Thit Kho*), 227–29

Chinese Barbecued Pork (*Char Siu*), *142*, 165–66

Clay Pot "Black Pork" (*Hong Bak*), 263–64

Crispy Fried Meatballs (*Bakso Goreng*), 166–67

Easy Lechón, 232–33

Filipino Meatloaf (*Embutido*), 266–67

From-Scratch Pot Stickers (*Guotieh*), 236–39

Grandma Miyoshi's Dumpling Soup (*Dango Jiru*), 268–69

Healing Pork and Shrimp Rice Soup (*Kao Tom Moo*), 92–93

Hot and Sour Soup (*Suan La Tang*), 80–81

Layered Vegetable Stew (*Pinakbet*), 111–12

Mixed Medley Stir-Fry, 112–14

pork belly, deep-fried (*chicharron*), 112

Roasted Pork Tenderloin with Mustard Sauce (*Kao Zhu Li Ji*), 171

Shanghai Soup Dumplings (*Xiao Long Bao*), 64–67

Shiu Mai (Pork and Shrimp Cups), 68–69

Somen Salad, 220, 242–43

Stir-Fried Mung Bean Sprouts with Tofu and Chives (*Pad Tao Kua Tao Ngae*), 125–26

Stuffed Egg-Crepe Rolls (*Yu Gun*), 211–13

Sweet and Savory Rice Noodles (*Pad See Ew*), 284–86

Sweet and Sour Pork (*Gu Lao Rou*), 172–73

Thai Basil Pork (*Pad Gkaprow Mu*), 174, 175

Thai Stuffed Omelet (*Kai Yad Sai*), 70–71

Vietnamese Crab Noodle Soup (*Bun Rieu Cua*), 286–88

Watercress and Pork Rib Soup, 99

See also sausage

Pot Stickers, From-Scratch (*Guotieh*), 236–39

Potato Flatbread, Stuffed (*Aloo Paratha*), 281–83

poultry

Amma's Rice (Biryani), 225–27

Brandied Chicken and Mushrooms in Oyster Sauce, 178–79

Caramelized Chicken with Lemongrass and Chilies (*Ga Xao Sa Ot Cay*), 179–81, 180

Chicken Adobo (Vinegar-Braised Chicken), 182–83

Chicken and Egg over Rice (*Oyako Donburi*), 260–61

Chicken and Eggs in a Golden Curry (*Kuku Paka*), 184–85

Chicken Coconut Noodle Soup (*Ohn No Khauk Swe*), 254, 261–62

Chicken Coconut Soup (*Tom Ka Kai*), 84

Chicken Delight, 229–30

Chinese Chicken Salad, 230–31

Colonial Curried Chicken Soup (Mulligatawny Soup), 85–86

Fat Noodles in Miso Soup (*Miso Udon*), 264–65

Filipino Fried Noodles (*Pancit*), 233–35, 234

Filipino Meatloaf (*Embutido*), 266–67

Herb-Scented Chicken Soup (*S'ngao Chruok Moan*), 94–95

Homemade Chicken Stock, 42–43

Honeyed Chicken Wings, 240

Lao Chicken and Herb Salad (*Larb Gai*), 185–86

Leftover Thanksgiving Turkey–Rice Porridge (*Jook*), 274–75

Lumpia (Filipino Eggrolls), 61–63

Mochiko Fried Chicken, 187–88

Rick's Chicken Curry, 188–90

Sesame Seed Chicken Wings, 53–54

Sichuan Chili Chicken (*Gung Bao Ji Ding*), 193–94

Special Indonesian Fried Rice (*Nasi Goreng Istimewa*), 279–81

Teochew Braised Duck (*Lo Ack*), 195–96, 197

Vietnamese Chicken Curry (*Ca Ri Ga*), 198–99

White Chicken with Ginger-Garlic Sauce (*Bai Chit Gai*), 248–49

Pumpkin Custard (*Num Sang Khya L'peou*), 315–16

R

Raita, 227

red pepper paste, Korean (*koch'ujang, gochu-jang*), 17

red pepper powder and flakes, Korean (*koch'u karu, gochu-garu*), 18

resources, 335–36

rice

Amma's Rice (Biryani), 225–27

Bibimbap (Seasoned Vegetables over Rice), 259

Black Glutinous Rice Porridge (*Bubur Pulot Hitam*), 317–18

Chicken and Egg over Rice (*Oyako Donburi*), 260–61

Garlic Fried Rice (*Sinangag*), 33

ground roasted rice, 186

Healing Pork and Shrimp Rice Soup (*Kao Tom Moo*), 92–93

Japanese Rice Cooked in a Clay Pot (*Gohan*), 34

Leftover Thanksgiving Turkey–Rice Porridge (*Jook*), 274–75

Lola's Sweet Rice Rolls (*Suman Sa Gata*), 330–31

Purple-Dyed Glutinous Rice, 35

Rice Cooker Casserole, 275–76

Seaweed-Wrapped Rice and Vegetable Rolls (*Kimbap*), 276–78

Special Indonesian Fried Rice (*Nasi Goreng Istimewa*), 279–81

Sticky Rice Stuffing (*Naw Mai Fun*), 244–45

Stove-Top Jasmine Rice, 36

types of, 15, 18–19

washing, 37

White Glutinous Rice, 38–39

Yellow Coconut Rice (*Nasi Kuning*), 249–51, 250

Rice Crackers, Seaweed and Sesame (*Furikake Mix Arare*), 52–53

rice flour (rice powder), 19

rice wine, Shaoxing (Shao-hsing rice wine), 22

rice wine, sweet, 10

rock sugar, yellow (rock candy), 19

rolling pins, Chinese, 238

Roti (Indian Flatbread), 191–92

S

sake, 20

salads

Chinese Chicken Salad, 230–31

Green and Golden Zucchini Thread Salad (*Hobak Namul*), 134, 135–36

Lao Chicken and Herb Salad (*Larb Gai*), 185–86

Somen Salad, 220, 242–43

Soybean Sprout Salad (*Kong Namul Sangchae*), 138

Spicy Korean Oyster Salad (*Kul Kimchi*), 139

salam leaves (*daun salam*), *14*, 20

sambal, 4, *28*, 29

Santos, Gloria

    Filipino Sweet and Savory Cake (*Bibingka*), 301–2

    Lola's Sweet Rice Rolls (*Suman Sa Gata*), 330–31

    profile, 332–33

sauces and dips

    Black Vinegar Dipping Sauce, 67

    Chili Dipping Sauce, 152

    Chili-Lime Dipping Sauce, 196

    Chinese Broccoli in Oyster Sauce, 107–8

    Dipping Sauce (*Tik Chror Louk*), 95

    Green Onion Oil, 60

    Homemade Black Bean Sauce, 210–11

    Indian Cucumber and Tomato Relish (*Kachumber*), 137

    Mustard Sauce, 171

    Raita, 227

    Soy-Ginger Dipping Sauce, 239

    Soy-Sesame Dressing, 243

    Sukiyaki Sauce, 271

    Sweet and Sour Sauce, 63

    Yogurt Dip, 283

sausage

    Chinese sausage (*lap cheong, lop cheung*), 20

    Lao Sausage (*Sai Oua*), 168–69

    Rice Cooker Casserole, 275–76

    Sticky Rice Stuffing (*Naw Mai Fun*), 244–45

saw-tooth herb (saw leaves, culantro), 6, *14*

screwpine leaves (pandan leaves), *14*, 17

seafood

    Spicy Korean Oyster Salad (*Kul Kimchi*), 139

    Teriyaki Squid, 216–17

Vietnamese Crab Noodle Soup (*Bun Rieu Cua*), 286–88

See also fish; shrimp

seaweed, types of, 20–21

Seaweed and Sesame Rice Crackers (*Furikake Mix Arare*), 52–53

Seaweed-Wrapped Rice and Vegetable Rolls (*Kimbap*), 276–78

See, Merla

    Hearty Beef and Vegetable Soup, 87–88

    profile, 100–1

sesame oil, 21

sesame seeds, toasting, 21

shallots, Asian, 21

shallots, fried, 22

Shaoxing rice wine (*Shao-hsing rice wine*), 22

shiitakes, dried (dried black mushrooms), *xx*, 1, 11

Shiu Mai (Pork and Shrimp Cups), 68–69

shrimp

    Crispy Fried Meatballs (*Bakso Goreng*), 166–67

    Crispy Shrimp Rolls, 57–58

    dried shrimp (*ha mai, hae bee, goong haeng*), *xx*, 1, 22–23

    Healing Pork and Shrimp Rice Soup (*Kao Tom Moo*), 92–93

    Korean salted shrimp (*saeujeot*), 132

    Shiu Mai (Pork and Shrimp Cups), 6°–69

    Shrimp and Mung Bean Sprout Omelets, 207–8

    Shrimp and Pineapple Red Curry (*Kaeng Kue Sapparod*), 209

    shrimp chips (*krupuk udang*), 281

    shrimp paste, black (*petis, hae ko*), *xx*, 1, 23

    shrimp paste, dried (*belacan, trassi, terasi*), *xx*, 1, 23

    shrimp paste in soybean oil, 288

    Shrimp Toast (*Banh Mi Tom Chien*), *46*, 55–56

    Shrimp with Homemade Black Bean Sauce, 210–11

Special Indonesian Fried Rice (*Nasi Goreng Istimewa*), 279–81

Tangy Tomato Shrimp, *214*, 215–16

Vietnamese Crab Noodle Soup (*Bun Rieu Cua*), 286–88

Water Spinach with Shrimp Paste and Chilies (*Kangkung Belacan*), 118–19

soups and stews

    Black Glutinous Rice Porridge (*Bubur Pulot Hitam*), 317–18

    Chicken Coconut Noodle Soup (*Ohn No Khauk Swe*), *254*, 261–62

    Chicken Coconut Soup (*Tom Ka Kai*), 84

    Clear Soup with Red Spinach and Sweet Corn (*Sayur Bening*), 74, 79–80

    Colonial Curried Chicken Soup (*Mulligatawny Soup*), 85–86

    Fat Noodles in Miso Soup (*Miso Udon*), 264–65

    Gingered Oxtail Stew, 150–51

    Grandma Miyoshi's Dumpling Soup (*Dango Jiru*), 268–69

    Healing Pork and Shrimp Rice Soup (*Kao Tom Moo*), 92–93

    Hearty Beef and Vegetable Soup, 87–88

    Herb-Scented Chicken Soup (*S'ngao Chruok Moan*), 94–95

    Hot and Sour Soup (*Suan La Tang*), 80–81

    Japanese-Style Beef Stew (*Nikujaga*), 273–74

    Layered Vegetable Stew (*Pinakbet*), 111–12

    Nepalese Nine-Bean Soup (*Kawatee*), 96, 97–98

    Red and White Miso Soup (*Awase Miso Shiru*), 89–91, *90*

    Shanghai Soup Dumplings (*Xiao Long Bao*), 64–67

    Spiced Red Lentil Stew (*Palida*), 128–29

    Sweet and Sour Fish Soup (*Canh Chua Ca*), 82–83

Vietnamese Crab Noodle Soup (*Bun Rieu Cua*), 286–88

Watercress and Pork Rib Soup, 99

See also stocks

soy sauce, 23–24, *28*, 29

Soy-Ginger Dipping Sauce, 239

Soy-Sesame Dressing, 243

Spice Blend, Aunty Kaisrie's (*Masala*), 190

Spinach, Red, and Sweet Corn, Clear Soup with (*Sayur Bening*), *74*, 79–80

Spinach with Shrimp Paste and Chilies, Water (*Kangkung Belacan*), 118–19

spring rolls

Brown Sugar Banana Spring Rolls (*Turon*), 324–25

Chinese spring roll wrappers, *15*, 27

Crispy Shrimp Rolls, 57–58

Lumpia (Filipino Eggrolls), 61–63

See also dumplings

squash

Burmese Pork Curry (*Whethar Sebyan*), 163–64

cutting techniques, 114

Green and Golden Zucchini Thread Salad (*Hobak Namul*), *134*, 135–36

Layered Vegetable Stew (*Pinakbet*), 111–12

Pumpkin Custard (*Num Sang Khya L'peou*), 315–16

Spiced Chayote and Peas (*Safed Kaddu aur Matar ki Sabzi*), 115–17, *116*

Squid, Teriyaki, 216–17

star anise, *xx*, 1, 24

steaming techniques, xv–xvii

stir-fries

Beef, Tomato, and Pepper Stir-Fry, 147–49, *148*

cooking techniques, xvii–xviii

Eggy Stir-Fried Cabbage, 110

Mixed Medley Stir-Fry, 112–14

Stir-Fried Beef with Mustard Greens, 160

Stir-Fried Glass Noodles (*Japchae*), 246–47

Stir-Fried Mung Bean Sprouts with Tofu and Chives (*Pad Tao Kua Tao Ngae*), 125–26

Sweet and Sour Pork (*Gu Lao Rou*), 172–73

vegetable cutting techniques, 114

stocks

Dashi (Japanese Kelp and Fish Stock), 40–41

Gelatinized Stock, 64, 65

Homemade Chicken Stock, 42–43

Korean Beef Stock (*Komt'ang*), 43

Stuffing, Sticky Rice (*Naw Mai Fun*), 244–45

sweet and sour dishes

Eggplant Curry (*Bagaara Baingan*), 108–9

Sweet and Sour Fish Soup (*Canh Chua Ca*), 82–83

Sweet and Sour Pork (*Gu Lao Rou*), 172–73

Sweet and Sour Sauce, 63

Teochew Braised Duck (*Lo Ack*), 195–96, *197*

T

tamarind, *xx*, 1, 24–25

Tangerine Peel, Steamed Meatballs with (*Niu Rou Yuan*), 158–59

tapioca starch (tapioca flour), 25

taro stems (*bac ha*), 83

Tea, Ginger (*Wedang Jahe*), 318–19

Tea, Spiced Milk (*Chai*), 320

Tea Eggs, Marbled, 51–52

tofu (*dofu, dauhu*)

Clay Pot "Black Pork" (*Hong Bak*), 263–64

Deep-Fried Tofu, 122

Deep-Fried Tofu Simmered with Tomatoes, 123

Hot and Sour Soup (*Suan La Tang*), 80–81

Japanese Beef and Vegetable Hot Pot (*Sukiyaki*), *270*, 271–72

Japanese-Style Hamburgers (*Wafu Hamburgers*), 153–54

Pan-Fried Tofu Simmered in Sweet Miso Sauce (*Tofu no Misoni*), 124–25

Red and White Miso Soup (*Awase Miso Shiru*), 89–91

Stir-Fried Mung Bean Sprouts with Tofu and Chives (*Pad Tao Kua Tao Ngae*), 125–26

Tofu Omelet with Sweet Peanut Sauce (*Tahu Telur*), 126–27

types and preparation, 25–26

Tomato, Beef, and Pepper Stir-Fry, 147–49, *148*

Tomato Relish, Indian Cucumber and (*Kachumber*), 137

Tomato Shrimp, Tangy, *214*, 215–16

Tomatoes, Deep-Fried Tofu Simmered with, 123

Turkey–Rice Porridge, Leftover Thanksgiving (*Jook*), 274–75

turmeric, 26

V

vegetable cutting techniques, 114

Vegetable Hot Pot, Japanese Beef and (*Sukiyaki*), *270*, 271–72

vegetable oils, xiii, 16

Vegetable Soup, Hearty Beef and, 87–88

Vegetable Stew, Layered (*Pinakbet*), 111–12

Vegetables over Rice, Seasoned (*Bibimbap*), 259

Vietnamese balm (*kinh gioi*), 288

vinegar, cane, 183

Vinegar Dipping Sauce, Black, 67

Vinegar-Braised Chicken (Chicken Adobo), 182–83

W, Z

watercress, 26

Watercress and Pork Rib Soup, 99

Wong, Nellie

profile, 218–19

Stuffed Egg-Crepe Rolls (*Yu Gun*), 211–13

wrappers, 7, *15*, 27

zucchini. *See* squash

ABOUT THE AUTHOR

Photo by Iris Peppard

Patricia Tanumihardja is a freelance writer who covers food, travel, and lifestyle through a multicultural lens. She was born to Indonesian parents, grew up in Singapore, and after living on and traveling across three continents, she now considers the United States home. Tanumihardja lives on the Monterey Peninsula in California with her husband. Please visit her Web site, www .ediblewords.com, and blog, www.theasian grandmotherscookbook.wordpress.com.